Simpson and

Simpson and the Donkey

THE MAKING OF A LEGEND

PETER COCHRANE

MELBOURNE UNIVERSITY PRESS
1992

First published 1992
Printed in Australia by
Brown Prior Anderson Pty Ltd, Burwood, Victoria, for
Melbourne University Press, Carlton, Victoria 3053
U. S. A. and Canada: International Specialized Book Services, Inc.,
5602 N. E. Hassalo Street, Portland, Oregon 97213–3640
United Kingdom and Europe: University College London Press
Gower Street, London WC1E 6BT, UK

Designed by
Lynn Twelftree

National Library of Australia Cataloguing-in-Publication entry

Cochrane, Peter, 1950–   .
   Simpson and the donkey.

   Bibliography.
   Includes index.
   ISBN 0 522 84502 9.

   1. Kirkpatrick, John Simpson, 1892–1915. 2. Kirkpatrick, John
   Simpson, 1892–1915—Correspondence. 3. Kirkpatrick, John
   Simpson, 1892–1915, in fiction, drama, poetry, etc. 4. World
   War, 1914–1918—Campaigns—Turkey—Gallipoli Peninsula.
   5. World War, 1914–1918—Medical care. 6. Soldiers—
   Australia—Biography. I. Title.

940.47594

Please note: the captions
on pages 129 and 132 have
been transposed.

Contents

Illustrations

Acknowledgements

This book began in earnest in 1989 when I came across a large collection of letters written by John Simpson Kirkpatrick. Had Simpson never become a legend, the letters would still constitute a significant record of the life of a working man, an immigrant in his newly adopted land, an itinerant whose home town and family travelled with him in his memories and his dreams. I was by no means the first researcher to make use of these letters, but my predecessors had not been interested in sorting biography from legend, nor in seeing the making of a legend as an historical process. I was interested in both, and the letters became a small but important part of this larger project.

The letters are held at the Australian War Memorial along with other collections that contain written records, photographs and memorabilia on Simpson and his family. These led on to source material in other States, in New Zealand and England, material that was equally rich in 'Simpsonia'. It became obvious that the legend's history was recoverable, and the plan for an essay became a plan for a book.

Historical research and writing is supposed to be a solitary occupation, but the acknowledgements page usually suggests another side to that story. Along the way many friends and colleagues were helpful and stimulating. I want firstly to thank the staff of the Australian War Memorial, in particular Stephen Allen, Jenny Bell, Joyce Bradley, Ron Gilchrist, Michael McKernan, John McQuilton, Pam Ray, Anne-Marie Schwirtlich, Ian Smith, Peter Stanley and especially Marie Wood, whose knowledge and enthusiasm helped me through the documentary labyrinth on numerous occasions. The War Memorial also helped financially, with a grant-in-aid in 1989 and 1990. I must express my gratitude for the research assistance I received: Frank Zammit was able to comb the *Daily Malta Chronicle* for me when he was in Valetta, while Shirley Banks was an extremely efficient helper in the archives in 1989.

I was also fortunate to be a departmental visitor in the History Department of the Research School of Social Sciences (RSSS) at the Australian National University in 1989, and a visiting fellow in the Humanities Research Centre (HRC), ANU, in 1991, where a lot of writing was done and the manuscript completed. My thanks for the practical help and good company of staff at these institutions: in particular to Professor Ken Inglis, Anthea Bundock, Bev Gallina and Helen Macnab at RSSS, and to Professor Graeme Clarke, Wendy Antoniak, Jodi Parvey and Heather Grant at the HRC. At the Red Cross Society (Victoria), Rodney Youens and June Taylor were most helpful, as were Colin Fairweather at the City of Melbourne Archives, and Peter Fraser and Peter Venn at Anzac House in Melbourne.

In my pursuit of the Moore-Jones paintings and various related photographs and texts, many New Zealanders were generous with their time and expertise: thanks to Roger Blackley, Nicholas Boyak, Howard and Fenola Chamberlain, Jim Henderson, Ewan Hyde, George and Betty Johnstone, Puti Kindon, Jock Phillips, Chris Pugsley, Kevin Stewart, Ian Thwaites, Jane Tolerton, Luke Trainer and Jane Vile.

Many other friends and colleagues helped along the way—those exchanges in the corridor or on the stairs in the library, off-the-cuff references and other advice, freely and ever so casually given, little things perhaps, but they mounted up and at the end they were indispensable. For every one of those exchanges I am most grateful. The late Graeme Sturgeon and the late Lloyd Robson helped in this way on several occasions, and these are debts that I dearly wish I could repay.

I am also indebted to those friends and colleagues who read and commented helpfully on draft chapters at various stages of incompletion: thanks to Chris Cuneen, Ann Curthoys, Ralph Elliott, John Herouvim, John Hirst, Ken Inglis, Allan Martin, Drusilla Modjeska, Andrew Moore, Ros Pesman, Gail Reekie, John Rickard, Penny Russell, Geoffrey Serle, Barry Smith, Julian Thomas and Barry York.

Renata Howe and Anne Richter were also most helpful on points of detail regarding Irving Benson, as was Michael Sharkey for David McKee Wright, Beverley Davis and Helen Bersten on Rabbi Danglow, Gavin Souter regarding certain details from the Fairfax archives and Norm Sinclair on the recent commemoration of Simpson at the Shrine of Remembrance in Melbourne.

Tim Bonyhady, Robert Darby, Bill Gammage and Humphrey McQueen read the complete manuscript with their typical care and sharpness. Their valuable criticisms and insights were gratefully adopted and adapted.

For permission to quote from records in the City of Melbourne Archives I would like to thank Mr Colin Fairweather. Mr Rodney Youens organised permission for me to quote from material in the Red Cross Archives (Victorian Branch). For permission to reproduce illustrations I am grateful to the Australian War Memorial, Canberra Times, Hocken Library (University of Otago) and Queen Elizabeth II Museum (Waiouru). I also wish to thank Sir Sidney Nolan for permission to reproduce his 'Simpson and the Donkey', which appears on the cover, and thanks to the Bridget McDonnell Gallery (Carlton) for permission to photograph the original.

I cannot conclude without a word to those good friends and relatives who have been puzzled by my sudden and persistent interest in soldiers and donkeys, but who have been polite enough to say nothing and indulge me. When the book is in their hands, I hope they will see that it is primarily the history of national culture, its politics and symbolism, that concerns me here—not so much of a diversion after all. Legends are a way into this domain, and to understand a legend we must know the story of its making and remaking as well as we know the tale itself. Finally my thanks go to Alison Free who took in the legend when I brought it home, and never once said that it had overstayed its welcome.

They were a quaint couple. The man was a six foot Australian, hard-bitten and active. His gaunt profile spoke of wide experience of hard struggle in rough places. The donkey was a little mouse-coloured animal, no taller than a Newfoundland dog. His master called him Abdul . . .

Their partnership began on the second day of occupation of the Anzac zone of Gallipoli. The man had carried two heavy men in succession down the awful slopes of Shrapnel Gully and through the Valley of Death. His eye lit on a donkey. "I'll take this chap with me next trip," he said, and from that time the pair were inseparable.

When the enfilading fire down the valley was at its worst, and orders were posted that the ambulance men must not go out, the Man and the Donkey continued placidly at their work.

At times they held trenches of hundreds of men spellbound, just to see them at their work. Their quarry lay motionless in an open patch, in easy reach of a dozen Turkish rifles. Patiently the little donkey waited under cover, while the man crawled through the thick scrub until he got to within striking distance. Then a lightning dash, and he had the wounded man on his back, and was making for cover again. In those fierce seconds he always seemed to bear a charmed life. Once in cover he tended his charge with quick skilful movements.

"He had hands like a woman's," said one who thinks he owes his life to the man and the donkey.

Then the limp form was balanced across the back of the patient animal, and, with a slap on its back and the Arab donkey boy's cry of "Gee," the man started off for the beach, the donkey trotting unruffled by his side.

Sun, *11 October 1915*

Introduction

There rests the Heroicall, whose very name (I thinke) should daunt all back-biters; for by what conceit can a tongue be directed to speake euill of that which draweth with it no less Champions than Achilles, Cyrus, Aeneas, Turnus, Tideus, and Rinaldo? who doth not onely teach and moue to a truth, but teacheth and moueth to the most high and excellent truth; who maketh magnanimity and justice shine throughout all misty fearfulnes and foggy desires . . . For as the image of each action styrreth and instructeth the mind, so the loftie image of such Worthies most inflameth the mind with desire to be worthy, and informes with counsel how to be worthy.

Sir Philip Sidney, *An Apology for Poetry* (1595)

With its creation, circulation and passage across time a simple tale can acquire a complicated history. The complications will be greater still if the story happens to be among the most celebrated tales from the Great War, if it has come to occupy a place in a nation's rituals of remembrance, figures prominently in commemorative literature, sculpture and memorabilia and, having passed into the collectivity of our culture, has become an instantly recognisable icon. This is what happened to a simple tale about John Simpson Kirkpatrick, the Man with the Donkey. In the time between his death at Gallipoli on 19 May 1915 and the evacuation of troops nearly seven months later, Simpson became a national hero in Australia. His story was told and retold in newspapers across the country; it figured in school texts, in published memoirs and reminiscences, and even in film in 1916. The simple tale has been with us ever since—the pre-eminent legend of Australian heroism and self-sacrifice.

To grasp this fast-won fame we look to the tale itself. Simpson was a humble water-carrier, a rescuer of wounded men, and he was also the man with the donkey, with all the rich associations that partnership carried. Militarists and pacifists, imperial patriots and socialists alike could appreciate his deeds, agreeing that he was a selfless hero. Both Christians and secular humanists could see their reflection in his image. Again and again he went 'unarmed, fearless and smiling' through a mess of torn flesh and a hail of shrapnel, seeking out the wounded and bringing them to safety on the back of a donkey. It was a story of inspiring courage matched by pathetic vulnerability, an irresistible dualism; thus interpreted, his fame and its many forms of representation seem plausible. But this reading of the tale is confined to the surface narrative with little hint of the allegorical riches beneath, no reference to the producers and the peddlers of the legend, or to the politics of the home front. If the legend is to have a history, the search for its inner meaning must be linked to the context in which the tale flourished, so that at the end we are left, not with the universal appeal of a tale for all factions, but instead with a knowledge of its place in our culture—why Simpson and his donkey were 'sold' with such vigour, why his image lodged in so many minds. For the hero was disinterested but the makers of his legend were not. The function of the legend was to instruct and inspire in the nature of heroic virtue, to will men to similar action. Simpson thus fits squarely into the epic tradition and, since the tale could be told in a few minutes, its essentials tailored to a mere paragraph or a modest stanza—an inducement to its repetition—it might best be described as a little epic.

The epic tradition began in the ancient world when poets turned their attention from supernatural powers and contests to specifically human capacities and virtues. Though some relics of the earlier outlook might be retained, the epic focused on heroic man—on males who surpassed others in qualities that all possessed to some degree. The transition to the epic has been rightly described as a 'descent from heaven', whereby the new protagonist is distinguished by his physical prowess rather than his hermetic knowledge, magical powers or supernatural associations. As Thomas M. Greene put it: 'The epic is the poem which replaces divine worship with humanistic awe, awe for the act which is prodigious but yet human'.[1]

To induce heroic awe there were literary prerequisites to be met: the hero must be acting for the community; what he does must be dangerous; it must involve a test of strength, courage and will; and it must make a difference. Beyond these basic requirements, the 'heroic' has varied according to time and custom, its expressions and meanings given by different stages of social development and by culture. The barbaric Achilles could no more find an honoured place in the age of chivalry than the Arthurian type could be taken seriously in the modern period.[2] Although heroic literature dealt with men of prowess (and occasionally with women, such as Joan of Arc who it was said 'forgot her sex' and whose leadership was notable for its supernatural connections), there was no rigid formula.[3] The one thing that epic heroes had in common, apart from their variously defined prowess, was the ideological purpose of the genre, a purpose that linked them across time and culture.

The epic tradition was meant to be inspirational. By imprinting images of the heroic virtues on the mind, the epic poet hoped to spur others to courageous exploits. As Sir Philip Sidney put it in his *Apology for Poetry,* the 'Heroicall' must 'teacheth and moueth', it must 'inflameth the mind with desire to be worthy' and, equally notable and relevant to the Simpson legend, it must deter the 'back-biters'.[4] The function of the epic heroes was to set a stirring example; they were the role models for powerful castes and war-like aristocracies preoccupied with the martial activities of consolidation or conquest, and later for the citizen armies of the revolutionary period and the modern era which followed. Modern warfare may disappoint one's sense of epic setting, but the need to 'inflameth the mind with desire to be worthy'—the desire to fight, to put it bluntly—was as great as ever. With the new citizen armies relying heavily on volunteers, who fought for ideals rather than monarchs, the common soldier experienced a startling rise in status and found himself contrasted with the 'mercenaries, criminals, vagabonds and destitutes' of previous contingents. He was now the object of a cult that had previously centred on gallant officers, aristocrats and kings.[5] From 1914 the scheme of action would be transformed by technology and strategy, but the ideological conditions for the epic tale remained. Journalists and newspaper editors, politicians and wartime censors would replace the epic poets; the heroes, far from being exemplars for some warrior caste, would be models to stir the common man. In Hegel's words they would be rendered as 'total individuals who magnificently concentrate in themselves what is otherwise dispersed in the national character'.[6]

One temptation is to concentrate in the hero all the necessary conditions for his fame, to see it spring direct from his own elevated character. Simpson's courage and compassion are unquestionable; his stoic persistence, brave deeds and tragic end are beyond dispute. Yet his fame is nourished by other sources, for while heroism is an individual act, heroes are a social creation. They are made by a configuration of circumstances and needs that lie outside the heroic moment. The setting for Simpson's fame was not the battlefield but the recruitment crisis on the home front. He died as this crisis was getting under way, and his legend was one of the symbolic resources created and mobilised by the imperial patriots, the 'Yes' men and women behind the subsequent campaigns for conscription and the recruitment drives made more urgent by conscription's repeated rejection. The need to 'inspire and move' became a coordinated effort that linked government, censors, newspaper editors, correspondents and others in the business of persuading men to enlist. The tales of Simpson were part of their epic venture. A searching interpretation uncovers those themes that lent themselves to the case for enlistment and later coercion. Between the hero and his audience, therefore, are the mediators: the makers of heroes, the peddlers of epic deeds, the interested parties who 'inflameth the mind with the desire to be worthy', who claimed a lien on the meaning of that term, and who found in Simpson a stirring moral exemplar and a neat diversion away from the immense suffering of the war.

Simpson entered History in a similar fashion to Madoc, that fantastic figure from Welsh mythology—as an instrument of imperial conflict. He became a powerful idea that was used to back an imperial claim on young men for military service, in the same way as the Welsh prince, said to have beaten Columbus to the Americas by some 300 years, became the basis for an imperial claim on a new land. As Gwyn Williams reminds us, a legend can be more than mere amusement for simple folk; it can acquire a power from situations entirely independent of itself. What makes it important are its political usefulness and its fascination for people at specific points in time.[7]

The canonisation of the English poet Rupert Brooke is a more recent case that is equally compelling: when Brooke died on his way to the Dardanelles in March 1915, his death, as John Lehmann has written, was 'a god-send to the politicians and generals who used him . . . to create a legendary inspiration for the national cause'. That he died of blood poisoning from an insect bite before he reached the fighting was an intolerable fact that Churchill and others refused to acknowledge in the public lamentation that followed, choosing instead to stress the nobility of the sacrificial hero.[8] Simpson can hardly be compared with Brooke in individual terms, for he was no poet, nor did he have friends at the highest levels of the Admiralty, but the angelic flights of his afterlife are not dissimilar. The tales told about him are no straightforward guide to a life spent and lost. Their language is replete with meanings that he could never have expressed or intended, meanings that can be derived only from the mediations between one man's experience of war and the global contest for power. A history of the Simpson legend, therefore, is not primarily an exercise in biography but a study of allegorical meaning—to fathom the tales in their setting and their iconography, and the popular enchantment with both. As Yeats put it: 'How can we know the dancer from the dance?'[9]

Simpson was a historical figure, not a fictional invention. Yet so little was known of his life that his anchorage in history was not secure, and the limits to what the legend-makers might do with his death were few. They would not turn him into a light-horseman. They would not make him a killer. They would not raise him in social class or education. Such transformations were hardly needed because the lofty virtue and pathos of his ventures, as well as his appeal to ordinary people, depended on none of these things. Thus, apart from the obvious limits, one fascinating feature of the legend is the freedom its makers enjoyed to disregard the historical figure and create a Simpson who would fit their ideological needs as generated in the first instance by the Great War and by conservative politics thereafter. As Winston Smith discovered in Orwell's *Nineteen Eighty-Four*, it is easy to invent the lives of dead men.[10]

Out of the Simpson legend comes a dutiful man committed to his King and his country, a volunteer, one of the 'nomad tribe' whose experience in the Australian bush had prepared him for the trials of war. He is pictured as a prototype of the Australian soldier—the 'digger' or the 'Anzac'. Patsy Adam-Smith described him as being 'as redolent as a gum tree, as Australian as a kangaroo, a real colonial spirit'. Even his entry in the *Australian Dictionary of Biography* was unable to avoid the grab-bag typecasting of nationality: 'He was a typical digger: independent, witty and warm-hearted, happy to be indolent at times and careless of dress.'[11] These assertions about Simpson's typicality merely reiterated an established tenet of the legend which both naturalised and depoliticised him. From the beginning, the legend departed from the man, as the historical figure disappeared under the accretions of myth. The principal inventions depended on the omission of certain facts about the real Simpson which are set out here as a prelude to the history of the legend itself: Simpson was a Pommy, a 'new chum' in Australia; he was a political radical; he was hardly the willing soldier; and he saved few, if any, lives.

Although his Anglo-Scottish origins figure in the legend at its outset in 1915, they were soon lost in the refining process, in the quest for an authentic digger hero, and it was only the interest of the English in claiming Simpson as their own that sustained the occasional reference to his immigration before the war. The *Queensland School Paper*, in 1917, observed the antipodean character of his head: 'The man was a six foot Australian, hard-bitten and active. His gaunt profile spoke of wide experience of hard struggle in rough places'.[12] Not until the Reverend Irving Benson wrote his 'biography' in the 1960s were Simpson's ethnic origins firmly established, which is an irony since Benson's rendering was in other respects the most dishonest of all. As for Simpson's volunteer status—a vital part of the legend in the context of the recruiting and conscription campaigns—he was an inadvertent, possibly reluctant Digger. He was planning to return home before the war broke out and enlisted to get back to England on the cheap, where he hoped to join the English army. He was disappointed by his sojourn in Egypt and regarded Gallipoli as another obstacle to his plans.

While there, his commitment was indeed exemplary and he *did* work in a perilous setting—the most important thing about him which the legend did not forget. Yet there is no doubt about what he did: with the help of a donkey he transported *slightly* wounded men—those with leg wounds, men who were conscious, some who could chat or smoke, even stop for a photograph—to Anzac beach. Years later, when the sculptor W. L. Bowles produced for the Australian War Memorial a maquette depicting Simpson at work, official historians insisted that a soldier on board the donkey in a state of collapse was, from a medical service point of view, 'absurd'. The soldier had to be conscious and capable of helping himself to some degree. He was not to be 'sitting jauntily up smoking a cigarette, and looking as pleased as Punch', but equally he had to be 'alive to the situation and able to take an intelligent and purposeful interest in what is being done for him'. Otherwise he would be on a stretcher. This view prevailed, the maquette was altered and a not-so-dramatic statuette was finally cast.[13]

From the folklore about Simpson comes the suggestion that his acquisition of the donkey was a 'lazy dodge', for many stretcher-bearers worked closer to the firing line, carrying the most exhausting and awkward loads, but that aspersion misses the key points. The donkey freed Simpson from a stretcher-bearer squad of four (Anzac heroes come in ones not fours); its presence implied a wounded soldier who would be renewed. Later, it made for a pathetic icon with powerful Christian associations, and for a classic children's tale. The donkey also signified the nature of Simpson's work on the battlefield for in this respect, too, he was not a typical digger: he never fired a shot, had no love of the bayonet and his work was akin more to nursing than fighting. Yet far from reducing his epic status, and thus his standing as a *man*, we shall see how these absences enhanced it.

Finally there are Simpson's politics to consider. After his death the legend-makers were free to enlist the memory of his deeds in their recruitment campaign, but there is no evidence that he supported what *Labour Call* described as the 'sooling-on business' by the 'safety brigade', those who were not intending to enlist them-selves.[14] His political outlook was radically social democratic, and his feeling for the English ruling class was one of deep mistrust and hatred. He believed Westminster to be a talking shop where the rich pursued their interests at the expense of the poor. The accretions of myth have covered over his personality and his politics. The profile in the *Australian Dictionary of Biography* is not alone in trying to protect the memory of Simpson from his class consciousness, but it serves as an introductory case in point. In keeping with the conservative claim on the legend, and despite access to Simpson's angry letters, the *Dictionary* author gave no hint of the hero's radicalism. Indeed, the account fits with Benson's bowdlerised blending of fact and folklore. Just as Rupert Brooke would be remembered for a few war sonnets rather than his South Seas phase or his lively parodies of Christianity, so Simpson would be remem-bered for a few weeks of uncharacteristic ministration.[15] The insistence upon a conservative simplicity in which 'what is desirable is unambiguous, firm [and] unchanging' has been a feature of the legend from its origins in the war up to the present day. The elements of the life that would spoil this simplicity have been overlooked or disregarded.[16]

In other ways the Simpson legend is not so simple. It can claim a place among wartime tales as one of the richest in symbolic suggestion, as there are a number of powerful motifs that are gathered and unified around its sectarian core. As Paul Fussell has suggested, the most popular wartime legends can be distinguished by the presence of meanings that have great cultural significance or emotive power.[17] The Simpson legend carries us into the deep reaches of collective memory much as a dream conveys us into the subconscious. The Man with the Donkey was a symbol saturated with emotional significance, packed with meanings that sprang from the material circumstances of Australia's war.[18] In the belief that every legend has a history, I have tried to identify and unravel these meanings in order to explain this legend's political significance *and* popular appeal, its permanent place in Australian folklore and its periodic appearance as an official icon. The underlying theme is the legend as epic, a concentration of conventions drawn from battlefield journalism, a highly political creation that is remade with changing circumstances.

In the following chapters there is a continual play, mostly unannounced, between the known facts about John Simpson Kirkpatrick and the expurgated versions of his life, between the material conditions of war and their transformation in the press, and, of course, between the tales of Simpson and the historical circumstances that produced them. For the most part this interplay is not a means of contrasting falsity with truth but a method of writing the history of a legend. History's claim on a past reality is always qualified by the bias and method of the historian, the limits of the records, of the imagination and of language. Yet if the bias, the record, the imagination and the language are the mediations that cannot be surmounted, they are also the means by which we can know more about what happened.[19] History can deepen our knowledge of material conditions, politics and power, of the experience of war, of its fabricated representations, and of the hearts of men and women. It might even convince us of the *secondary role* of 'texts' in shaping the course of events, for the Simpson texts were undoubtedly a historical force in themselves.

The Simpson legend began as a few scraps of news but was soon institutionalised, cut and tailored for mass consumption. Beyond the official legend was the folklore, which included the occasionally subversive versions of the tale, the not-so-forgetful subterranean whispers.[20] The official legend prevailed in wartime because it was based on Simpson's obscurity and sustained by the imperial establishment. Had he been a *cause célèbre* in his own lifetime, his character familiar, his deeds scrutinised and widely reported, the legend we know would have been impossible. The fact that he was little known provided the scope necessary for the invented afterlife, as though he was lost, distorted and magnified in the mists of time, like so many of the epic heroes. Much of the folklore about him also depended on this elusiveness, since it gave rise to engaging questions, to the guesswork and hearsay that is characteristic of folklore, to a flow of 'revelations', and to significant disputes about his appearance. The legend was always simmering, threatening its own legitimacy, giving off more tales from the heroic past, perhaps revealing a new photo portrait, or suffering from troublesome questions about an old one.

What has changed over the years is not the story but the political settings that have prevailed whenever the legend has rejoined popular culture and public ritual, and the contemporary shift in its meanings. The legend was launched in 1915 on the need for military manpower; in the 1930s it was mobilised against pacifists and an increasingly jaundiced memory of the war; in the cold-war period it re-emerged as a model of single-minded commitment to the Christian (anti-Communist) heritage, a heroic formula that linked physical courage to the loftier virtues of gentleness, compassion and self-regulating obedience (the high ground of mateship). This is the formula that has underwritten the power and persistence of Simpson's afterlife: the core motif is obedience; bravery, gentleness and compassion are organised around it. Whether Christian hero or not, Simpson was always portrayed as a loyal servant of empire, a model worker, 'even unto death'. His legend was an allegory on allegiance, part of a massive exercise in state-directed persuasion. And like all allegories what really mattered were the messages beneath the literal surface of the text. That an apparently innocent tale was harnessed to the slaughter in this way is an irony befitting the carnage of the Great War. Above all else, the image signified what Winston Churchill approvingly described as 'self-surrender'.[21]

Chapter One

To Hide
the Man

He that recounts the life of another, commonly dwells most
upon conspicuous events, lessens the familiarity of his tale
to increase its dignity, shows his favourite at a distance,
decorated and magnified like the ancient actors in their
tragic dress, and endeavours to hide the man that he may
produce a hero.

Samuel Johnson, *Idler*, no. 284, 24 November 1759

Unlike the abundant relics of the early Christian martyrs, which, as
Gibbon remarks, 'have replenished so many churches', the relics of
the Man with the Donkey are convincingly meagre.[1] His younger
sister, Annie, donated what little there was to the Australian War
Memorial: his identity disc, his service medals, his oak leaf and
scroll, a bronze medal presented posthumously by King George V,
and a tin of cigarettes (Wills' Woodbines) that Annie had sent to
Gallipoli in May 1915, not knowing that Jack, as she called him, was
already dead. She donated the relics in April 1965, to coincide with
the fiftieth anniversary of the Gallipoli landing. The family had also
possessed a collection of Jack's letters but Annie was unable to
include them with her donation, for the letters had travelled a very
different path, a path that leads back into the life before the legend
and then forward into the process whereby legends are made and
remade.

The family had treasured the letters since Jack's death. They were
kept in a vault at the local bank in South Shields in the north of
England, the town where Jack had grown up. The letters had been
in that vault for nearly forty years when Annie entrusted them to the

Reverend Clarence Irving Benson, an Australian who was planning to write a biography of her beloved brother. That was 1956. Benson returned to Australia with the letters and published the biography almost a decade later, relying heavily on the precious documents in his care. The published letters occupied nearly a third of the entire volume and gave the book its authenticity. They allowed readers to feel closer to their hero than ever before. This story became the definitive account of Jack's life and made Benson a distinguished keeper of the legend. What readers could not possibly know was that the published letters had been so carefully censored that the Simpson they met in Benson's book was nothing like the Simpson of the letters in full.[2]

The Reverend Benson had emigrated from Yorkshire to Victoria in 1916. He was a novice clergyman burdened with what was thought to be a terminal lung disease. While his two brothers fought in France, he was taking up a quiet parsonage in Hamilton. But Hamilton could not contain him any more than his breathing difficulties could slow him down. Benson soon established himself as a man of inexhaustible energies and a leader of the Methodist Church in Melbourne. For decades he was known to thousands as the presenter of 'A Pleasant Sunday Afternoon' on radio 3LO and later radio 3DB, and as a regular columnist for the Melbourne *Herald*.[3] He was a watchful anti-Communist, a keen supporter and acquaintance of Robert Menzies, a collector of signed first editions by Winston Churchill, a celebrant of England's green and pleasant land and a man who spoke of the 'soul of the empire'. Benson was present when Menzies, retired from politics, was installed as Lord Warden of the Cinq Ports in 1967. He was an enthusiast for English pomp and ceremony and was eager to have a cup of tea at Walmer Castle, Sir Robert's new home.[4] With his biographical sketch of Simpson he aimed to sustain a good Christian tale, a tale of a man's devotion to his mother, his family and his empire.[5]

In pursuit of the man behind the Simpson legend, Benson travelled to England in 1956. As he tells it, he had some success researching at the South Shields municipal library where there was a bronze statuette of Simpson in the foyer and assorted material within.[6] Through an advertisement in the local paper he got in touch with boyhood friends, including one who long before had swapped pet rabbits with the boy Jack, and another who had been at Gallipoli with him. Better still, he had been rescued by Jack, in the thick of battle, on 3 May 1915. 'He was unconscious,' wrote Benson, 'but he remembered being taken down to the beach on a donkey.'[7] Eventually, through the good offices of the local librarian, came the richest reward of his search. The Reverend Benson was introduced to Annie.

> It was one of the great experiences of my life. More than anything I gleaned from her, she in her own personality helped me to feel and realize the spirit of the Man With the Donkey. They had grown up together, they were knit in close bonds of origins, growth and affinity. Her generosity of heart, practical ability, sound sense, and instinctive kindness made Jack live for me. Here was the mind and heart that had come from their Scottish parents planted in an English North-country home. I saw it all. I was at the fountain head of a hero's life.[8]

In the few days remaining in South Shields a firm friendship was struck with the sister who, Benson had decided, would be a model for Jack. Annie and her husband Adam invited him to stay with them, though it appears that Benson did not want to impose and so remained in his hotel. Then came a little adventure that changed the whole project. On the evening before his departure, Annie asked him to meet her outside Barclays Bank next morning. 'This was a mysterious request' [he wrote] 'and I went to sleep and awoke early speculating on what it might portend'. As arranged, they met outside the Bank at ten, and Annie asked him to wait while she went inside.

> The minutes dragged achingly. Then she emerged and handed to me a large handkerchief tightly knotted. I stared at it wonderingly. "Here are all the letters Jack wrote to his Mother from the day he sailed on the *Heighington*!" I had no words. I was dumb with incredulity. Here was Eureka beyond my brightest hopes. Had the kerchief been full of hoarded golden sovereigns they would have seemed less than the dust in the gutter. Now I could know the man I had crossed the world to find—the man behind the legend.
> I stammered out what I could from a heart full of gratitude. This was Annie's response to a man who had come from Australia for the sake of "Our Jack". There in the street I kissed her, for in three days I felt as if I had known her for a lifetime. I agreed with all that Jack thought of her—"Wonderful Annie!"[9]

Later he untied the knots and opened the precious bundle to find 'a pile of letters and post-cards, many of them worn with much handling, some crumpled and stained—almost illegible—and others mere tantalizing scraps'. Now he was sure he could trace what he called 'the unknown story'.[10]

The trip to Simpson's home town, the interviews, the encounter with Annie, and the jackpot—the letters—can all be found in Benson's little book, *The Man with the Donkey. The Good Samaritan of Gallipoli*. The letters appeared as an impartial presentation (the man's own words) with very little commentary. Benson's preface was brief:

> [They] have no literary merit—they are the writing of a plain man of limited education to report his doings to the folks at home. Shining out of them is his great love of his Mother and almost all of them reveal his concern for her. He constantly sent her money even in times of hardship when he had little himself. Every day was Mother's Day for Jack Simpson.[11]

Benson published 42 of some 70 letters, in part or in whole, and he referred briefly to three others—an apparently generous serving. Covering the period October 1909 to February 1915, they provided a serial impression of an itinerant working life in Edwardian Australia. But this was not just any life, this was Simpson. The excitement of the letters derived from the fact that until they were published in 1965, nothing was known of the man before he went to Gallipoli. The tales from the legend, rich as they were, were confined to those grim days after the landing on the peninsula, the last days of Simpson's life, whereas the letters that Benson published take us back several years. They are the only record of Jack's travels and his time in Australia.[12]

From the published letters we learn how young Jack left home just two days after his father's funeral. 'The sea that was in Jack's blood began to call,' wrote Benson. We follow the young seaman from Madeira to Genoa. By mail he receives a photo of his mother with which he is not entirely pleased, and he learns that Annie has lost her job. He is in London and then in Leith before he is home for Christmas. The letters resume early in 1910 when he is again away at sea, this time bound for New South Wales. They are as rich as ever, describing his movements, his diet ('plenty of good grub and eating any Gods amount of it'), his weight which he carefully monitored ('I have not got any sloppy fat about me but bone and muscle and the things that weigh'), and other clues about family dialogue and assumed roles.

Jack tells his mother that he is working with 'a fine lot of men and respectable'; another time he assures her he is not a 'tramp', but has a change of underclothing as well as a billycan, and that in Australia 'the best of respectable men', even homeowners, pack their swag and go off looking for work; he reveals that he has signed over half his pay to her and that she can draw it as her own; he wants another photo of her, one that he especially liked, but had forgotten to take with him: 'I think you look best on that one and I meant to fetch it away with me but forgot so mind and be sure and send it . . . P.S. Now dont forget that Photo and write Sharp'.[13] Several years of wandering, and seafaring along the Australian coast, followed.

The letters—the apparently generous serving that Benson fed to his readers—were rich in several ways. Here is a working man on the track, picking up the tricks of the itinerant trade, living on his wits as well as his muscle, learning to read the labour market, and occasionally to act collectively. Jack became adept at jumping ship when it suited him. In one case he hung on until the 13th of the month, knowing that his mother would draw her half pay on the 12th. At one point he is on the goldfield at Yilgarn in Western Australia, but the field is overrun with men and 'work was hard to get. There was men working for three and four bob a day'. He departs as quickly as he came, looking for a better chance. There is a letter in which he laments the coal miners' strike at home and wishes the union had been stronger. In another one he sends word to a friend 'that he is silly to waste his time loading hay for his old man he wants to keep his eyes open for a ship coming out this way'. Jack was another celebrant of the working man's paradise.[14]

Even the regular reports on his weight are part of the comparison between his new life and his old. Jack constantly balances his old and new self and is very pleased to have attained twelve and a half stone or thereabouts. He is eating 'any Gods amount' of food and this, he lets slip, is a lot more than he got when at home. In his second letter from abroad he informs his mother:

> I think I have eaten more in this fortnight than I have eaten for the
> last six months. I eat enough for two men at meals still I am always
> feeling "ungry" I am getting an appetite like a horse but there is one

John Simpson Kirkpatrick on his 21st birthday
A photo portrait taken in Australia and sent to his mother in South Shields: his suit was probably supplied by the photographer, as he had no need of one while seafaring and labouring in Australia.

consolation there is plenty of grub more than is used, they do live high in this mess room they are fed like fighting cocks I can tell you.[15]

Benson also published a letter about a Christmas Eve brawl on board a coastal trader, the S.S. *Kooringa*. The brawl followed the goose and plum pudding and brandy sauce. Jack came out of it with one eye closed. He reported it to his mother: 'You couldn't see anything for blood and snots flying about until Mates and Engineers came along and threatened to log all hands forward'.[16] Jack seemed to enjoy a brawl, or at least he enjoyed telling his mother he did. Benson must have judged that his readers would make allowances.

By 1914 Jack was homesick and his enthusiasm for Australia somewhat blunted. He planned to return the following year, believing wages had improved in the old country, while prices in Australia were a real problem ('the money goes sharp out here'). With the outbreak of war Jack saw his chance to get home sooner. He arrived in Fremantle, deserted his ship and, thinking he would get a free passage home to England, enlisted in the Australian army on 25 August 1914. The next letters were from Egypt, where he was languishing, sick of the drill, sick of the grub and sick of the sand. They were his last letters home.[17]

The student of texts

In his pursuit of Simpson, Benson had placed himself in a peculiar position. On the one hand, he was a celebrant of the legend and his purpose was to inject it with new life, to make it glow. On the other hand, he had taken on the scholarly task of biography and promised his readers 'the man behind the legend'. But his commitment to the latter was all bluff:

> The legend began even while he (Jack) lived and it grew apace after his death so that it has become necessary to sift the facts from the fiction. Indeed, any student of texts will find the Simpson legend an excellent exercise in distinguishing the man from the legend and the realities from the imaginative afterglow.[18]

The legend did not begin before Jack's death and Benson does not at any point investigate how it got under way, though that is beside the point for now. The point is that Benson declared the necessity of sifting fact from fiction'. He travelled half the world in his endeavour to find more facts. He covered some ground in Australia, too, and consulted with several key figures in the making of the legend. He called for help over the air waves and he got a sheaf of replies.[19] And, as we know, he uncovered the letters and revealed them—some of them, partially—to a world of curious readers who would never have guessed how much Benson had amputated.

A reading of the original letters reveals that Benson made cuts to fit a sanitised legend. He sifted crucial facts, and what he published constituted his own fiction. That so many of the letters were published testifies, ironically, to a highly selective sifting. The cuts and omissions fit a pattern. They fit with Benson's outlook on life, his politics, and his preference for a moral tale of his own making rather than an historical one.

There are two sorts of omissions. The first are those that revealed Simpson the radical labour man, reflecting on his attitude to the 'old country' and on his working life in the new. The second are those that displayed his wilful temperament and his short fuse. In both cases the man of the letters-in-full is a more complex and fascinating character than the sanitised Simpson of Benson's book. The pattern is too consistent to have been accidental. Benson threw out Simpson's politics and his invective. In so doing he also dispensed with most references to the economically grim and friction-ridden side of existence at 'home'. The Reverend left his readers with a Simpson who could describe where he was going and what he was doing, who talked a lot about food, who joked with his sister, suggesting she had 'the worrums'—'Peur wee Annie . . . tell her to try wormcake'—and who sent money to his mother. He left us with half a man.

The Jack of the letters-in-full (he always signed 'Jack') is a much livelier figure than the 'pleasant Sunday afternoon' Jack of Benson's book. It wasn't that Benson buffed all the rough edges, but that he cut out Jack's view of the world, his 'native' philosophy, his instinctive responses in everyday life, his politics of neighbourhood and class. He cut out testimony that makes the letters important in their own right, regardless of the legend that would later attach itself to this immigrant labourer 'on the track' in his new country. The paradox is that Jack of the letters-in-full fits so much better with the rough-hewn masculinity of the Anzac legend.

Annie often said Jack's heart was in Australia, and he would be getting out there some day. Benson reports this,[20] but the letters he cut, and the ones he left out altogether, make it clear that Jack had equally strong views about the England he had left behind and about contemporary events there, which he followed in the newspapers he liked to read in the evenings. In 1912, while working as a fireman in the stokehole of the S.S. *Kooringa*, he wrote to his mother about industrial troubles in the 'old country'. This letter reveals a Simpson who is cynical about industrial and political affairs at home, who sees politics as a stacked deck, and who wants radical change. He is a man of strong opinions, to say the least:

> I see that the railway men who get 24 bob a week have got a rise of $3\frac{1}{2}$ percent. I suppose that they must have caught the owners when they were drunk and I [*sic*] a generous state of mind to have got such a hell of a rise. I suppose that the railway men will be going about like Lords now that they have got a shilling a week rise but I suppose the Lords and Dukes will take it off them next year again as the expenses will be too big for them to keep up. That is just like the style in the old country . . . I often wonder when the working men of England will wake up and see things as other people see them. What they want in England is a good revolution and that will clear some of these Millionaires and lords and Dukes out of it and then with a Labour Government they will almost be able to make their own conditions. I am enclosing a PO for a quid.[21]

This was one of several letters in which Jack spoke his mind. In another, a kind of political testament, Jack told his mother about working conditions in Australia and again commented bitterly on industrial life back home. Benson chose to cut out the heart of this four-page letter, to publish only the opening lines and a slice from the closing page. But from its opening lines he did allow his readers a tantalising snippet:

> I see that the miners have started work and by the accounts in the papers out here they have not got what they came out for. It is damned hard when you come to think of it the way they have been treated it is a pity they had not waited for another two or three years until they had plenty of money in their union so that they could have hung on a bit longer then the Government would have forced a settlement one way or another [22]

For once, Benson's readers were allowed to glimpse a union man who could talk strategy and who felt for the miners whose circumstances he knew so well. But they were not allowed to see the heart of Jack's letter; they were not to know he linked the working man's sufferings to class privilege and political structure and then back to the limits of the working man's outlook. And they were not allowed the opportunity to sense that Jack enjoyed propounding his parliamentary socialism to his mother. Here is the heart of his letter, beginning in mid-sentence at the point where Benson lopped it off:

> but then it will always be the way in that Louse bound country it is not like Australia for we have not got any house of Lords where a lot of empty headed fools have the right to throw out any bill no matter how much benefit in would to the working classes just because there fathers sat before them. But then England has always been like that and always will be until the people do away with they lords. Look at the railways at home for instance they all belong to private companies that pay very large dividends every quarter through having the men with constant jobs work 10 hours a day for the huge sum of 1 pound one shilling a week then other people think that they are very well paid the Government workers on the railway out here were growling about a pay rise of wages so they went to Arbitration Court and the award they got was that no man that was working for the government connected with the railways the least he could work for was 9/6 per day and of course paid higher wages according to your job. Now on the NER at home a porter gets 22 shillings a week one week and 18 shilling the next week and if he is extra civil to the passengers he might if he has got a bit of good luck he might get a stray threepenny bit so you will see the difference between the two countries the working man out here votes for a labour Government out here but the men at home has not got the sense for that he must go and vote for the first big Liberal Capitalist that puts up for the seat. Now mother I hope you and Annie are keeping alright . . . [23]

Jack could not punctuate a sentence but he had no trouble pouring out his angry words, stringing together a diatribe against 'the Lords and Dukes'. His view of England as a 'Louse bound' country was closely tied to the rate of wages there, to the degree of inequality and class privilege. The phrase is repeated in another letter where, referring to an old friend, Jack suggests he would be 'better off out here than slaving in that lousebound country for a quid a week'.[24] Benson was a careful political censor—he gave his readers the entire letter, minus that rude sentence.

Jack's experience in the 'colonies' provided a new perspective, an opportunity for comparison that seemed to overlay a lifetime of gathered intuition. So it is no surprise to find him on the colonial labour market with his wits about him. In Queensland after a short spell on the canefields he is bargaining over the price of his labour on a cattle station, but he won't work for less than '30 bob a week', and so moves on. At Coledale, south of Sydney, he is sacked for dragging his heels. 'A gang of us got sacked for slackness,' he tells his mother, 'I was on stonework and damned heavy work it was.' Then he is unemployed for three weeks surviving 'the best way I could', until finally he gets work in the pits at South Bulli. Benson left this letter out altogether. Not only does it talk of slackness and unemployment, but it is also critical of working conditions in Australia. Here and there the letters in full reveal that Jack's preference for Australia is complicated by distinctions between one job and another, one region and the next, by the poor quality of some lodgings and by higher prices which were blunting his enthusiasm for higher wage rates in the 'colonies':

> I have 8 bob a shift 9 hours and all nightshift it is rotten I can tell you. Now mother you will be saying he is doing well but what a mistake the people at home make the hear they make good money out here, true but the what is the good of it you have it all to pay away. Now look at me for instance. I work for about £2 2s a week and the it is not constant it is very seldom the pit works the full ten shifts a fortnight if so you get about 4.4.0 out of that I have got a pound a week to pay for lodgings for you can't get them any cheaper and no washing done so that is 2 quid and by the time I send you something each pay you will see I have not much left. I am about sick of it although it will not be too bad if this job is anyway constant for I can always be looking round for something better.[25]

Lodgings could be a problem in more ways than one. A number of times Jack reported on his experiences as a boarder in strange parts. There is another letter, not used by Benson, undated but from his coalmining period, in which Jack talks about the lottery of taking lodgings. He tells his mother she ought to be in Australia taking in boarders for she 'would make a fortune in a quarter less than no time'. The rates were high and the food not much good. His previous lodgings had been rotten and a mess of trouble. 'There was very little grub and what there was it was dead crook.' Hardly a drop of water for a bath and at night 'when the man and wife were drunk they used to scrap like hell'. One of these nights the man started on Jack:

That put the tall hat altogether for he smote me across the head with the poker and put a cut in my head about an inch long after that I sailed in and then you could not see anything for dust I broke a chair over his head and in the struggle we upscuttled and broke a good few things so me he got a summons out against me for assault and "abreaking hup of the appy ome" but as both him and the wife was drunk and I wasnt the case was dismissed I was only there a fortnight altogether and then I came stop with Parks and I have got a good lodge I can tell you plenty hot pies and onion puddings them the things you want to get your back up.[26]

Jack's contempt for the rich was not matched by any inclination to glorify the poor. His first-hand experience did not seem to allow for that. He could be as dismissive of the working man—and of working women—as he was resentful of the lords and dukes. When his mother tells him she is going to open a sweets shop, a plan that did not eventuate, he writes to tell her she is in the wrong district, reminding her that he used to deliver milk to that lot and they

would rob "Old Nick" himself if he gave "Tick" [credit] and I suppose you will know there is no hope unless you give the good old "Tick". I wasnt four years going round with the milk without finding out a little of there weak points.[27]

Jack was eleven or twelve when his four-year stint delivering milk began. His father, Robert, had been badly injured at sea in 1904 and lay bedridden at home until his death in 1909. Jack's mother had wanted to apprentice the boy to an engineering firm, being determined to keep him out of the pits, but engineering was in the doldrums at that time and apprentices earned too little. He took to the milk cart instead, to help support the family.

Annie was also at work when Jack left England in 1909 on the S.S. *Heighington*, and the letters reveal that his mother was taking in lodgers to help make ends meet. In her letters to Jack, she would expound on life at home, on relations with friends and with lodgers, and Jack would reply with his own opinions. Two recurring themes are the intermittency of work for men at home and the health of young women (Annie included, for she was often 'poorly' and may indeed have had 'the worrums'). Jack regularly sent his 'hope' that Annie or Peggie or Sarah would soon be feeling well, and that Sam or someone else might get work again. These sorts of comments put another complexion on Jack's sense of home and family altogether.

Benson cut them from the letters he published, though he did tell readers there had been three other Kirkpatrick children who had died of scarlet fever: 'She had lost three boys with scarlet fever and had a dread of losing him'.[28]

When Benson wanted to sum up Jack's personality he said 'Durham men can be dour but no portrait of Jack would be true to life without a sense of his ready wit, gaiety of heart and infectious cheerfulness'.[29] There are times when one letter or another suggests these characteristics, and Benson's selections are skewed in their favour. He wanted to hide the more substantial and complex personality, to conceal an insistent, sometimes wilful and fiery temperament, a man whose letters are as bossy and belligerent in some parts as they are loving or playful and teasing in others. In so doing he omits evidence about frictions at home and the circumstances of family and neighbourhood that might have helped to explain Jack's contempt for a 'Lousebound' England. Perhaps all this was also evidence about the source of Jack's raw courage, something Australians had pondered for half a century. Benson preferred the light banter of some letters to the hard words of others, the hints of homesickness to clues about poverty, the fond thoughts of family to the bossy advice Jack would occasionally dish out to his mother, and the hints of misogyny in his threatening references to other women in South Shields.

Benson would intervene whenever Jack got heated. He didn't like the signs of a short fuse, the sting of a pugnacious temperament. Jack had grown up near the Tyneside dockyards in a depressed coalmining region that was periodically seized with strikes—big strikes on the docks, in the pits, on the rail or in the engineering shops.[30] His mates were miners' sons, ironworkers' boys and lads like himself whose fathers were at sea, or dead. He left school when he was eleven or twelve and was at sea himself at seventeen. It should not have been hard to accept the idea that neither Jack nor his mother minced words. During the war she wrote to him in Egypt to tell him about the Pork Shop man who'd been caught sending carrier pigeons to Germany. She said hanging was too good for 'naturalised British subjects' who did things like that. 'They should be roasted alive to make an example of them.'[31] Jack followed up with a letter lamenting the German attacks on England and the suffering of 'womenfolk and kids at home'. He thought 'it would not be so bad if they dropped a bomb or two on some of those chaps at home that won't volunteer'.[32]

We can assume there was nothing genteel about the Kirkpatrick banter. It was hard language which was sometimes deadly literal and sometimes ironic. One other thing was certain: theirs was not the sort of language that Benson was going to reproduce:

> I am glad you and Peggie are getting on allright [wrote Jack] and hope it will last and if Peggie gives you any lip give her a thick ear to be going on with till I get home, and mother don't let your temper get the better of you or I will tell Peggie to give the same to you till I arrive.[33]

Jack was not how Benson wanted him. He was full of rough talk, and Peggie got the brunt of it a number of times. 'If I was to get a wife like her', he told his mother, 'I would be getting hanged inside a year.' And there was a warning:

> She would not have a good word to say about you even if you gave her your all, and as regards her talking about you you can tell her that I will wring her neck if I get home before she gets away.[34]

Benson used another letter, one that was written soon after Jack's departure from England. He allowed Jack to report on his movements and to commiserate with Annie on the loss of her job—a significant event for a family whose breadwinner was barely tried in his new occupation—but he cut a handful of lines from the middle section. They seem harmless enough, though they may be a reminder that young men leave home for many reasons apart from having a cliché (the sea) in their blood. Soon after his departure Jack had received a letter from the luckless Peggie:

> Pegg tells me she has never seen you in a bad temper since I went away. Now that is what I call a good change. Now tell Sarah I received her letter allright and I am glad that you are keeping allright and sorry that she is not getting plenty of [word] at work and tell her that I hope Sam is working and fetching her plenty of quids.[35]

Jack had left home in a hurry, just two days after his father was buried. Another deletion reveals his mother was in a terrible state when he went, not wanting him to go and wracked with worry. Jack left so fast he did not even say goodbye to Annie, though he wrote from Genoa to apologise and blamed the ship's strict schedule. He wrote to his mother, too, telling her she had no need to worry now for he was as happy as could be, 'and I don't see why you shouldn't be the same'. To avoid these frictions Benson cut out the last one and a half pages of a three and a half page letter, and then linked up the first part with the final lines of a postscript.

The uncut letters also show that Jack was a hard judge who routinely found fault. A letter dated November 1910 mentioned a South Shields couple he was lodging with at Corrimal. They had sold up and were going home to England, he tells his mother, 'but I am not sorry for she was full of slacking and tales she is a proper gossip she will very likely to [*sic*] call on you when she gets to Shields again full of gossip as usual but you want to give her the cold shoulder'.[36] And when he meets up with a Tyneside man in Melbourne, another who will probably call on his mother when he gets home, it is a similar story:

> He is a hell of a liar for he told me he was 2nd engineer in the old Southmoor with my father then he said he had served his time to be a blacksmith and now he is going to sea as a donkeyman. Now he was telling me his oldest son is second engineer on one of the home boats and that his youngest son was apprentice at sea and had two years of his time in he must have thought that I had been out here ten years instead of two and did not know his sons he is a bigger liar than Tom Pepper.[37]

It is not clear if these remarks were Jack's idea of casual gossip or if they were considered warnings. If it was the latter, then who was Jack trying to protect—himself or his mother? What is more certain is the way they fit into Jack's wider commentary, into the dismissive and judgemental thread that runs right through his correspondence. This could be coincidence. If another fifty letters surfaced there might be new threads and a different pattern. But it does fit with Jack's grim memories of home, with the gossip and spleen that was part of cheek by jowl life in South Shields, and with the experience that led to his rejection of 'lousebound' England.[38]

The irony is that the letters in full do reveal that Jack was, in his own way, a devoted son, something Benson emphasised by means of censorship and the rendering of Jack into a pleasant lad. The letters in full make the point by a more faithful route. It is in the cuts, for example, that we find a lad who is protective towards his mother and sister and sometimes fiercely clannish in the course of it. Jack's language is that of a protector and he deals stern words in response to news of troublemakers at home. One of the problems for Benson was that Jack was fiercest when speaking in defence of

Ashore in Melbourne: John Simpson Kirkpatrick (right) and fellow seamen, March 1912

Portrait postcards were a popular means of communication before the Great War. This one, post-stamped 2 March 1912, was addressed to Simpson's mother in South Shields and carried a brief message on the reverse side. Much later sister Annie marked the photo with a cross, to indicate her 'dear brother'.

his mother, the same mother he deserted so quickly once his father was dead. (Perhaps he could only love her at a distance?) That was when he talked of wringing necks and of thick ears. When his mother told him about bothersome lodgers he replied with words that Benson could not bear to publish:

> I see you have given Sam his marching orders just like his damn cheek trying to rule the roost he would not have done it if I had have been home I bet or it would not have been any fault of mine if it had not stopped. I also see that you have given Antonio his notice to 'Git', but then it was just like that pig to try and boss it when he got the chance. I wish I had only been at home I would have made the Russian Jew bugger dance a hornpipe on his ars but never mind better luck with the next lodger.[39]

More than once the young itinerant refers to the deprivation his mother has suffered, presumably in those years before he left England, when his father was bedridden after the working accident, and there was no compensation to be had. He takes a considerable interest in Lloyd George's Insurance Bill because it should help working people, but he is skeptical about that prospect: 'I expect it will be some of the ten thousand a year men that will get the benefit of that,' he tells Annie, on a picture-post letter from Melbourne. 'In the long run one thing that is sure it will not be the working people.'[40]

Benson wanted Jack to be bland and inoffensive, like his 'Pleasant Sunday Afternoon' radio programme. He wanted an even-tempered Jack, a Jack who had grown up in some agreeable setting, untroubled and unmoved by the world around him, a Jack who came from a make-believe family wherein there were no tensions and no spleen. Most of all he wanted a lad who was a good solid imperial patriot like himself. He chose his letters and excerpts accordingly. Did he never ponder the source of Jack's courage and compassion? Did it not occur to him that a 'pleasant' lad might not do what Jack would attempt in Shrapnel Gully?[41]

Jack was well aware that he and Annie meant the world to his mother, and his mother, in turn, meant a great deal to him. At times when he was homesick, he would playfully render her Scottish accent in phonetics: 'Ah weel wel hae tae mak the best oo it so dont forget to write pretty often'. In his postcards to Annie he routinely advised her to be a good daughter and hoped that others were also helping out. While still a fireman on the S.S. *Kooringa* which was plying the east coast of Australia, he again reminded Annie to be kind and suggested how much he missed their mother:

> So be good to her while you are at home for if you ever happen to be knocking about on your own then is the time that you will miss her.[42]

Jack and Annie were very close. She would write to him about her work, her health and about her boyfriends; about their mother, and about how much she missed him. Jack would reply in the language of the lads. Young women were killjoys or good sports, and Jack regarded Annie as a good sport because she could take what he dished out. She could laugh when Jack said 'Poor Bugger' and sent his 'deepest sympathy' to a friend who had got married. Once he wrote to his mother wondering how tall Annie had grown. He guessed she would be 'like all tall young "Women" of her age Long, Lean and Razerfaced, and all legs and wings but never mind things was never that bad but what they couldn't be worse'.[43] There was the joke about 'the worrums', and when he heard she had dumped her 'sailor boy' he wrote to her playfully, with some good advice:

> If you must have something in the watery line well then take my advice again and have a fireman. For they are a much quieter sort of an animal than the sailor and when properly tamed will feed from the hand of their keeper that is if she is a nice girl. But never mind kid I suppose that it is a bit of a change to have someone in the ironline.

Annie liked being 'the kid' to Jack. She had wanted to send him a watch, but he told her no. It was Egypt, 1915, and there were '99 chances out of 100 that I will not get it'.[44]

Several other family letters from Annie and his mother have survived from that period because Jack never got them. He was in transit at the time, and a little later he was dead. The letters were returned to the family with the rest of his belongings, the relics of a hero. Annie's last letters were like a devotional. She was so proud and so worried as well. 'Oh Jack [she wrote], we do pray for you to be spared a safe return to us . . . Oh to have you home again. "Home" will not be complete until you come back again'. Annie told him she and his mother both felt they had no right to be happy as long as he was in danger. 'I haven't entered a place of amusement since Christmas,' she wrote, on 24 May 1915. And in a postscript she

His younger sister, Annie

Once he wrote to his mother wondering how tall Annie had grown. He guessed she would be 'like all tall young "Women" of her age Long, Lean and Razerfaced, and all legs and wings . . . '.

Mrs Sarah Kirkpatrick
An undated photograph, probably taken after the war
His letters home routinely included a 'PO for a quid', or a 'PO for fifteen shillings',
made out to his mother, and occasionally a much bigger instalment. He seems to have
sent her a quarter to a third of his weekly wage over five years.

begged him to send just a few lines 'for Jack it would make your heart ache to see her waiting and watching for the post'.[45] Annie was wearing an elastic band around her hat in the colours of the 'Combined Australians', and a brooch made out of a medical corps badge. 'Of course you'll understand that I would wear anything that had any connection with you. I only wish you had sent me one of your buttons off your coat and I would have had a pin soldered onto it for between mother and I.'[46]

There was another test of Jack's devotion to his family, one that Benson rightly emphasised. Jack was committed to supporting his mother (and sister) as best he could, and he rarely failed. The letters home routinely included a 'PO for a quid', or a 'PO for fifteen shillings', made out to his mother, and occasionally a much bigger instalment. Although the record is not perfect, the amount seems to average out at a quarter to a third of his weekly wage over the five years he is writing. He was only a youth and he was a world away, yet he did not like to write unless he had something to send. 'But never you will not be dependent on any son in laws for anything if I can help it', he told his mother. That was a reference to the husband of his elder sister, Sarah, to whom he never wrote. Why Benson would cut that line out is not clear. Perhaps he did it in order to be consistent, as anything that smacked of friction had to go.[47]

When Jack went to war he made arrangements for his mother to draw fourteen shillings a week from his pay, through the Commonwealth Bank in London. That was a third of his soldier's wage. But word arrived that it was not available to her as Jack had opened the account in his own name, thinking at the time that he was going straight on to England, and only later finding instead that he was stuck in Egypt where the Commonwealth Bank had no branch. His letters from Egypt are somewhat preoccupied with the problem. He tells his mother he tried to get a loan from his colonel thinking he could send this on, but his colonel would not help. He has an officer write to Sir George Reid on his behalf 'to see about getting the money paid over to you', and he reminds his mother that he is now going under the name Jack Simpson and his pay, when the problem is sorted out, should be made over to Mrs Sarah Simpson. Benson approved of these efforts and so published some of them, but he did not like the change of name and so left that out, with no indication that a cut had been made.[48] Perhaps he did this because he had seen

Jack's birth certificate and suspected he was illegitimate, or he may have thought that taking the name Simpson, his mother's maiden name, signified a rejection of the father whom Jack never mentioned? It is impossible to say, but the latter would be consistent with Benson's censorship of all family tensions.[49]

The power of the legend

When Benson left South Shields, late in 1956, he and Annie were on the best of terms. A correspondence began that was to continue, intermittently, over eleven years. Benson was overjoyed at having found the letters. Annie was flushed with his promise of a book and his talk of friends in high places. They each believed in respectability, they expressed a mutual desire 'to walk humbly with God', they both loved Winston Churchill and a nice cup of tea. Annie wanted Jack to be remembered and she hoped to find a place in the legend for herself. Benson wanted all the help Annie could give. It seemed a good basis for collaboration.

Soon after his departure he wrote to her from the Howard Hotel in London, asking for family photos. She replied: 'I am so honoured to grant your request for the photos'.[50] Then he made the most extraordinary proposal. Benson asked for the precious letters, suggesting he could take them to Australia as a gift from Annie to the nation Jack loved. He could present them to his friend the Prime Minister, and Annie would get a personal letter from Sir Robert thanking her for the gift. Annie hesitated, but only for a moment. Then she packaged up Jack's letters with great care and according to Benson's instructions: first they were to go into tissue paper bags fastened with Sellotape; then they must be enclosed in a biscuit tin about 2 or 3 inches deep, also sealed with Sellotape. And they were to be registered at the post office.

Annie wrote separately. She had faith in the Royal Mail. Beyond that she would put her worry in his hands:

> You just do as you think best regarding their safety aboard ship. I know that you regard them as a sacred trust to you until you present them to your dear Prime Minister.

She reminded him of what a fine cup of tea her husband Adam made and signed off in a way that suggested the privilege of Benson's visit: 'I wish you God speed and a safe return to your beloved Australia and thank you again for giving us the honour of such a close friendship through my beloved brother'.[51]

Once home he began work on the book. He was reading war diaries at the War Memorial and was quite perplexed at conflicting reports about Jack 'but still expect a magnificent story to come out of it'. He told Annie the PM had been absorbed with the Suez crisis but was now advised of the gift of letters: 'He asked me to thank you in advance and to assure you that he will write and thank you on behalf of the Nation when my task is complete and I can hand the letters over to him'. Annie had to be patient because Benson's task would take almost a decade.

He visited England again, in 1961, but the flow of letters was not renewed until 1964 when he wrote to say the book was almost complete, and Annie replied, delighted and looking forward to the three copies that Benson had promised her. It was to be launched in Melbourne and Sydney to coincide with the 50th anniversary of the Gallipoli landing. Benson wondered if Annie was well enough to travel; perhaps he could arrange for her to visit Australia as a guest of the government on this great occasion. He could talk to his friend the Prime Minister about it. He had heard about the bleak weather in England. He told her about 'perfect sunshine and blue skies' in Melbourne.[52]

The invitation stirred Annie to great excitement. Her daughter would have to come—would that be all right? She went off to the photographers to have a portrait done, to send to Benson for advanced publicity. The black dress did not come out at all well, so she had another photo session in a brighter coloured outfit. She hoped the photos were to his liking. Then she went off to see her doctor and win his approval for the trip. The visit would make her very proud, she told Benson. She would bring Jack's medals and his identity disc and give them to Sir Robert herself:

> I had intended giving them to Sir Robert when he was here for dear Sir Winston Churchill's funeral but he was so busy and so far I haven't heard any further from the High Commissioner at Australia House.[53]

Benson was shocked. It seemed Annie had written to the PM, direct. She was going to hand over Jack's things herself, in his absence. Why had she not gone through him? He felt like a middleman cut out of the trade. He was compelled to point to her *faux pas*: 'I was a little surprised,' he told her, 'that you had written direct to Sir Robert during his crowded days in London re the disc and medals which we discussed carefully on my last visit.'[54] Benson knew the right way to go about it, for he had, he told her, 'specifically refrained from approaching Sir Robert on the matter until he had returned to Australia'. He wanted to know what she had said. He was quite upset. He dealt with the PM. The PM was his friend.[55]

What Benson failed to realise was that Sir Robert Menzies did not see things in quite the same light. Sir Robert had been sidestepping Benson's unctuous overtures for more than thirty years. Benson was always asking favours, offering gilded praise, recalling promises not kept, badgering for an autographed photo or a copy of a speech, and yearning to be seen at lunch with his dear Prime Minister: 'I am sorry that we have not been able to manage that lunch. It is now five years since we had a meal together!' Benson wrote, in 1952. Three years later he reminded Menzies that eight years had now passed and that lunch 'still awaits your leisure', and in 1967 he was begging for a mere 'twenty minutes' in Walmer Castle.[56]

Menzies treated his latest proposal—for Annie's visit—as he did most others that came from Benson without any significant political advantage attached.[57] The episode fits neatly into the evasive pattern. Early in March 1965 Benson had to tell Annie that he had written twice but heard nothing from Sir Robert. 'The dear man is so overwhelmed with affairs that mail banks up on him.' The Duke and Duchess of Gloucester had been invited but that, of course, was a visit of another order. A fortnight later he told her that hope was fading and he was a disappointed man. (He had in fact been unable to get past Sir Robert's secretary.) And then came the final answer: 'For some reason he is apprehensive about the strain and risk of your visiting Australia . . . However he has asked the High Commissioner to invite you to the celebration at Australia House [London] for the 25th April'.[58]

Annie was mortified. She took it as a slight. Why had this happened: 'Surely you would get a reason?' she asked him. Her disappointment bordered on despair at times; at others it flooded into anger. She had wanted to be there to honour her brother. 'I am very very hurt but will still hope at this late stage that something will happen to clear away the doubts.' And there was a dramatic note beneath her signature: 'P.S. cannot write more as I'm so very upset at this treatment'.[59]

Benson wrote back reminding Annie that there was a good reason—Adam had died late in 1964 and Annie's health had been poor ever since. At the time Benson had written to comfort her: 'I like to think of him spending Christmas in heaven', he said.[60] But the trip that might have lifted her from the doldrums never happened. The publishers, Hodder and Stoughton, sent her a copy of the book and she did go to Australia House for the Jubilee commemoration in London. But more than two years passed before she wrote again to Benson.

There were two sharp letters, one after the other, each revealing that a sourness had been stewing for a long time. Annie wanted her photographs back. She had not had a thank-you note from the Prime Minister which she had been so looking forward to. Why had they rejected her in 1965? That was still hurting. And why did he still have Jack's letters when he had promised to hand them over?[61] She heard he was doing more research, possibly a second book. She would have none of that. Her daughter would object, and her son, and she would too: 'So please DON'T and also PLEASE place those sacred letters in the Archives—as promised and return my possessions'. Annie said her letter would be duplicated and the copy sent to 'someone in Authority in Australia'. Her patience had run out.

Worst of all, the book itself had been a great disappointment. 'You did not stick to the truth,' she told him. There were devious and upsetting distortions in the book. In her second letter, five handwritten pages, Annie set them down. She had never given those letters to Benson outside Barclay's Bank. 'NEVER for a moment could I have visualised you would write such a FAIRY STORY—of how you received those letters', she told him. Their encounter outside the bank was a complete invention. And she had never handed the letters to him in the street: 'You made me appear a simpleton handing such sacred letters in an open street to a complete stranger. I trusted you and NEVER thought you would have written such a STORY'.

Annie's version of the handover was very different to the version Benson had published. She reminded him of the facts: he had arrived at her house with his niece, Marjorie. (Benson had also omitted to mention his travelling companion who was probably the Marjorie who became his second wife some years later.)[62] He had asked many questions and lamented that there were no letters. Annie had told him there were some letters and the following day she had been to Barclay's Bank to get them from the safe, whereupon she took them straight home. Benson and Marjorie had then spent two days at Annie's home, reading the letters, taking notes and supping on the hospitality: 'Don't you remember me taking a tray through into the front room for yourself and dear Marjorie? I certainly haven't forgotten'. Annie quoted his letters back at him, full of requests and effusive thanks. She had complied with his every wish. 'None of this was even hinted at in your book', she said. Not one word about her fruit cake; not a whiff from Adam's pot of tea. 'And I would like to add we did not request you to leave your Hotel to stay with us—as we were then living in a small two bedroomed Council house and could NOT have accommodated either yourself or Marjorie.'[63]

There seems to have been no doubt in Annie's mind that she was defending the important things that Benson had neglected: 'You did not stick to the truth,' she repeated. Yet other truths were missing, truths that did not concern her in the slightest. She never once touched on the truth in Jack's letters that Benson had obliterated altogether—about his politics, his temper, the strains within the family, the bitter memories of home. When Benson took away Jack's politics, all that was left was an apolitical itinerant who slogged for King and Country and who appeared to love his mother dearly, a conservative hero for a conservative legend. That suited Annie just fine. She did not object to the utter misrepresentation of Jack because appearances and respectability were important to her. In fact, in some respects, she wanted a more severe censorship than did Benson. She wanted Jack's mis-spelling corrected; she hoped Benson would delete the bit about Jack's change of name; she objected to any mention of the amounts Jack had sent home to his mother; she thought the Christmas Day brawl on the ship should be cut out, and she wanted no references to his swearing.

Benson obliged her by correcting the mis-spelling, but he would not concede the other requests. Jack's generosity to his mother was a key part of the story, while his change of name and his 'kerbstone English' were already part of folklore, so he argued. As for the Christmas Day brawl,

> I should be sorry indeed to cut this out because it reveals his fun and frolic and manliness. We must not make him look like a saint with a halo, because he was not . . . In my view they [the letters] make the man of the legend all the more human, manly and attractive . . . Please trust me because the total effect of the book will be to

make him more attractive and lovable than ever. And you are the heroine of the story . . . I softly whisper that the Queen [has] conferred a Knighthood on me.

The knight prevailed. Annie did not press these matters any further, though she continued to be most unhappy about the heroine she found in Benson's story.[64]

The forces that shaped Benson's version of Jack continued to be powerful after the author hurriedly handed over the letters to Prime Minister Holt in 1967—spurred on no doubt by Annie's talk of 'someone in Authority'. They have been in the War Memorial library in Canberra ever since. Journalists, historians, poets and playwrights have pored over them on many occasions. They have been perused every April as Anzac Day has drawn near, and frequently have been cited or quoted in books and newspapers. The best-known account based on the letters is to be found in Patsy Adam-Smith's *The Anzacs* where Simpson becomes part of the bush mythology of Australian nationalism, one of the 'boozers and brawlers and ships' deserters and blokes who hump their blueys'. The *Australian Dictionary of Biography* entry, as noted earlier, is merely a reiteration of the conservative myth. A recent play, *Simpson J. 202*, by Richard Beynon, managed to portray its subject as a lovable half-wit, although the author had read the letters. Anzac Day in 1990 gave rise, specifically, to a review of the letters by Petra Rees in the *Australian*, which revealed that Simpson was a bit of a larrikin, but censored the politics and invective of the letters completely.

None of these distortions was a case of what Bernard Crick has called 'the gentler question of the biases found in all history'. The late Sir Lewis Namier and Eric Hobsbawm gave rather different accounts of the past, but they did not consciously falsify.[65] Of the four examples cited, however, only Adam-Smith's account can match Benson's for pure craft: Adam-Smith had a special place for Simpson in her gallery of knock-abouts for he was one of 'those toughest, roughest of all men, the ships' firemen, shovelling coal with a bullocky's tongue [*sic*] . . . Jack Simpson was a *real* man'. A tongue used in that way must have been a diverting notion, but it can hardly excuse Adam-Smith's selective use of the letters. Simpson's class consciousness was ignored in preference for the barely disguised sexual appeal of the legendary itinerant. Not content with censorship, Adam-Smith claimed to have revealed the

Extract from a letter to his mother dated 5 August 1911

Jack wrote of England as a 'lousebound country', and he commiserated with Jack Fenwick who had got married: 'Poor Bugger tell him I am sorry to hear it'.

'*real* man' and denounced the 'official' version of Simpson as fictional. Her fiction was as complete as the official one, made worse by a trench of clichés and the zeugmatic figure of speech. In her preface she went further, claiming that the popular distortion of Simpson reminded her of the 'affected paintings in churches of St. Thérèse' which bore no resemblance to the real woman as revealed in the diaries held by the Vatican. Adam-Smith summoned up some indignation: 'None of your men who "walk down Piccadilly with a poppy or a lily" could have done what Simpson did. I was sick at heart at the proliferation of simpering words for schoolchildren about this delightful man's man'.[66]

It would appear that all subsequent accounts conform to the conservative limits, set by Benson and approved by Annie, as though a hypnotic spell has been at work. Again and again Simpson's allegiance to class, his vehemence and anger, have been erased, in favour of the simple tale centred on his alleged loyalty to mother, nation, empire and, in the last instance, to his manhood. In another context it is the kind of censorship that Benson would have branded 'Bolshevik'.

Benson's crusade

The question remains of how Benson could square such a violation of his texts with his professed aim to uncover 'the man behind the legend', or, for that matter, with his Christian principles? His disposition in this regard was probably set long before he encountered the letters, having its origins in his love of northern England and his identification with the physical landscape and social world of Simpson's childhood, for he too had grown up in northern England and his memories, unlike Simpson's, were fond ones. When Benson was researching Simpson's life he was also recovering his own childhood. This affinity with Simpson, and thus the furtive presence of autobiography, might have been strengthened by the loss of his two brothers in the war, and by some barely recognised need to merge something of himself into the Gallipoli hero's life. But the deep background is necessarily sketchy and tentative. A more tangible answer comes out of the connection between Benson's religious principles and his politics, which cannot be separated from the Cold War and his fear of Communism.

Benson had grown up with Kipling's jungle books beside his bed. In the post-war period, knowing the bard was out of fashion, he was fond of quoting T. S. Eliot in Kipling's defence. Like Menzies he loved the empire with a great fervour, believing it was the bearer of 'new visions of service and self-government'. Its coming apart saddened him, as he was still an advocate for colonialism in the 1960s, fond of quoting Cecil Rhodes, and denying that empire had anything to do with 'imperialism' because, he said, the only imperialists in the world were the Communists. For Benson the fight against Communism was paramount as its 'relentless aim is world domination'. Benson saw the democracies besieged by Russia whose objective was 'to convert our grandchildren into communists', and by China 'which sought war to finish the job' in his lifetime. Against such evil he advocated 'a crusading fervour for the things we believe', and it was here that the legend of the Man with the Donkey converged with the politics underpinned by his Christianity.[67]

Benson believed Australia needed Christian heroes to inspire the fight against Communism. Post-war prosperity had led to a 'drowsy apathy' and a 'reluctance to develop and defend this great heritage'. Everywhere he looked he saw indifference or hostility to the values that mattered to him and he believed Communism would thrive on this. He railed against what he called 'the flabby, easy-going Christians'. He saw himself amongst a small rearguard of leaner types whom he called 'The Saving Remnant' which was a reference to Isaiah's belief in a chosen few who would save the people of Israel, a 'loyal, dependable, clear-visioned minority . . . the seed of the future':

> When the race had lost its sense of direction—their hearts were fat, their ears [*sic*] heavy, their eyes shut—in such a time the prophet saw a small remnant that could be gathered amid the godless mass.

This small remnant would save the world from Communism. By way of analogy he expressed the view that less than one hundred people had produced the Renaissance in Europe.[68]

The Anzacs were also a saving remnant. What Benson espoused was a biblical version of the editorial line of the conservative press which argued that just as diggers had fought against tyranny in two world wars, so they would carry on that tradition in South East Asia.[69] He was finishing his book when conscription was reintroduced for the purpose of sending troops to Vietnam. Benson wrote and spoke about the Anzacs regularly, for they fitted neatly into the 'saving' tradition as he wanted it to be understood. They had turned military disaster into noble and meaningful defeat. When he likened them to martyrs, he also spoke of 'the spiritual affinity in the nearness of Good Friday to Anzac Day for the Crucifixion and the Resurrection speak to us of the success of failure'. The Anzacs had confronted what Benson referred to as 'the worst influences that had assailed civilisation', and they had prevailed in 'a baptism of blood that was to weld us into a nation'.[70] Their ordeal suggested the dignity and purpose that a defeat could bestow. They were moral exemplars the likes of whom could again renew the nation and save the world. From here it is hardly surprising that Benson singled out the Man with the Donkey whose image was rich with Christian associations, who had surely been 'loyal, dependable and clear-visioned' and whose work rate for the cause was second to none. Simpson, for Benson, was a free-world Stakhanov; the letters that spoke of slackness and unemployment must have chilled him to the bone.

Benson conjured up his own moral conception of heroism and went looking for an epic figure for the fight against Communism. What he found was someone who might well have ended up on the other side had he survived. Yet there is no evidence that Benson agonised as he wielded his censor's blue pencil. His political convictions and alignments were too firm. He and the legend had a higher calling in the fight against 'drowsy apathy' and Communism.

Chapter Two

'And Life is Perfected by Death'

I was a child and sickly in those years.
But I have read the histories,
have learnt the things I was too young to know.
I feel my memories
crystallizing into myth.

Bernard Bergonzi, *Reading the Thirties* (1978)

Soldiers' diaries are rarely compiled with historians' purposes in mind. The diarist is under no obligation to place his entries in context, to say whether they are his observations or those of someone else, or to be true to the calendar. The date of an entry is no sure sign of when the writing took place and what appears to be first-hand evidence may well be hearsay. 'The further personal written materials move from the form of the daily diary, the closer they approach to the figurative and the fictional.'[1]

These cautions are important if we are to understand how the legend of the Man with the Donkey began because we must distinguish genuinely contemporary accounts from those that merely look contemporary and, once the eyewitness record is established, we must weigh it against the later tales. For years after Simpson's death scores of men sought to secure a place in the legend with accounts of their own part in it, describing how they worked with him or saw him at work, watched him walking calmly among the bullets and wondered if his life were charmed, told him to take more care (to no avail), called him over for a cup of tea, or foraged rations for his donkey. There were a few who claimed to have taken a photograph of him, and some who said they had stood over his lifeless body, fashioned the cross, buried him, or watched others put flowers on his grave.

In the years that followed the war the tales told of Simpson often closed with the news of his death spreading among the soldiers, and the hush that set in that night as they realised their loss. In some accounts it is claimed that the entire peninsula fell silent as his death was mourned by all. The Indians, it was said, were so upset that they wailed and threw dirt on their heads, while some Anzacs risked their lives to gather flowers for his grave. One distant branch of the folklore suggests that even the Turks acknowledged him in their own dramatic way by shooting the sniper who had fired the fatal shot.[2] 'Poor fellow, every man on the Peninsula knew and mourned his loss,' wrote Sister Evelyn Davies in a letter to her mother from a hospital ship in the Mediterranean in January 1916.[3] The inference in all these accounts is that Simpson was a legend in his own time, a Gallipoli hero before he was a hero anywhere else, and that the sheer force of the military celebration carried the legend beyond Gallipoli to the civilian sphere and thence into the collective memory of the nation. The question, however, is whether the *contemporary* record supports this inference. We should not be surprised to find that the answer is no, for the Simpson legend is an allegory and, like all allegories, its accuracy is of less importance than the message that lies beneath the literal surface of the text.

A hero in his own time?

Many apparently first-hand accounts of Simpson at work have survived in the historical records. Most are preserved at the Australian War Memorial as part of the national collection of documents and relics relating to the deeds of the diggers. The collection is a record of the martyrs, a modern, secular, antipodean version of the *Acta Sanctorum*.[4] It seems to be rich with witnesses to the legend in the making, but a careful examination of these records reveals that only two are indisputable. The entry for 1 May 1915 in the War Diary of the 3rd Field Ambulance singles out seven men by name, the *last* of whom is Simpson:

The behaviour of the men in view of their rude introduction to the circumstances of war was splendid . . . No 202 Pte Simpson has shown initiation [*sic*] in using a donkey from the 26th to carry slightly wounded cases and has kept up his work from early morning till night every day since.[5]

The second authentic record is from a personal diary, the original, which shows no sign of rewriting or retrospective alterations. This is the diary of Sergeant J. E. McPhee of the 4th Field Ambulance, which mentions Simpson twice; the tenses are right and it has the ring of immediacy:

10 May: Re—Simpson—English name, called Scotty and speaks with thick brogue—doing great work—bringing wounded from trenches, dressing stations etc., on little donkey which he calls Murphy— Deserves VC. during the first push he brought couple of men from beyond the firing line. Works by himself.

Nine days later,

19 May: Poor old Scotty Simpson killed by machine-gun bullet in Shrapnel Gully *this morning* . . . Scotty Simpson will be much missed with his mates from Shrapnel Gully—his cheery face and droll ways known to a great many—particularly ambulance men. His unit was the 3rd Field Ambulance ('C' Section)—but he worked by himself and appeared to have a roving commission. His donkeys Murphy and Duffy were taken charge of by some of our 4th Field stretcher-bearers who happened to be near him when he fell. Buried in cemetery to right of Anzac Beach.[6]

Three other commentaries written soon after Simpson's death confirm McPhee's impression that soldiers noticed him and were impressed. Colonel Monash's commendation of 20 May was proof of Simpson's immediate impact, as was Padre Green's effort to get him a VC and the evidence taken by Simpson's commanding officer, Captain H. K. Fry, for the same purpose. Fry's note, dated 3 June, indicated his purpose and identified his witnesses: 'Saw ADMS re Simpson and Goldsmith (Simpson for VC). Adams, Sharples and Jeffries and Conrick to give evidence.' A second note, dated 14 June, stated: 'Adams and Sharples evidence (re-Simpson) in morning.'[7] What happened at the inquest is not known, but it did not result in a VC for Simpson. The extant record that predates the circulation of the legend in Australia, and therefore could not have been influenced by it, contains no proof that Simpson was singled out to any greater extent than other soldiers mentioned in dispatches or commended for their bravery, and it does not suggest that he was known beyond the immediate range of his operations.

Although Gallipoli was an isolated theatre of war, Anzac troops were spread out along an extremely rugged coastline: steep, clay-faced hills and sharp spurs covered with dense scrub and dwarf 'holly' which fell away in many places to precipitous sandy cliffs. The ravines and gullies around 'Anzac Cove' teemed with units from every State in Australia, and from New Zealand, but the terrain isolated the various units. A soldier's experience of Gallipoli could be largely the experience of his own unit and its localities. There were men who arrived with a brother or a mate and then did not see or hear of him for weeks. News of their good or bad fortune might take even longer:

> 24/7/15 . . . Had a visit from Bert Boordman. He told me that Bill Taylor was killed a few weeks ago, also that George Hill got a nasty wound in the chest. Everything very quiet.[8]

Familiarity with Simpson was also localised in this way. In his own time there was no reason why he would have been *widely* known beyond his immediate surrounds for, in one sense, what he did was not unusual: as chapter five will show, his feats of daring were equalled by many others, on many occasions, all over the peninsula. (Far from being a problem this typicality is one of the keys to the making of the legend.) *If Simpson was a hero in his own time his celebration was brief and extremely localised.* He might have been a local or Shrapnel Gully hero, but not a Gallipoli hero. Colonel Monash's 20 May commendation is quite accurate in this respect: 'Private Simpson and his little beast earned the admiration of everyone at the upper end of the valley'—that is, 'everyone' who could see him at work from the vantage points overlooking the gully.

Another close encounter would seem to defy these limits, for Private Victor Laidlaw of the 2nd Field Ambulance wrote about Simpson as though he were a household name:

> Got official news today of Major General Bridges death, he was CO of our whole division, regret felt all round. Another fatality I found out today was a private in the 1st Field Ambulance [*sic*], he had been working between the base and the firing line bringing down wounded on a donkey, he had done invaluable service to our cause.

Between journeys: Simpson pauses at a dressing station
Most photographs of the men who worked with donkeys were taken in similar circumstances—a leisurely moment at the end of a journey, usually close to a dressing station. This photograph was taken at the lower end of Shrapnel Gully. The soldier is not distressed; his wound appears to be slight.

One day he was bringing down a man from the trenches and coming down an incline he was shot right through the heart, it is regretted on all sides, as this chap was noticed by all, and everybody got to know him, one couldn't miss him as he used always to work with his donkey, cheerful and willing, this man goes to his death as a soldier. Heard officially that there is to be an armistice tomorrow.

Laidlaw was a Shrapnel Gully man who had been carrying water up the gully early in the campaign. When he said 'everybody got to know him' he can be speaking only of his own locality, and even in Shrapnel Gully it took him four days to find out the man was dead.[9] What is more, the available record is not the diary itself but a typescript of the diary, a remove that makes it impossible to know what the original said about Simpson, if anything.

This problem of rewritten diaries is highlighted by a rare instance where the original and the rewritten version are both available: the value of trooper Ion Idriess's testimony is much reduced once the two versions of his Gallipoli experience are examined carefully. As published, his diary entry for 22 May says: 'The infantry are quite cut up—not over their terrible losses, but because of one man, Simpson Kirkpatrick I think his name is.' But Idriess was sapping 'right up at Quinn's Post' at that time, and Quinn's Post was local—it held Shrapnel Gully in full view. Worse still this is Idriess in 1932. In the original diary, now held at the library of the Australian War Memorial, there is not one word about Simpson.[10] Idriess is the case that proves the point: the legend could influence men to alter their diaries, to colour their wartime jottings by adding information they learned later or by mentioning people who subsequently became famous, and even to use ploys, such as feigned uncertainty ('Simpson Kirkpatrick I think his name is'), for contemporary effect. Simpson was an embellishment that Idriess could not resist. He wrote himself larger, with the help of a national hero.

Another diary, an original, seems to be an eyewitness account of Simpson at work. Trooper A.S. Hutton's entry for 14 May reads:

> There is a fellow named Simpson in the 3rd Field Ambulance who walks among the bullets—he is said to have a charmed life.

Hutton's entry for 18 May, however, notes Simpson's death, an entry of unfortunate prescience considering that Simpson died on the 19th:

> Simpson is shot through the heart at last, about a dozen bullets through him.[11]

Trooper Hutton's entry for 14 May seems authentic if we consider just the words, as quoted above. But if the writing in the diary is examined it is clear that it was written some time later, squeezed into a tiny space next to the date, in unusually small handwriting, to ensure a fit. The boundaries of the new text are the original entries for 13 May and 14 May, an uncongested script characteristic of the whole diary. Hutton's only other mention of Simpson is his death, the entry dated 18 May, and that is also squeezed in, again in much smaller writing. The compressed script and the dating mistake are easily explained. Hutton decides *later* that Simpson deserves an entry or two; he has the story, but perhaps not the exact dates, so he returns to what might be the appropriate pages and makes the entries in the tiny spaces that are left. He might have done it next morning, several months later, or perhaps after the war. Since we cannot establish when, we cannot accept Hutton's report as a contemporary account.

Possibly the most hopeful, and thus most disappointing, record is the diary of Private J. H. Turnbull of the 8th Battalion. This contains a long entry for 19 May which mentions Simpson twice and includes what appears to be the only eyewitness account of his death to survive on paper:

> The stretcher bearers were busy in Shrapnel Gully. Many bearers and wounded were killed. There was one man called 'Simmie the Donkeyman' who was doing good work. He had a donkey with a red cross band tied across his forehead. He had one wounded on the donk & was helping another chap along with his arm around him. He returned with his donk singing and whistling along that awful shell swept gully. He was going backwards and forwards all night . . . At mid-day Simmie the Donkeyman was killed. He had a wounded man on his donk and was about to enter a sap leading over the ridge to the Dressing Stn. when a sniper on Dead Man's Ridge got him. We were watching him from our camp across the gully. He spun around and dropped. An Indian who was at a well near by rushed out and picked him up and carried him to shelter in the sap. But poor Simmie was gone.[12]

If these words were from a diary written on the spot, the report could be accepted as authentic and first-hand. Unfortunately, the diary as preserved is a rewritten version which includes pasted-in press cuttings about Simpson from the 1930s. The press cuttings make it clear that Private Turnbull was a fan, a follower of the legend. Whether he was faithful to his original record, whether, like

Idriess, he was influenced by the legend and used Simpson to embellish the diary, or whether there were innocent mistakes arising from the copyist's error of dittography (repetition) or haplography (eye skip), we cannot know. His account of Simpson's death might be authentic, but the rest—the Red Cross brassard, whistling and singing, working all night, supporting a second soldier on his shoulder—are all motifs that recur in the legend and therefore could have been learned from the legend. Put bluntly there is simply no telling as to whether Turnbull is doing an Idriess.[13]

An anonymous diary from the 1st Field Ambulance is another possibility. Its entry for 24 May reads: 'One man is doing splendid work with two of these wee donkeys bringing in wounded. Simpson of the Third Field Ambulance better known as Murphy. I saw him later shot dead'.[14] This is written five days after Simpson's death, yet his work is described in the present tense, as though it is still happening on 24 May and Simpson is still alive. Why should the tenses be in order everywhere in this diary except here? How close was this anonymous diarist to Simpson? Is it possible that he did not know Simpson was dead on the 24th, and that he added the last little sentence later, when someone filled him in on the death and its significance? We do not know, and the point is not to question the diarist's sincerity but to recognise that a diary's aura of immediacy can be deceptive. Such awareness is important here because it bears directly on the origins of the Simpson legend, on the process whereby one simple story among many becomes special. Even if these diary entries could be shown to be authentic, they would do no more than confirm Simpson's status as a local hero, one of numerous brave men whom soldiers chose to mention. In its telling and retelling the legend insists that its origins are military and that Simpson was a special kind of hero in his own time on Gallipoli. He was not.

There were soldiers over the ridge in Walker's Gully who had never heard of Simpson. His death was unnoticed by most men on Gallipoli and, had they known of it, it would have had no special meaning anyway. Bravery, like death, was everywhere. Diaries are packed with the names of brave men and their feats, terrible wounds and matter-of-fact accounts of death: 'Snowy Riddell was killed 4/5/15. Sgt Major Bowers on 7/5/15 (head blown off). Ditchburn was blown to pieces on the 5th with 5 others'.[15] Amongst the contemporary accounts, Simpson is just another name. Bill Gammage's study of Australian soldiers at war confirms this. He found no evidence for the proposition that Simpson was widely acclaimed in his own lifetime. Replies to a questionnaire, sent to surviving Gallipoli veterans in 1991, confirm this conclusion.[16]

Very few Gallipoli diaries or letters mention Simpson. Most of the diaries of men who were close by, some in Shrapnel Gully, in May, contain not a word about the man with the donkey. A New Zealand stretcher-bearer who worked with Simpson for five days made no mention of him at all. As well as a diary, this Kiwi carried a camera and was prone to take snaps when he could, but it never occurred to him to photograph Simpson and his donkey, though, looking back some twenty years later, he wished he had. By then the legend was in full flight and various photographs had enjoyed a moment of glory before the authenticity of their image was disputed, but this soldier withstood the temptation to claim one of them as his own. In a letter to the director of the Australian War Memorial, he spoke of the chance he had let go:

> Well Major, I would like to be able to say that I took a photo of Simpson and his donk, but although no one could disprove it if I said that I did, I will be honest and say that I did not.[17]

Victor Laidlaw, whose diary was quoted earlier, also had a camera, but there is nothing to suggest that he took a snap of Simpson. Another diarist was in charge of working parties in Shrapnel Gully from 17 May, two days before Simpson's death. His narrative, based on his diary, records many familiar experiences—the hard slog up and down the gully, lots of sniping, running round dangerous corners, dodging shrapnel, passing the cemetery near the main sap leading up the gully—all of which images were potential 'triggers' for association with, or narrative devices leading into, the Simpson story. There is not a word. This might seem surprising, but reflection will reveal it to be quite predictable: for the diarist like many others was running the same risks as Simpson.[18]

The multitude of published letters from the same period and in the same vicinity also fail to mention Simpson. Some tell of sniper dodging in Shrapnel Gully; one even discusses the most dangerous spots, the skill of the snipers and the numbers killed; there are letters that single out other soldiers for their good fortune or misfortune, but none mentions Simpson. Among contemporary records—the diaries on the spot at the right time and the letters that pre-date the legend—one is more likely to find mention of the wounding of General Birdwood, the sniping of General Bridges or the death of a certain Patterson, a soldier who seems to have caught the attention of a good few.[19]

Wilfred Doe wrote home to his family on 14 May 1915. He told them about his infected foot and how he had been brought down to the beach on the back of a donkey. 'You would have laughed to see me', he said. 'I had to ride a donkey not much bigger than a goat, I should have carried the donkey, not the donkey me, as my feet could touch the ground . . . ' A substantial portion of his brief letter is about the little beast, but there is not a word about the man who led it.[20] The official history of the New Zealand medical services in the Great War is also laden with donkeys, but it goes so far as to suggest that Simpson might not have existed. Its author, A. D. Carbery, has a fascinating passage about these serviceable creatures, yet he describes 'the famous donkey man Simpson' as 'possibly apocryphal'.[21]

The Australian press representative on the peninsula, C. E. W. Bean, contributed to the Simpson legend from the outset, but some of his claims are dubious. Bean told the Simpson tale to the reading public in a despatch dated 12 June. His opening lines invoked that part of the legend which claims that on Simpson's death the word spread far and wide:

> It was the evening after the Turkish attack of May 19 . . . Some of us were sitting yarning that evening while the sun set over the sea, turning the craters of Imbros into the dull grey of an elephant's hide set against a background of the most delicate rose—when someone passing said, "I suppose you have heard that the man with the donkeys is dead." It came as a real shock. Everybody knew the "man with the donkeys," and everybody knew that if ever a man deserved honor in this war it was he.[22]

'Everybody.' Bean relates the tale at length, singling out Simpson as the hero of the stretcher-bearers. The odd thing is that in his earlier dispatches, written between the evening of Simpson's death—the evening when he was sitting yarning—and 12 June, Bean does not mention Simpson at all. His dispatch dated 20 May, the day after the word allegedly spread so rapidly, includes a long passage on the work of the medical corps; this would seem an ideal opportunity, but there was nothing about Simpson. The same is true of his dispatch of 3 June, which described an attack on Quinn's Post, a spot near Simpson's beat.[23] The inescapable conclusion is that word of Simpson's death did not spread far and wide and that Bean used

literary artifice to give his story 'first hand' authority and, incident-
ally, to inflate Simpson's standing with the troops. Bean turned his
attention to Simpson not long after he declared in the *Commonwealth Gazette* that there would be times when military secrecy would
require him to deal with 'safe subjects quite apart from news'.[24]

The afterlife abroad

Bean's account of Simpson was one of the earliest published in the
Australian press. It appeared in the *West Australian* on 20 July, then
in other major dailies around Australia and in New Zealand. In
Melbourne it was printed in the *Age* on 24 July, barely more than two
months after Simpson's death, and just a week after the Melbourne
Argus had reproduced another story, this one lifted from a Maltese
newspaper, the English-language *Daily Malta Chronicle*. Purportedly
written by a wounded soldier who remained unnamed, the *Chronicle*
story appeared on 12 June. It was the first published account of
Simpson's deeds, the very earliest printed source of the legend, and
it concluded with the customary reference to Simpson's universal
acclaim on Gallipoli:

> Everybody knew Simmy and 'Barney' (the donkey) and when news
> of his death became known expressions of profoundest regret were
> heard from one end of the lines to the other. And many were the
> vows of vengeance sworn.[25]

The paragraph on 'Simmy' came at the end of a full-page article on
the storming of Gaba Tepe heights. Not all readers would have
waded through a full page of unbroken print to reach him, but the
Argus reproduced only the Simmy paragraph, this time under a new
title—'The Donkey Man. A Humble Hero'. Simpson had been
moved from the wings to centre stage and for the first time Mel-
burnians learned of his work at Gallipoli:

> All hours of the day or night whenever there was any fighting going
> on, Simmy, (with his little whip in his hand) and 'Barney' were to
> be found right in the thick of it. Simmy would lift the wounded man
> onto Barney's back, and if he couldn't sit there he'd tie him on, and
> with a 'Gee Barney' away they would go to the nearest dressing
> station. This went on day after day and night after night, and where
> you would see others running for their lives across dangerous spots,

Simmy and 'Barney' would walk calmly on as if they were going along some City thoroughfare in times of peace instead of travelling through a tornado of Shot and Shell.[26]

In the months that followed, the *Argus* published letters from soldiers about Simpson and then, in November, a letter from Simpson's mother, Sarah. A soldier had sent her an *Argus* press cutting, and her brief reply was published: 'Tell the Australians from me, his mother', she said, 'that my heart is bursting with sorrow, and with pride, to know that my beloved son and the light of my life, died with the brave Australians'.[27]

The *Sydney Morning Herald* also helped to launch the legend. One of its journalists was writing dispatches from a dugout at Shell Green, a spot to the south of Shrapnel Gully. He was Lieutenant Oliver Hogue who wrote under the pen-name 'Trooper Bluegum'. On 20 July the *Herald* ran his eulogy of Simpson, and on 26 July it ran a photograph of a man leading a donkey carrying a wounded soldier, though neither soldier was identified. 'Novel Way to Carry the Wounded', read the caption. Next, the *Herald* announced that a feature photograph of the man with the donkey would be appearing in its affiliate, the pictorial *Sydney Mail*.[28] The *Mail* was one of several papers, popular with the troops on Gallipoli, in which Simpson made numerous post-mortem appearances. One soldier has recorded his memory of having read about Simpson in a newspaper while he was on Gallipoli. No doubt many did, but this rare piece of evidence has the value of suggesting that, if Simpson's was one of many tales with some currency on Gallipoli, he was no *legend* there until after his tale had left the peninsula and returned in the form of headlines, high diction and feature photographs.[29] Only then did his story circulate *as legend* among the soldiers, and from this secure base it shot into a permanent orbit, with military and civilian cycles entwined, mediated or connected by correspondents and propagandists, and spread further by the chit chat of the convalescents who liked to read newspaper accounts of their own doings.[30]

Once established, these cycles acquired their own momentum and mythical power. Like everyone else, soldiers spoke of Simpson *through* the legend. He became an archetype, the product of previous writings, reminiscences or commemorative rituals; of interventions by correspondents and the creative fancy of the tale tellers. These mediations *were* the legend; they were what Simpson became. Simpson talk, from the trenches to the classroom or the pulpit, was mostly a repeat, a variation or a refinement. The real man was eclipsed by the tales, by the image and by the associations that accompanied this process. It is remarkable how quickly the tales acquired their civilian dimension, how persistent they became, how they began to appear in other places such as school texts or sermons, and in other forms, such as poetry, bronze and film in 1916, in soldiers' published memoirs, and in the form of photo-lithographic prints which sold in large numbers in England, Australia and New Zealand in 1918.[31]

Many of Australia's heroes were mentioned in the press once, perhaps twice, but none of these were picked up and sustained by repetition, or embellished and transmuted into other forms. In the seven months between Simpson's death and the evacuation of Gallipoli, his story was retold in newspapers around the country. And it went on being told: press coverage was the legend's motive power. Correspondents talked to the wounded about Simpson in hospitals as far apart as Epsom in England, Valetta in Malta, and Randwick near Sydney.[32] The Australian press, alerted in many cases by Bean's authoritative dispatch, was quick to annexe their accounts and pursue new ones. In its enthusiasm, the Sydney *Sunday Times* inadvertently revealed the gathering momentum: 'The story of the devotion of the pair—man and animal—came through several times before it was first announced . . . that Murphy was a donkey!'[33] Soldiers read about him and responded to the newspapers with their own thoughts. In October the Sydney *Sun* ran the story as told by Albert Currie, a wounded stretcher-bearer then recuperating at the Epsom Hospital in Surrey. Currie said that he had told the story to the *Epsom Times*. The *Sun* ran it again, under the title 'Men Held Spellbound'.[34] The next day there was more Simpson. The *Sun* ran a sizeable photograph of a man with a donkey at work in Shrapnel Gully. The photograph was from London's *Daily Mirror*. '"Murphy" brings home one of the Boys', ran the caption. It appeared along-side a full column article on 'Our Wounded Heroes: Army Medical Corps and Red Cross. Great Silent Service'.[35]

The *Sydney Mail* ran the Simpson story as a sort of serial which followed the earlier 'instalments' in the affiliate *Herald*. The same photograph that the *Herald* ran in July appeared in the *Mail* as a feature photograph on 29 September, but by late September the legend had done its work. Many newspapers had already carried tributes and tales of Simpson. The caption was bold and sure:

A legend on the silver screen

The film Murphy of Anzac was one of Fraser Films' last gasps before it passed into liquidation due to powerful rivals and the economic difficulties produced by the war. One reviewer in Theatre Magazine *(1 June 1916) wrote that 'the returned soldiers who "acted" in this film probably had a good time. I'm sorry I can't say that I had the same'. He praised the actor who played Simpson, but was appalled at the casting of 'the most ridiculous villain that ever smoked a cigarette'. The film has not survived.*

"Murphy." Who has not heard of Murphy?

asked the *Mail*, confident of the reply, but not so confident that it failed to retell his story in small print beneath the caption.[36] Early in November the same paper followed up with a long account of Simpson, 'the true story of one of the noblest heroes of Gallipoli', written by Private J. J. Fraser, a 3rd Field Ambulance compatriate. The preamble mentioned that there was considerable conflict as to who Simpson really was, and as to his real name. Was it really 'Murphy'? Had they got the man mixed up with the donkey? Private J. J. Fraser would clear all this up.

There is no doubt that Fraser knew Simpson since he had landed in the same boat and laboured over the same terrain. An official report, dated 19 May, indicates that Fraser was wounded at the spot where Simpson was killed, and on the same morning. Fraser was a genuine acquaintance; he knew the work that the man with the donkey was doing, yet he made it clear that Simpson had no special standing during his own life:

> He was not exactly an idol, nor did we look on him then as anything of a hero. He was just—well, just Simpson, our Simpson, stretcher-bearer of C Section, 3rd Field Ambulance.

The reminiscence emphasised Simpson's good humour and antics as much as his bravery. Fraser remembered him especially for his entertaining ways on board ship. At more than two thousand words, his account filled a page and a half of text, but not all readers were satisfied. On 24 November the *Mail* referred to the mystery as continuing, and this time said that the man was known to his comrades by many names, including 'Murphy, Simpson, Simmy, Scotty, etc.' It concluded that the real name was John Simpson Kirkpatrick and it reproduced the letter that Captain H. K. Fry had written to Simpson's sister about her brother's death and the heroic work that led to it.[37]

Subsequent letters to the *Mail*—at least those that were published—suggest that readers were picking up snippets of information about Simpson from various newspapers and were puzzled by their inconsistencies. One of them claimed that Simpson's real name was Latimer and that, according to a 2nd Field Ambulance man, he was an Irish-Scotsman who had worked at the Alfred Hospital in Melbourne, and then at 'the Asylum', before enlisting in the 2nd Field Ambulance. More photos followed of the man and of a donkey called 'Duffy No.1'. These were challenged too. There was a letter from a hospital in Egypt complaining that the *Mail* had got the identity of the man and the donkey wrong. This particular donkey was not born until after the death of Simpson; it was a very young donkey, as the photo clearly showed. The correspondent claimed to be part of the group that had put the Red Cross brassard around its head and named it 'the Lemnos donk', adopting it as a sort of mascot. As for the man—he was not Simpson, he was a mate who was rarely seen with donkeys.[38]

The *Mail*, along with many other papers, laid such a lively trail that one suspects a deliberate policy to promote the story. It was the loyal newspapers of the empire that ensured that the Simpson story became a national and imperial legend. The creative process whereby, in Elizabeth Barrett Browning's words, 'Life is perfected by Death', began in Malta, was picked up in England, figured at least once in the Indian press, and came to Australia where it circulated widely, an indication of its symbolic power and its political utility. In Australia the spread of the legend was helped by the informal folkloric elements of culture: soldiers and civilians were keen to make a contribution to the story or to sort out its confusions. Although the legend was orchestrated by politically motivated imperial patriots, it was not a purely political invention for the success of a tale like Simpson's depended on its power to reach into the culture and collective experiences, on its relevance to the ordeal of the war and on the necessity of living with its memories.[39]

Long after the war Lieutenant General Sir Stanley Savage recalled his battalion going ashore at Gallipoli and hearing the story of the man with the donkey. He and his troops went ashore in September (1915), so some in the battalion almost certainly knew the story *before* they landed; they thus took it *to* Gallipoli and perhaps told their own version to soldiers already there.[40] We then have the paradox of second division men talking of Simpson to curious 'veterans' of the first division or, alternatively, bearing the brunt of the 'real' story which, according to first division men, they could not possibly know because they were not there. Late in the campaign Private Andy Carnahan wrote home to his family in New Zealand:

> The stretcher-bearers have perhaps the hardest duty of anyone in the service . . . I have seen them coming over the ridges and along the tracks continually swept with schrapnel and rifle bullets; one reads of individual acts of this nature earning VCs in Europe . . .

> A young Australian took possession of a transport donkey
> and travelled back and forward to the firing line night and
> day . . . killed while making a trip; he used to bring in the wounded
> that were conscious enough to sit on the "donk". The little donkey
> is still with us with his red cross brassard tied across his head. The
> Australians are going to take him home he certainly deserves a good
> pension.[41]

Despite its vitality, immediacy and detail, the account contains
nothing that proves this soldier ever saw the man with the donkey.
What Carnahan says is that he saw stretcher-bearers, and it is not
even clear whether these were Australians or New Zealanders. He
goes on to retell the Simpson story as he might have heard it or read
it, and then mentions a little donkey which is supposed to have been
Simpson's. Carnahan's testimony might be an eyewitness account,
or it might be the legend talking. One senses the simple tale
slipping into the realm of folklore at this early stage, as the soldiers
read about him and talked about him, as photographs of a man with
a donkey began to circulate among them on Gallipoli and in the
hospitals, and as the popular imagination set about interacting
with the accretions of myth coming out of the press and further
embroidering a humble tale.[42]

Benson wrote that Simpson 'had been so much a part of Peninsula life that it was hard [for soldiers] to realize that he had gone',
but that was in the 1960s when Australians had a governor-general
(R. G. Casey) who had been on Gallipoli in 1915 and who also
claimed to have seen Simpson at work. Casey had his own swag of
Simpson tales, including one about him and Simpson being present
when General Bridges was mortally wounded. Casey and Benson
were at the far end of a long line of claims, begun well before the
war was over, which included stories about Indian soldiers
who called Simpson 'Bahadur' (bravest of the brave) and about
Australians who risked life and limb regularly to gather flowers for
his grave; stories that came later and could never be authenticated.[43]
In 1917 the *Argus* reckoned that 'Every Australian at the Anzac
landing knew "the Man With The Donkey" and when he died . . . his
last resting place was pointed out to newcomers with a thrill of
admiration'.[44] In England, where Simpson's mother and sister had
already been invited to the first Anzac Day commemoration at
Westminster Abbey in 1916, the first issue of a sixpenny newspaper
for convalescing diggers carried an account of the man with the

donkey that alluded to the spread of Simpson talk and in a way endorsed it by pointing to the cross-currents that are characteristic of folklore:

> It is said by some that Simpson was not so crazy about rushing to join up . . . and that his girl chided him for his slowness. However that may be, Simpson was away with the first contingent, and was among the first crowd ashore at Anzac.[45]

Although there is no evidence that Simpson ever had a 'girl', the implication in this account was clear: one could always make up for a slow start. Ditherers, prevaricators or 'cold-footers' could regain their honour by enlisting.

E. C. Buley's *Glorious Deeds of the Australasians in the Great War* is another case of the tales confusing, or being enlisted to confuse, the origins of the legend. Buley's book was based on hundreds of interviews with wounded soldiers which he conducted in London while the Gallipoli campaign was still in progress. The first edition was published in October 1915 and it was in its third edition by December—an instance of the extraordinary speed at which the Anzac legend was formulated and spread in hard cover. The book was immediately adopted as a school text in Victoria, as was Buley's *Child's History of Anzac* in 1916. Other States followed Victoria's example by teaching straight from the books or using extracts published in their respective *School Papers*. In his Preface to *Glorious Deeds*, Buley wrote that he would resist the temptation to identify the doers of the many deeds of remarkable bravery he had encountered in conversation, but that there would be one exception: Simpson. As Buley put it, 'No Australasian ever speaks of him without saying, "He earned the VC. a dozen times"'. Possibly some soldiers did say something like that to Buley; possibly he was doing his own embroidering. Either way, the Simpson legend was growing apace.[46]

Whatever the accuracy of Buley's account of his sources, Simpson had clearly become a talking point among participants, including some who could not possibly have seen the man at work. Sister Evelyn Davies from the hospital ship *Oxfordshire*, in Mudros Harbour, wrote to her mother in January 1916. In the course of a five-page, handwritten letter, Simpson enters the text in the midst of a passage on mateship:

> The saddest part of all is to hear men talk about their mates who have fallen. I didn't think men became fond of each other as they

really do, they are fine even the roughest of them . . . You heard of the man named Simpson belonging to the Field Ambulance. He did such excellent work rescuing the wounded under fire with the aid of a donkey, Mum he was a 'White Man' as the Boys say, ' he worked night and day going from the firing line down to the Beach taking two patients sometimes on the Donkey and perhaps supporting two or three others he wouldn't pause even for meals the men would try and get him to take tea he would take a few sips and then get back to work, he worked two Donkeys resting them alternately and seemed to have a charmed life and did most daring deeds and was known as 'The Man with the Donkey' however he at last was killed by a sniper, poor fellow every man on the Peninsula knew and mourned his loss. His grave was decorated beautifully and a cross erected inscribed with 'The Man with the Donkey' and 'Greater love hath no man than this etc'. He was one of the many Heroes who deserve but do not get Victoria Cross.

We do not know how Sister Davies learned about Simpson. It is possible that she picked up the tale from wounded soldiers, she may have read about him in a newspaper, or heard about him through the Red Cross, or perhaps she had acquired one of the photographs of Simpson that were circulating in the Middle East.[47] She shared the tale with her mother who may already have known it: 'You heard of the man named Simpson . . . ,' writes Miss Davies, suggesting either that her mother has already mentioned Simpson in an earlier correspondence, or that Davies thought it likely that she already knew. Either way, the letter is evidence that stories about Simpson were already in wide circulation. The content of Davies' version indicates the same thing. Her tale conforms to the 'essential Simpson' which, by January 1916, has already been repeated many times over: that he worked incredibly hard and fearlessly amidst hundreds, sometimes thousands, of wounded men; that he would not pause for meals; that he led a charmed life; and that he was killed. The story takes on a twist of its own when Sister Davies describes soldiers forcing a cup of tea on Simpson (perhaps that is what she would have done), but then it returns to the accepted pattern, with the image of 'every man on the Peninsula' mourning his death.

The traditional assumption has been that the legend spread by a sort of natural progression from Gallipoli, where Simpson is a legend in his own time, to Australia and then to the empire and the

Lemnos, 1915: Sister Evelyn Davies (AANS) on a donkey

A letter from Sister Davies to her mother, dated January 1916, mentions the Man with the Donkey. Her version of the legend suggests that tales of Simpson were already circulating on hospital ships and in other convalescent zones around the Mediterranean. She repeated the main themes of the legend, including the erroneous idea that he was a hero in his own time on Gallipoli. In her view Simpson was 'a White Man'.

world. But as the examination of Gallipoli texts and the loyal press has shown, this was not how the legend originated. It was a civilian legend, and to miss this fact is to miss the real significance of its making. The problem now posed is how to make sense of the Simpson legend in its own time—in the circumstances of the war and its aftermath. It is the problem of interpreting the legend historically, of trying to grasp the social and political context of its commemoration, of reading the symbol as it merges into national and imperial culture, and thus into History.

Chapter Three

An Instrument of Imperial Purpose

Not as one fallen in battle shall I die.
I feared the battle and shall die ingloriously
O my friend, he who falls in battle is blessed.

From the Gilgamesh epic

The idea of national character, however false or flawed, has been a powerful force in Australia's history. In the Great War imperial patriots could not have done without it. They represented the conflict as a chance for Australia to prove itself by confirming the superiority of the British race and showing that the colonial fighting man was at the forefront of race evolution. This outlook dominated the daily news. The fierceness of Australian soldiers acquired mythic proportions in the reports of the first battles at Gallipoli, and from there the heroic myth grew as it followed the troops to France and Palestine, concentrating on 'the thrill of battle, rather than the terror of the fight' and changing 'the unpleasant particulars of modern combat into the epic model of national achievement', the adventure, that we have since called the Anzac legend.[1]

The editorial exponents of this point of view said the 'baptism of fire' at Gallipoli marked the nation's coming of age and made for a glorious opening to its new responsibility as an adult member of the British family of nations. Within a year the date of the landing would be marked as an annual day of remembrance just after Easter—a meaningful proximity for the imperial patriots—and just as sacred.

When C. E. W. Bean wrote his official history of the Gallipoli campaign, his two volumes were organised accordingly. Volume One was devoted to the preparations for war, to the first day and the first month of a seven-month campaign. Volume Two dealt swiftly with the rest. It was the beginning that mattered for, as anthropologists have suggested, mythology is typically obsessed with origins.[2] Bean's emphasis confirmed the belief that the first weeks of battle were the most important time of the war, Simpson's time. His military career, from his enlistment in Perth to his death in Shrapnel Gully, marked the outer limits of the so-called 'national beginning': the ordeal of fire, the proving and its recognition at home. For the making of an Australian hero, Simpson's basic credentials seemed perfect: he was quick to volunteer, he took part in the landing on 25 April, he was in the thick of the action, and he was dead—a fundamental requirement for martyrs—within a month.[3]

Reading about his heroic deeds it is easy to forget that Simpson's greatest role was on the home front, where the conscription controversy began to unfold in mid-1915 soon after his death; he was never so busy as in his afterlife. Australia was the only combatant nation that did not have compulsory enlistment or conscription. It was the only country to reject it by referendum, and it did so twice, in 1916 and 1917, and each occasion was fiercely contested against a background of declining enthusiasm for the war and a continuing shortage of recruits. The legend of the Man with the Donkey unfolded as the bitter conflict over conscription got under way, at a time when the immediate past was an immensely rich field to draw upon; scarcely had Gallipoli slipped from the present when it was recast as the great blood sacrifice, the dawning of true nationhood. The Anzac legend played a part in lifting the morale of Australian soldiers, many of whom died living up to it in battle but, on the home front, Anzac was a political weapon, a heroic example directed at the men who *were not* in uniform.

Newspaper readers could have been forgiven for thinking that Australian soldiers were responsible for just about every allied victory they took part in; but when these readers scanned the death lists or followed the barely perceptible movements of the battle fronts, they must have wondered what victory meant. By mid-1915 the big problem facing the central committee of the imperial patriots—otherwise known as the Australian government—was the lack of recruits for a war that was not going well. As the imperial demand for colonial troops grew more insistent, censorship became an important instrument in the recruiting campaign. The Commonwealth Censor's Department, previously concerned with keeping military secrets secret, now acquired the additional task of a watchdog protecting government policy, promoting recruitment (and then conscription), and stifling critical comment.[4] This transformation was made easier by an overlap in personnel, for the senior ranks of the Department in each State were to be closely associated with recruiting drives and the conscription campaign. The new brief conforms to Orwell's description of political language as being 'designed to make lies sound truthful and murder respectable, and to give an appearance of solidity to pure wind'.[5] The irony was that a symbol of compassion and deliverance became part of this calculated exercise in word control, that an apparently innocent tale was harnessed to the juggernaut.

From mid-1915 onwards official censors, like-minded editors and correspondents took more care with their words. References to the incidence of small pox, meningitis and venereal disease in the armed forces were suppressed; newspapers were required to refrain from publishing war pictures of 'a gruesome character [as] such pictures would tend to prejudice recruiting'. Even photo portraits of men who had been killed or wounded would soon be discouraged. Correspondents had commonly falsified dispatches to disguise military strategy, but now they routinely distorted events in order to maintain optimism. (Field censors, chaplains included, did the same with soldiers' letters.) The misery of a disastrous attack was transformed when readers were told it was 'incompletely successful'; futility beyond any human scale of measurement was ignored when heavy losses were justified with the headline: 'But Not a Foot was Yielded'.[6] When the controversial English correspondent Ellis Ashmead Bartlett announced a lecture tour of Australia in 1916, he was allowed to proceed only after his speech had been judged likely to create recruits.[7]

The epic formula

Once these limits were in place what remained was a blinkered coverage of war that worked to a simple epic formula. In the words ascribed to a wounded soldier trapped in its spell: 'War is hell, but it is splendid'.[8] This was the message coming out of the 'print

circus'—the editorials, letters, leads, photographs, even advertisements, that made up the political line, the case for enlistment or
coercion. To go to war was the true test of character; to risk death
for the empire was the ultimate rite of manhood. *It was meant to be
an ordeal.* 'Terrible losses', 'ghastly wounds' and 'shocking sights'
were the nub of the test. So were 'tremendous fusillades', 'continu-
ous tempests', 'fearless charges' and 'impulsive dashes'. Abstract
adjectives dealt with the horrors, romantic turns of phrase covered
the action, many of them drawn from the language of 'boys-own'
literature and of nineteenth century pseudo-medieval romance. For
males of fighting age there was no escaping the choice on offer:
honour or shame, glory or ostracism. The newspapers that spoke for
the imperial patriots rang loud with this choice, in the new, clipped
language that disguised the real war as a chance for sissies to be
transformed and boys to become men. It was similar to the choice
that Shakespeare's *Henry V* posed at the siege of Harfleur: 'He that
hath no stomach to this fight,/Let him depart . . . /We would not
die in that man's company/That fears his fellowship to die with us'.[9]

In October 1915 the *Argus* told the tale of one 'Jim' (otherwise
unnamed) of the 14th Battalion, a rather transparent allegory but
important because it had all the ingredients of the epic formula. Jim
had been a shop assistant in a '*soft* goods' store, a fellow who wore
fine clothes, travelled first class on the train, was always home on
time, had a mother to care for his linen and a sister to feed him
breakfast and shine his shoes. When he enlisted he was partly
transformed in training camps at Broadmeadows and in Egypt, and
the transition to manhood was completed in battle at Gallipoli:

> When a door slammed on a Sunday Jim used to jump with a start,
> and perhaps contract a nervous headache, but shrapnel shells [now]
> rained pellets about him, high explosives caused the air to smack his
> chest and guns boomed everywhere, and he took no notice.

Jim went without sleep, endured a 'torturing thirst', ate biscuits that
were 'harder than his teeth', and all without complaint, because the
men about him did the same. 'He was beginning to develop wonderfully.' He bathed in the midst of shellfire, went after fish with a
bomb, stopped shaving, became skilled in the care of firearms,
strolled about half naked, got a suntan 'as brown as that of a
Chinese', acquired such skill with his bayonet that he could put it
to a dozen different uses, and became a model for newly arrived
troops. Perhaps most important of all, he joined the collectivity of

heroes by teaming up with an artist, a drover and a miner, the social range of these comrades presumably completing his 'development'.[10] Not a word about shirking and yet the story from beginning to end is about wimpishness and the disgrace of not going to war.

This connection was frequently more explicit, as in the headline 'Australians in Action. Soldiers' Thrilling Letters. A Knock for the Loafers'.[11] In 1915 it was still easy to find soldiers who would pen such letters for the press. One wrote to the *Sydney Morning Herald* to say how frightful the war was and how he hoped never to see its like again, but he added: 'Our boys have been simply marvellous and I am proud to be wearing the Australian uniform. I would not be one of the shirkers over there [Australia] for all the tea in China'. Another soldier told of how he had been among the first into battle: 'First come, first served—and take it from me it was served to our boys in bulk, for they got it hot and strong; but they took it smiling'. Before the battle he had been reading a weekly newspaper in which he saw pictures of 'big good-for-nothing loafers lounging about yapping to girls'. He and his comrades laughed about their 'brave brothers in Melbourne streets' and agreed that 'they should be sent to us in bags, to make cover for we who are willing to fight'.

A correspondent for the *Argus* also managed to set shirking against the passage to manhood on the battlefield. He claimed to have gone searching for a frightened man, before a charge, and told readers that he had found none. 'No one feels afraid before battle', he wrote. One pale-faced lad, quietly reading a letter, seemed to be a possibility, but the correspondent found that he was upset with news of his mates' weekend camping expeditions near Melbourne. 'They're wanted so bad here!' said the lad. Then he went into battle and the dispatch concluded with a striking image of his transformation, an image of the soldier preparing to kill again: 'Next time I saw that boy he was pressing sparks out of a bayonet and joking about more grim work ahead'. The search for masculine imagery also produced some extraordinary analogies, such as that found in a published letter from a wounded soldier who likened his charge into Turkish territory to 'a vicious ram winning and butting his way into the middle of a pack of hungry dingoes and suddenly realising that valour could sometimes carry one too far'.[12]

Death and ghastly wounds were incorporated into this grotesque exercise as a matter of routine falsification. The newspapers could have said much less about these things, but they were part of the heroic ordeal, the test of manhood, so readers were not spared.

Registered at the General Post Office, Sydney, for Transmission by Post as a Newspaper.

Vol. 36.—No. 1856.   THURSDAY, JULY 29, 1915.   PRICE 6D.

THE CALL TO THE OTHERS.

'The Call to Others'

A Red Cross nurse conjures up the last-ditch heroism of the diggers to shame the shirkers.

They were the risks that *real men* would knowingly confront. Suffering and dying were associated with conventions that were widely advertised: dispatch after dispatch told the tale of men 'giving out' or 'expiring' with a smile on their face, some of them managing to make a heroic little speech in which they indicated their contentment. *Men* did their duty regardless of the cost. The smiling wounded and the smiling dead were everywhere. An Australian doctor working in No.1 Australian General Hospital in Heliopolis wrote home about his pride in the wounded:

> The stories they tell of the charges in the face of a hailstorm of that fearful shrapnel; the rescue of each other; the bravery of their mates—(never themselves do they mention)—the suffering, and the pain, and misery—all told with bright, eager faces and cheery smiles. Oh! mother, I am proud to be Australian.[13]

Letter-writing medical officers were a great source for material on heroic inspiration. One of them, an officer who must have been extremely perceptive or incredibly mobile, or both, was able to say that in his hospital 'the only groans were from unconscious men'. Special correspondents insisted that none of the wounded was melancholy, and the *Argus* simply lied when it said 'all of the letters from the front are full of the heroic spirit'. It may have been stretching the truth (or inventing a lie) on another occasion when it told of a soldier who lost his hand, sauntered in to have the stump of his arm dressed, and then went off to search for his watch and rings. Apparently the only miserable fellows were those who had not yet got into battle, the initiates eagerly awaiting their transformation into men. A colonel whose foot was blown off while he slept in a dugout overlooking Anzac beach is said to have regarded his stump with a 'quiet smile'. 'Now look at that', he remarked. 'The mean, miserable wretches; and I wasn't doing a thing to them'. A private with his chin blown off and unable to speak writes: 'I never was a beauty, but this won't help my looks'. Another soldier wrote to his brother-in-law (a rent collector in Fitzroy) to say he had been shot but not to worry, 'bullets don't hurt much'. As David McKee Wright put it, in his Rupert Brooke Prize poem of 1920, 'Bleeding and wearied to their task they stood,/And laughed at pain amid a thousand ills'.[14]

Even death had a hard job wiping off these smiles. One report, headed 'Captain Dies Smiling', told how the captain still had that smile on his lips when he was buried.[15] A soldier was quoted as saying he would rather face death than a dentist any day. A correspondent said he got the impression that death was 'apparently nothing' to the Australian soldier, 'compared with having to stand up to words of praise from a high official'. He, too, had seen nothing but smiling faces wherever death was present:

> I saw hundreds of our lads pass out, and never saw the sign of a cloud on their faces. They just keep on smiling to the last. Their splendid pride and courage seem to remain imprinted upon their faces even after death. One almost imagines the proud though cold lips saying, "I did all that was possible, and if my death has been part of the price of the good win the boys are sure to have, I'm delighted to die".[16]

Men about to die were mostly, if not universally, content because they knew their duty as men was done and so, it seems, were happy to expire. A soldier on Anzac beach enquired after his wounded cobber:

> 'Any chance?' he asked the doctor. 'No', came the reply. 'Well, it don't matter', continued the soldier. 'I know he's had ten of 'em [Turks] so he's quite ready to go; and as for meself', remarked the man as he turned to go up the gully, 'I've had seven of 'em, so I don't mind passing out now'.[17]

Another dying hero was reported to have said: 'What matter? I've had my fun. I did all I could', he smiled, 'I've tried to be a man'. And as a man he died.[18] Death in the print circus was not always swift, for there was often time for speeches and smiles, but it was usually clean, unflinching and heroic. If they were truly men, soldiers would turn to death passively, as though the war was not for fighters but martyrs; they would turn to death, in Rupert Brooke's chilling words, 'as swimmers into cleanness leaping'.[19]

The *Argus* dealt with death editorially on 3 May 1915, following the first published lists of Australians killed and only a week after Winston Churchill wrote in *The Times* of a soldier's death bringing 'the sure and triumphant consolations of a sincere and valiant spirit'. The *Argus* spoke of the 'grim severity of the struggle in which our Empire is engaged', of 'grief tempered with that noble pride which old Spartan fathers and mothers felt when their loved ones fell in obedience to their country's call', of the 'glory of wounds and death incurred in their country's cause'. It directed Australians not to dwell on the sadness of loss, but 'on the stirring story of duty manfully performed and undying fame won by courageous self-sacrifice'. For those who died there was no better way to go, as Arkwright's wartime poem, 'The Supreme Sacrifice', made clear: 'Tranquil you lie, Your Knightly virtue proved'. For those who lived there was the chance to share in the camaraderie of heroes and the opportunity to avenge their comrades. Vengeance was a potent theme in the epic formula.[20]

By early 1916 the fast-growing unease with the war was reinforced on the home front by declining standards of living, profiteering and industrial unrest. The government responded by further tightening censorship practices, by prosecuting soapbox critics and hounding the editors of 'unpatriotic' journals. 'People who speak against recruiting at this time are committing treason', said the Victorian Chief Secretary in December 1915, a convenient statement because it so neatly expressed how the recruitment drive had become an assault on democracy, and how censorship had been transformed from a military tool into a political bludgeon.[21] The 'soolers-on' did not want to hear of defeat or debacle or unadorned death. They wanted heroes, exemplars in the epic mould, and they intended to have them. The Deputy Chief Censor put it brazenly in August 1915:

> There is no better way of stimulating recruiting than the publication of spirit-stirring stories, fresh and unconventional, of the gallant lads now fighting at Gallipoli.[22]

A 'spirit-stirring story, fresh and unconventional'

The Simpson legend was created by newspapers committed to the recruitment offensive and wanting conscription. Major components of the 'Yes' case in conscription propaganda were the claims that men were dying for want of reinforcements and that infections and fatigue were taking a heavy toll because of prolonged trench service.[23] Simpson became part of the epic hype that so dominated the major dailies in the Great War. He did not figure in the labour press or those papers of the left that defended the volunteer system or opposed the 'sooling on business' by the 'safety brigade'.[24]

In the establishment press, where the need for more men was an incessant theme, the tales of Simpson fitted in neatly as a dramatic example of the shortage of fighting men at the front. They featured

Simpson labouring relentlessly in those first terrible weeks. They told how he acquired a donkey and used it to carry the wounded at a time when stretcher-bearers were in critically short supply, a time when wounded men suffered horribly from exposure and neglect, while others were left to limp or crawl to the beach. A scarcity of stretchers meant that torn bodies were being carried down the gullies in greatcoats and blankets. Innovators like Simpson were desperately needed. He broke ranks, used his initiative, revealed his independence and did great service, though some said he was carpeted for his actions having been 'practically a deserter from his unit'. By then it was too late, for the value of his work with the donkey had already been acclaimed, and his superiors saw the wisdom of his ways. As one account would have it, Simpson was accosted by an officer on the morning after the landing, but he soon put his superior straight:

–Why Simpson what's this? Where did you steal these donkeys?
–It's oll right, sorr, [replies Simpson with Irish brogue], this is Duffy No.1 and Duffy No.2. They're useful, sorr.[25]

The consequence, as the storytellers were quick to emphasise, was that Simpson worked alone. He had a 'roving commission', said one soldier; he was the only man on the peninsula who was under no one's immediate command, said another; he was the most dutiful and the most independent soldier at Gallipoli. In these respects the nature of his labours was about as sharp an expression of the Anzac legend, emphasising the individual initiative and resourcefulness of the digger, as we might find. He was supposedly too human to be a parade-ground soldier; he was a handful for his sergeant; and he shirked the drudgery of forming fours and other irksome military tasks. The Simpson legend thus fitted neatly with headlines such as 'Fighting without Leaders' and 'Everyman his own Officer'. It highlighted the archetypal qualities that made Australian soldiers great in battle, and it dramatised their call for help.

Private J. J. Fraser's eulogy tells of 6000 wounded men lying on Anzac beach, waiting for attention or evacuation: 'Simpson was there. He was everywhere'. Next thing he's got hold of a donkey, then two donkeys. In the days that followed, 'as the noise of battle grew louder and louder', wherever the wounded fell the call would go out: 'Where's Simpson?' In one instance, a colonel he rescues tries to give him a sovereign, but Simpson, this time in Scottish brogue, replies, 'Git on wi ye! Keep yer blanky quid. Ah'm not doin' this for the money, d'ye think?'[26] In Bean's account Simpson acquires the second donkey to keep up with the work, and he dies during the massive Turkish onslaught of 19 May while labouring feverishly among some 400 wounded comrades. Bean reports that Colonel Monash had reckoned that Simpson was worth 100 men to him.[27] For *Coo-ee*, a sixpenny newspaper for convalescing diggers, the numbers he had rescued would never be known; all that was certain was the image of a relentless Simpson with 'his donkey by his side like a big trained dog', searching for 'some mother's boy who might be lying bleeding to death'. Perhaps the most dramatic image of all is that in which Simpson, carrying a wounded man on his back or sometimes in his arms, trails behind his two heavily burdened little beasts, urging them onwards with a mixture of Arabic, English and Australian slang.[28] When Sister Davies wrote of Simpson in that letter to her mother in 1916, she said he worked day and night—in her view 'a White Man'—'taking two patients on the donkey and perhaps supporting two or three others'. As Davies told the tale he used two donkeys alternately because they could not keep up with his work rate.[29]

Oliver Hogue's account registered the same emotional plea for more men. There were too many dead to bury, and the wounded lay everywhere in want of help. Simpson would leave his donkey 'just under the brow of the hill and dash forward himself to the firing line to save the wounded. Murphy's [Simpson's] voice near them sounded like a voice from heaven', Hogue wrote. Ever smiling, of course, he worked on day after day:

> Then came a day when Murphy's mules came not. Stretcher-bearers were working overtime, and the wounded cried, 'For God's sake send Murphy's mules'. Later on they found the mules grazing contentedly in Shrapnel Valley. Then they found poor Murphy . . . He had done his last journey to the top of the hill.
>
> 'Where's Murphy?' demanded one of the 1st Battalion.
>
> 'Murphy's at Heaven's gate,' answered the Sergeant, 'helping the soldiers through.'[30]

Even in death Simpson is hard at it, but in his effort to be clever Hogue had produced a contrary image—that of Simpson leading soldiers through Heaven's gate, whereas his real role was to lead them away from it.

Children got the message too. Simpson first appeared in the Victorian *School Paper* (for Grades VII and VIII) in November 1915, a three-page account taken from the Melbourne *Herald*, and located between a poem about the heroes of ancient Greece and a version of Xenophon's speech to the ten thousand which began with an exhortation to his soldiers to perish gloriously if they could not conquer. Soon after, the tale of Simpson was in the *Boy's Own Annual* where young readers were told that he got hold of two donkeys because 'there were so many wounded to be fetched in', and that officers 'connived at the theft [of the donkeys] when they found what noble work he was doing'. There was also a poem that borrowed—as would others—from Hogue's account:

> Yes, friends, he's left us (evil fate!),
> Fresh duties to Begin,
> Murphy is up at Heaven's gate,
> Helping the soldiers in.[31]

The tireless E. C. Buley was also pressing on with a second book on the Gallipoli campaign. His *Child's History of Anzac* was a big seller in Australia and a recommended text in Victorian schools, as was his *Glorious Deeds of the Australasians*. The *Child's History* told of wounded men who have been all but abandoned, some of whom 'were lying in the bushes for days, and would never have been brought in alive but for the devotion of Simpson, and his little four-footed companion'. No one kept count, says Buley, but frequently he rescued more than ten or twelve souls a day.[32] Yet young men in Australia were still going to the football on weekends!

The limited circulation of the Simpson story internationally is consistent with this argument about its origins. It never made front-page headlines or appeared on a feature page, as it would in Australia; nor was it sustained by new versions of the tale and repeated tellings. Simpson's death was not a focus of *allied* outrage, unlike the death of Nurse Edith Cavell, who was shot by the Germans for 'spying'. There was obviously great mileage to be made from Cavell's case because she was a woman as well as a non-combatant, but her death figured in a different political setting. It became part of the moral campaign mounted by England to draw the United States of America into the war.[33] Simpson's fate in Turkey could not be part of this. The tales about him were largely confined to a *moral offensive* in Australia, the offensive that centred on enlistment, on going abroad to fight, and on shirkers who preferred to stay at home. Simpson figured in an outpouring of propaganda aimed at an Australian audience. Even the briefest report contained the motif in its bare essentials: the saintly bearer at work amongst the broken men, tireless, selfless, pressed beyond all reasonable limits. Simpson became an instrument of those who felt that the imperial bond was paramount and that 'cold-footers' had to be defeated. This was the Anzac legend at its core—unruly and independent working men, succumbing to the splendour of the epic idea, falling into line and giving their all for King and (another) Country.

The Simpson tales acquire their meaning not only from the messages carried in their text, but also from their location in the pro-conscription press, their part in the mosaic that made up the case for enlistment or coercion. The print circus recounted stories of wounded men crawling miles for want of a stretcher-bearer at the same time as it talked of 'pacifist intrigues' and 'yellow streakers'. While the *Argus* raged over the sinking of the *Lusitania*, the *Sunday Times* posed the option of enlistment at six shillings a day or conscription at six pence a day; the Sydney *Sun* celebrated the enlistment march of the Gilgandra men as the imperial press in one voice mourned the murder of Nurse Cavell; the sporting pages told of Les Darcy's fights, while the war pages suggested he had business elsewhere with dispatches on 'boxers at the front'; H. G.Wells was published on the 'khakification of England' as the *Bulletin* fed its readers with anti-shirker cartoons ('I was once hit by a shell./Really? Who threw the egg?'). And Ginger Mick went off to 'the flamin war to stoush the foe' at the same time as the press around Australia was preparing to run Bean's dispatch on the Man with the Donkey ('Was it fer glory or a woman's sake?/Oh, arst me somethin' easy, I dunno', wondered Mick). Such was the labyrinth through which poor Simpson, in death, would make his way. Simpson and Mick went into battle together.[34]

The cult of the wounded

In Australia the shortage of men at the front seemed to be confirmed by the repatriation of the wounded. The first soldiers to return from the fighting were wounded men who arrived in July

1915 to tumultuous welcomes. Shipload after shipload followed
them until the war was over. The first arrivals were Australia's first
real contact with the European war, and Australia's distance from
the theatres of hostility ensured that the wounded would continue
to be the one tangible sign of the awful devastation of war. The
wounded soldiers stirred the public imagination. Their return
coincided with the beginning of the recruitment crisis and, in the
two years following, the image of the wounded soldier was enlisted
in the recruitment campaigns. The tales of Simpson fitted neatly,
for they too evoked a powerful image—the wounded man on the
donkey, half conscious, badly injured in some versions, being led
out of the battle by the most humble and dutiful of Anzacs.

The representation of the wounded was relentless. Going to war
and coming home with a wound was to acquire a new status in
society. While the war still raged, the wounded experienced the
elevation of soldierhood to its purest form.[35] Wounds and scars were
now 'honourable wounds' and 'honourable scars'. The adulation
began at the wharves, where large crowds cheered hospital ships
from the Middle East:

> On Sunday last, Sydney turned out to welcome them home as she
> never turned out before. And it was wonderful how the spirit that
> dominates the nation was so strikingly reflected in our wounded
> men. Some limped, some were blind, some were maimed, yet all
> carried their injuries with a cheerfulness that must have lightened
> the pain of their suffering as well as brightened the hearts of the
> thousands who were there to greet them.[36]

They rode through the streets in a procession of open cars and
Red Cross ambulances, passing beneath temporary but elaborate
archways decked with banners honouring the 'wounded brave'.
Thousands lined the streets; hundreds of school cadets were enlisted to assist the police in keeping the line of the route open. Hands,
hats and flags were waved; floral bouquets and coins were thrown
to the soldiers as the procession followed its advertised course to
Randwick Hospital.[37]

Soldiers were well aware of the new category, 'wounded hero'. In
Melbourne a similar welcome awaited the troopship *Ballarat*. The
disciplinary and venereal disease cases were transferred to a launch
and whisked off before the ship docked,[38] so that only the honourably wounded would encounter the enthusiastic crowds on the pier.
Fighting men still at the front also grasped the new meaning of a

**A procession of wounded soldiers on their way to
Randwick Hospital**

*As the conscription campaign unfolded, the image of the wounded soldier became an
instrument of coercion in the hands of pro-conscriptionist newspapers.*

wound. A New Zealand surgeon recorded his sorrow at having 'to leave Anzac unwounded', but consoled himself with the thought that he had 'been getting worse for some weeks with dysenteric symptoms'.[39] In London Oliver Hogue wrote about the wounded in one of his love letters to his sweetheart: 'A sick soldier isn't nearly such an interesting proposition as a wounded soldier. Some of the lads who were wounded while landing and never saw the trenches were photographed and hailed as great heroes, while the men who bore the heat and burden of the whole campaign and then got enteric were merely classed as medical cases'.[40] Hogue himself had been evacuated from Gallipoli, 'unwounded' and suffering from enteric.

Once the shiploads began to arrive, Australia's cities were never the same. 'Our streets are full of wounded men', wrote the *Argus* columnist 'Vesta', in November 1915. Her message to all women was that attitudes would now have to change, that nothing would excuse them from the war's call upon their time and energy.[41] If there were wounded in the streets, there were many more in the newspapers. Daily the pro-conscription press in each State carried Honour Rolls of killed and wounded, letters from soldiers and doctors at the front, and correspondents' dispatches which told bloody tales of heroism, stoicism and tragedy.

Week in, week out, there were poems celebrating the deeds of Australia's men abroad, and there were the relentless photos depicting the convalescents. Around the country there were well-advertised cases of the rich opening grand homes to take in these men. Press photographers began snapping soldiers sitting in wicker chairs and wheelchairs in pleasant garden surroundings, on the grass chatting to nurses by slow moving rivers, waist-deep in thermal pools regaining their health, sipping tea at Anzac Buffets, being entertained in halls, getting all sorts of treatment in clinics for their wounds and their missing bits, fishing, reading in the shade, out for an airing in a pony chaise, 'sniping' pheasants, playing bowls, or chatting with relations.[42] Newspaper artists followed suit with their own impressions and loaded captions. In an effort to fund rehabilitation programs the *Sunday Times* sub-editors extended the meaning of the term 'shirker' to cover those who shirked their duty to finance the needs of the returning wounded.[43] Little boys who had been dressing up as soldiers started to wear a sling, or a head bandage with a bit of red paint on it. Little girls took to dressing up as Red Cross nurses.

The wounded man convalescing behind the lines made a heavy psychological claim on the 'stay-at-homes'.[44] A photograph revealed his location and inaction. It signified a gap at the front that had to be filled. In the feature photograph at the Sydney Railway Station, there is no sign of the process in which thousands of dead and mangled are being replaced by fresh legions, one vast anonymous mass by another. Instead we see an intimate masculine ritual, a heroic, individualised changing of the guard. The selective publication of soldiers' letters confirmed the idea that the wounded were eager to return to battle. They dramatised the need for help:

> Don't worry about me Mum, for I'm alright. It is a bit rough to come back in the trenches while the wound is still tender, but it only aches occasionally. I can 'stick it' alright until conscription goes through— as it surely will this time. I hear that all of us Anzac chaps get a rest then.[45]

In 1915 the head bandage became a regular feature in the press artist's dramatisation of the conflict in Europe.[46] The recruitment offensive now extended to drawings of the wounded man, strapped up, bandaged, bleeding, fighting on amidst a besieging enemy,[47] for nothing quite matched the pluck of the wounded soldier who fought on, or the eagerness of the evacuated casualty to rejoin his comrades in the trenches. The faces of the wounded stared out at readers, each one representing a gap at the front. 'These gaps have to be filled,' cried the *Sydney Mail*.[48] Officers in the field were frequently quoted to the same effect, and Oriel, resident poet with the *Argus*, in Melbourne, thought so too:

> Oh! duty is calling, and vengeance is calling
>> their cry shall never be stilled
> Till the last of the gaps in Australia's ranks
>> by Australia's sons are filled.[49]

As the conscription campaign unfolded, the image of the wounded soldier became an instrument of coercion in the hands of pro-conscription newspapers, a highly emotive motif in which sympathy and obligation were entwined. 'They're back with their Wounds, Their Glory, Their Helplessness', announced a headline in the *Sunday Times*. 'Something is up to Us.' Then another: 'Our Stricken Heroes Return Bringing Their Wounds and Messages—For More Men'.[50] Was it by accident of lay-out that the 1916 film *Murphy of*

Going to Take His Place At the Front.

"Good-bye, lad! I tried to do my bit; I know you'll do yours!"

A snapshot at the Central Railway Station, Sydney, on the occasion of the departure of a number of recruits for Holdsworthy Camp. Inset is a photograph from Egypt showing men who have recovered from wounds re-embarking for the Dardanelles.

'A snapshot at the Central Railway Station in Sydney'

Photographs such as this stressed the need to fill the gaps at the front, gaps left by the dead and wounded. The inset photo is powerful in a similar way, showing men formerly wounded and now restored to health, returning to the Dardanelles. The arrangement of the two photos is a careful one. It is not a casual 'snapshot', as the newspaper caption suggests.

The wounded soldier fighting on

The image of the wounded soldier fighting on rarely appeared in photographs. But in pencil drawings and watercolours, it became a powerful ploy in the conscription campaign.

Anzac was advertised in the Sydney *Sun* alongside another feature, 'Ashmead Bartlett's Pictures of the Dardanelles', which carried the rather unsubtle caption: 'You couldn't be there, Boy, but you can see what your pals had to do'?[51]

Deliverance and renewal

Pro-conscription newspapers busily reported on the care of the wounded, on their rescue, their repatriation and their convalescence. Simpson's register in this regard was immensely powerful. As legend, he can be understood as a personification of the anxiety that focused on the wounded, the national effort around them, and the recruitment campaign to fill the gaps at the front which they (and the dead) left behind. On the battlefield the selfless rescue of a comrade was the highest form of mateship; stretcher-bearers who routinely braved shot and shell to do this won high acclaim from soldiers and correspondents.[52] In the press at home the bearers were likened to saints. The rescue of the wounded soldier, his *deliverance* from the clutches of the enemy and from his wounds, was a process that linked the battlefront to hospitals behind the lines and, most importantly, to support networks at home. Newspaper photography frequently juxtaposed these three phases in the deliverance or salvation of the wounded soldier.

In fact, photographic journalism played an important part in the recruitment offensive and the conscription campaign of 1915–17. It consistently 'watched over' the wounded soldier, monitoring his convalescence, his renewal and where possible his return to battle. It charted his salvation at the hands of stretcher-bearers, hospital nurses in Egypt, Malta, France or England, and Red Cross workers everywhere. This visual dimension was amply supported by headlines, letters, editorials and sketches. There was a powerful interplay of text and imagery: the soldier's letter alongside the 'Roll of Honour' snapshots, the 'Comforts' column near images of weary stretcher-bearers or hearty nurses, the anti-shirker cartoon coupled with a sentimental poem from the front, the dramatic feature photo and its heavily loaded caption.[53]

In one instance, stretcher-bearers carry a man along a dusty road towards a waiting transport in the harbour at Alexandria. A nurse's letter, boxed beneath the photograph, offers a commentary and points the moral, telling of suffering in the trenches, terrible wounds, and the need for more men: 'There should not be one person in Australia not doing his or her part to save the burden of these men, for no one knows except those who see it how hard it is'. Beneath her words a second photo takes us on deck, where we see Australian soldiers tending to the wounded before they embark for Australia. The brassard bearing the red cross is prominent.[54]

The red cross on the white background was the symbol that most clearly linked the battlefront with hospitals behind the line and the care given to returned convalescents at home. As a shared symbol it featured in the photographic record of the war, since both the Army Medical Corps and the Red Cross Society employed it. Simpson's Red Cross brassard was an essential part of the icon and frequently figured in the tales. It linked him with the work of tens of thousands on the home front, for the symbol expressed, more powerfully than any other image of the war, the commitment to the men at the front and to the wounded at home where, as it happened, the Red Cross Society dominated the imagery of commitment. The Society became the outstanding symbol of human charity in the First World War because it was headed by imperial patriots from the highest levels and it had taken on the mantle of the major 'comforts' organisation in Australia.

The Red Cross had vice-regal patronage; its administration drew in powerful men (and their wives) from law, politics, sport and elsewhere. Red Cross operations relied on the enthusiasm and devotion of housewives—mostly middle class—in their tens of thousands, leading Michael McKernan to suggest that Red Cross women initiated 'what might be described as a completely new sector of the economy, the provision of comforts for the Australian troops and victims of war'. The visual record suggests that the Red Cross became a focal point for the immense desire to do something and the principal outlet for the pent-up emotions of anxious and patriotic people, especially women.[55] For those who took the lead, the Governors' wives and the senior office-bearers, the recruitment offensive was part of the brief. The Red Cross Society was represented at recruiting rallies, and its symbols—the cross, the nurse, the wounded soldier—were prominent in recruitment propaganda. Although the organisation was new in Australia (it was established in August 1914), in no time at all it was represented as the 'heart of Australia', the embodiment of commitment. Its flag was pictured flying from a depot on Anzac beach; its network was extending in Egypt and England and France; it flourished in towns and cities around Australia.[56]

The red cross symbol united the military and civilian spheres of mobilisation, linking soldiers with hospital ships' nurses and volunteer workers at home. The cross they shared stood for the salvation of the Australian soldier and figured prominently in the idea of national salvation; it signified the enlistment of the citizenry in the battle. The printed word backed up the photographs as the wounded acquired the label 'Red Cross Boys'.[57]

An extremely idealised account in the *Argus*, late in the war, indicates the nature of the reporting that had helped the Red Cross to become synonymous with getting the wounded home and nursing them back to health. 'Chilled to the bone with exposure' the wounded would drop back to 'what seemed like the portals of heaven', wrote the *Argus*. They would take hot drinks when half-frozen, cool drinks when full of fever. A primus stove from the Red Cross depot kept them warm, while surgeons worked in the light of acetylene lamps bought with Red Cross funds. The Society's bandages, bowls and beverages gave the wounded a new lease of life. They could now sleep in peace. When they woke they would be travelling to a base hospital in a Red Cross ambulance, 'fine, roomy, smooth-running vehicles fitted with electric light and beds with warm blankets'. Clean pyjamas too. In hospital the Red Cross supplied 'pipe, tobacco, cigarettes and matches; it placed invalid chairs at the soldiers' disposal, supplied them with artificial limbs, crutches and walking sticks, and furnished games and sporting material for their entertainment'.

Anything, from pianos to bath-heaters, might come to their aid, by courtesy of the Red Cross. The 'inexhaustible Red Cross chest' was at their service on the voyage home, and the organisation continued 'to shower its blessings on the men', once arrived, with recreation halls, laboratories, sanatoria, and hospitals provided as well as 'facilities for their education in toy making, netting, weaving, carpentering and type-writing'. There was the Red Cross volunteer motor corps and a furniture factory; there were comforts to provide for thousands of prisoners of war. Some penned letters of thanks to the newspapers; 'The Red Cross is really our mothers, our sisters, our friends in Australia, who are remembering us. God Bless them', wrote one of the thankful.[58] The Red Cross as a symbol of the unity of the military and civilian war effort, and notably of men and women, was expressed in a poem called 'The Red Cross Spirit Speaks' which merged the two spheres as though they were one and described that spirit as the 'avatar' of the nation's commitment:

FOR OUR WOUNDED SOLDIERS : PUBLIC SCHOOLS' DEMONSTRATION.

Red Cross Workers.

Representatives of Australia.

Nurse and Stretcher-Bearers.

ABOUT 10,000 pupils of the various Public schools in and around Sydney took part in a notable spectacular display at the Sydney Cricket Ground on Saturday in aid of the Australia Day Fund. The spectators numbered between 10,000 and 12,000, so that the fund will benefit materially. Unfortunately, rain fell during the afternoon, and several items on the programme had consequently to be abandoned. The Grand March, the "Australia" tableau, and the Maypole display did not, however, suffer, and in these events the splendid training of the young people was admirably manifested. About 350 squads took part in the Grand March. They formed a huge living map of Australia, with a Red Cross centre, and surrounded by senior cadets. In the March of the Nations, which followed, the armies of all the Allies were represented. There was a glorious volume of sound as the little ones sang "Rule Britannia," "Advance, Australia Fair," "Three Cheers for the Red, White, and Blue," and finally the National Anthem, in which they were joined by all on the ground.

THE RED CROSS IN THE HEART OF AUSTRALIA.

14.—The Sydney Mail, August 4, 1915.

'The Red Cross in the Heart of Australia'

Key symbols in the recruiting campaign were the red cross, the nurse and the wounded soldier. The visual record suggests that the Red Cross Society became a focal point for the immense desire to do something. These symbols were directed at children too.

I go wherever men may dare,
I go wherever woman's care
   And love can live;
Wherever strength and skill can bring
Surcease to human suffering,
   Or solace give.
  . . .

I am your pennies and your pounds,
I am your bodies on their rounds
   Of pain afar;
I am YOU, doing what you would,
If you were only where you could—
   Your avatar. [59]

On 'Australian Red Cross Day' in 1915, returned soldiers were paraded through the streets of Melbourne.[60] They figured in a pageant, a stirring jumble of national imagery and loyal intent. '*Recruiting musicians*' played in open cars; a horse-drawn pioneers float followed; there was a Ned Kelly platform; 'Australia and her maidens' floated along; there was a Gallipoli tableau with soldiers standing to arms. Beside the road women and men sold miniature Australian flags, the tricolor and Red Cross flags. Three elaborate Red Cross exhibits were in the motorcade, and Red Cross nurses were on hand to tend the parading wounded.[61] In other States the intent was much the same, though Perth called the occasion 'West Australia Day'.[62] In Sydney 'the streets were transformed into a gorgeous bazaar', wrote one soldier, who read about it from his dugout at Gallipoli. 'Hundreds of ladies became for the nonce bandits and thieves and robbers and levied toll on all and sundry. Mere man was fleeced shamelessly . . . He paid extortionate prices for miniature boomerangs and sprigs of wattle and blue-gum leaves and Australian flags, and patriotic colours and wild flowers and photos'.[63] The pageant signified how thoroughly the Red Cross had worked its way into the recruitment offensive and the imagery of the nation. More than a million pounds was raised in one day for the returned sick and wounded.

In 1915 the organisation set up an information bureau to provide an alternative source of news about men at the front, particularly those missing in action. This plugged into a long-established international operation, linking up with Red Cross bureaux in other countries. By these means the Society entrenched itself as a focus of incomparable solace at home, and the embodiment of commitment to the man in battle, as newspaper rhetoric in praise of the Red Cross confirms: when Vesta, the *Argus* columnist, issued her rallying cry that 'our streets are full of wounded men', she left no doubt as to how civilians must respond:

> The needs of Red Cross work stand out above all other needs: the call upon our pity and our gratitude is so insistent that we dare not let our enthusiasm flag for a moment . . . Thousands more are pouring into the hospitals daily. What they have done and what they have suffered no one needs to be told . . . The sheets they lie on, the dressings for their wounds, everything but the roofs above them and the food they eat, must come from us and be provided by our work.[64]

Vesta's commitment to the Red Cross was no more ardent than her enthusiasm for the 'sooling-on business', and no less blood-red than that exhibited by women in the higher reaches of the organisation itself. For imperial patriots, the recruitment campaign and the work of the Red Cross were like two sides of the same coin. To serve one and neglect the other was like going to church but putting nothing in the plate.

This complete dedication, linking recruitment with salvation, was exemplified in the work of Philadelphia Nina Robertson, a Presbyterian vicar's daughter from Wangaratta, who was Secretary-General of the Australian Red Cross from 1915 to 1938. Miss Robertson wrote regularly for the patriotic press. She was at home on the women's page chatting about knitting, diet, table manners or femininity. She loved the Empire with a capital 'E', and she loved Australia too, so long as it remained a loyal component of the Empire. She believed in the 'sacred charter of nationhood' and of 'valour's deathless page', and in 1916 she published a book of poems called *An Anzac Budget and Other Verses*. It included a poem for the dead at Gallipoli, and another for the returning wounded ('true lads and loyal/ . . . we bring you golden wattle'). There was a poem thanking God for Anzac Day, a day of 'aching pride, of piercing pain', which referred to the 'beauty of the soul through suffering tried', and 'the thorn crowned glory of the crucified'. There was a woman's prayer ('I am so placid as I sit/In train or tram, and knit and knit . . . '). There were also two other poems about enlistment that were anything but placid. For Recruiting Week in July 1915, Miss Robertson penned 'A Question for Australia':

> Do we deserve to win? England wants men,
> And thousands linger, heedless of her call,
> Treading the easy path of dalliance
> While on the field their gallant comrades fall . . .

About the same time she also wrote 'More Men, and Yet More, are Wanted':

> More men, more men, they want more men—it's
>   up to you to go!
> These were the words his horse's hoofs beat out on
>   the road below,
> Whether he trotted along the trail, or cantered
>   across the plain,
> Or galloped the length of the sandy track, it was
>   still the same refrain . . . .

The poem went on to describe how a shearer heard the call but at first resisted because he was soon to be boss of the shed. 'I've earned the billet and it's mine', he protested. But he continued to hear the sound of the call, 'More men, more men, they want more men—it's up to you to go!', and he thought of the boys at the Dardanelles, 'of all they'd dared and done/Of the silent graves on that blood bought cliff, and the battles not yet won'. He remembered the war in France and 'Belgium trodden low/And he looked it square in the face at last—it was up to him to go'.[65] Like Simpson in the *Coo-ee* version of his tale, the shearer had dallied, but not for long, because he was made of the right stuff. Simpson responded to his girl who chided him; the shearer heard the call of the rider and it seemed right. Each of them knew it was his duty to go.

Robertson's collection has a satisfying consistency. The principal motifs of the empire's cause are all gathered here—high imperial purpose (saving civilisation), the glorious dead, the honourable wounded, the urgent need for more men, and the contempt for those who, 'treading the easy path of dalliance', fail to go. She moved on paper as she did in her daily routines—from the politics of recruitment to the needs of the wounded, the cause of deliverance, which was simultaneously individual, national and imperial. It might seem too neat a contrivance to reveal that nearly two decades later Robertson championed the appeal for a monument to Simpson at the Shrine of Remembrance in Melbourne, or that her poem then would be a poem about the Man with the Donkey. But she did, and it was.[66]

In wartime Australia the wounded soldier and his saviour converged to become a key image in the recruitment offensive. In the print circus, the Red Cross Society and the red cross symbol merged, uniting the civilian and military spheres, signifying a commitment to empire and a love of nation, through its focus on the salvation of the individual soldier, the Anzac, the new symbol of national maturity. The red cross symbol featured prominently in the many stories of Simpson's heroism. He was frequently described, with initial capitals, as a 'Hero of the Red Cross'. In some stories the association was reinforced with Simpson falling dead close to a Red Cross flag; or the cross being clipped out of the long hair on the donkey's rump, then painted red; or some soldier claiming to have made the brassard. *The Anzac Book* did it thoroughly: written on Gallipoli, the relevant entry was entitled 'Murphy of Red Cross fame'.[67] Throughout these accounts the theme of deliverance and renewal was central, with regular reference to the number of lives Simpson saved. As an Anzac poet put it:

> Day in, day out, where the red death smote
> they carried their precious freight,
> And the sunshine glow is in hearts to-day that
> had else been desolate.[68]

Because the epic model was battle-centred, it should come as no surprise that a military, and not a civilian, figure became the most celebrated symbol of deliverance and renewal, nor that he was a volunteer and a 'model worker', the epitome of self-regulating obedience. The image of the Man with the Donkey—the unflinching stretcher-bearer, wearing the Red Cross brassard and leading a wounded soldier out of danger—was a powerful image of salvation. It was also an image that united disparate social forces behind a common imperial purpose: the red cross signifying the needs of soldiers, and especially of the wounded, expressed both commitment in battle and the vast mobilisation of people, across lines of sex, class and faith, on the increasingly dissent-torn home front.

Chapter Four

A Saintly Bearing

And his high death
Was more heroical
Than the most stoical
of fighting-men's.

John Oxenham, 'Only a Stretcher-Bearer' (1917)

Since the first moral criticism of Homer's epics in classical Greece, there has been argument about the nature of heroic virtue. While the epic tradition placed its emphasis on military valour, critics insisted that this ideal was deficient. They sought the essence of heroism in loftier virtues, arguing that a hero distinguished by military prowess alone was morally inadequate. The word 'hero', they pointed out, could be traced to 'eros' and so implied an epic formula in which fighting skills were matched by qualities that were life affirming rather than life taking. In the Christian tradition, argument about the better part of valour being compassion (rather than the conventional discretion) was connected to a wider debate as to the immorality of war and the ideal of non-violence. Anti-war teachings in the early Christian church acquired a considerable following until set aside by the authority of St Augustine's doctrine that war may be 'just' for Christians because its cause lay in man's sin and its prosecution was God's answering punishment.

The Augustinian doctrine was timely; once it was accepted, Christian kingdoms had less trouble justifying the wars they waged. They invoked God as their ally, blamed their enemy for the havoc and celebrated their soldiers as fighters and saviours. They could, in other words, eat their cake and have it too. The battlefield thus remained a theatre of heroic virtue, even though critics continued to reject the classical archetype of the soldier as a model of manhood. The Renaissance humanists (More, Colet, Vives and Erasmus) figured prominently among these critics, as did Milton and Johnson after them. Milton's savage assault on the epic tradition was a reaction to narrow and primitive notions of valour; Samuel Johnson spoke of 'vulgar greatness', praised Shakespeare for having no supermen in his plays and so expressed a preference for tragic rather than epic drama. Both were searching for 'the pattern of a Christian hero'.[1]

The modern period inherited St Augustine's justification of war, as well as an unresolved tension about the better part of valour. During the Great War both sides pictured themselves as the instrument of God's wrath and managed to find in their soldiers not only the fierceness needed to win, but also the compassion to be worthy of victory. As much as any other combatant nation, Australia gloried in ferocity, but compassion was still an important element in our epic formula. If compassion has since been ignored it is because historians have failed to point it out to us, a fact neatly illustrated by their preoccupation with fighting men at the expense of stretcher-bearers, for the latter were recognised as the organised expression of sacrificial goodness, and one among them became the pre-eminent symbol of Australian heroism. That Simpson never fired a shot and that his tasks were more akin to nursing than fighting enhanced his heroic status. The Simpson legend confirmed the traditional emphasis on military courage (if not military skills) and the Christian values that would justify victory, thus making, in John Oxenham's words, for a 'high death', a death 'more heroical/ than the most stoical/of fighting men's'.

The hierarchy of military manhood

Simpson was a member of the 3rd Field Ambulance, a stretcher-bearer whose task was to deliver the wounded from 'The Valley of Death'. Why he became an ambulanceman varies from one tale to the next, though his strength, his loyalty to a friend already in the field ambulance and even 'fate' have been evoked more than once. In some of the tales he works in the most dangerous zones, taking the donkey so far, then dashing forward under enemy fire. He returns with a man in his arms or over his shoulder, carries him to safety, then dashes back to help another. One version, retold many times, has him complaining of not enough work, for there are too few leg injuries and while stretchers are full he is idle. He courts death at any time of the day or night to rescue the wounded. On his way into danger he chats and smiles and cracks jokes. When soldiers warn him of the risks he is taking, his reply is always: 'My troubles!' He wears out two pairs of shoes in three weeks; probably never took them off, said one soldier. He bivouacs with the Indians to ensure forage for his donkey. On the day of his death he skips a meal in his keenness to get on with it. He rarely sleeps. According to the legend, the wounded soldiers know all this. They lie bleeding, semi-conscious, mangled, vulnerable, in that awful void called No Man's Land. In some accounts they actually call for him by name.

Through these tales Simpson became a symbol of the courage and dedication of the field ambulance man, the stretcher-bearer personified. Although its origins were political and civilian, the legend was underpinned by experience on the battlefield, by the importance of the stretcher-bearers in the psychology of the front-line soldier. Early in the war it became a convention among soldiers to say that bearers collectively deserved the highest praise, and after the war this kind of talk provided a military context for Simpson's commemoration. An official historian, A. G. Butler, claimed that Simpson had been singled out because his courage and the nature of the service in which he lost his life were typical of the stretcher-bearer, 'who must carry his case undeviatingly, without haste but without rest, through long periods of exacting and dangerous toil'. During the Simpson memorial appeal of 1933, Colonel L. E. Tinley wrote to the *Argus* to say that all stretcher-bearers would have a monument or a Victoria Cross if he could have his way. Major-General Brand said something similar: 'A memorial to Simpson would be a memorial to all who wore the Geneva badge, who never flinched, no matter how hot the rifle and shell fire, from giving first aid and then transferring the wounded to where skilled attention was available. Such a memorial would immortalise the AIF stretcher-bearers'.[2]

Such views had not always prevailed. Initially non-combatants in the newly formed Australian Imperial Force (AIF) were looked down upon, frequently chided and called names that implied that they were inferior to the fighting soldier. This was the military's hierarchy of manhood at work, giving shape and order to the gradations of 'manliness' within the ranks. Some fighting men thought stretcher-bearing was a good way to put on weight. C. E. W. Bean referred to a 'sort of general idea even in the force itself' that the stretcher-bearers were pretty safe. Back in Australia, he said, the friends of a field ambulance man might remark, 'I'm rather glad old Jones isn't in a fighting corps—he is a married man you know. He'll be better behind the firing line'. Bean said that people made much the same remark about the Army Medical Corps (AMC) details, and about men who were chosen from among the rank-and-file of battalions for stretcher-bearing duty.[3]

In 1916 Major Beeston, an Australian surgeon with the 4th Field Ambulance on Gallipoli, wrote of how the AMC was 'always looked upon as a soft job'; of how in peacetime 'we had to submit to all sorts of flippant remarks, and were called Linseed Lancers, Body-Snatchers, and other cheery and jovial names'. E. C. Buley recounted a moment on board ship before the landing at Cape Helles when a padre gathered the men together for a simple service. He talked about the band, who were also the stretcher-bearers, about how they had come in for 'a great deal of chaff' as non-combatants: 'And the time is at hand,' he added minatorily, 'when you'll want to bite off your tongues for every idle word you've said to the band'.[4]

This kind of chaff was not confined to the Australian army. In Egypt the acronym RAMC (Royal Army Medical Corps) was jokingly transformed to 'Rob All My Comrades'.[5] A New Zealander who worked as a hospital orderly in Egypt and England recalled later how, when on leave, he had no desire to draw attention to the fact that he was in the medical corps.

There was also a belief that the medical corps was a haven for pacifists and shirkers who would not take up the gun and do the man's work of killing the enemy. The belief was far wider than the reality warranted. It was the fate of only a very small number of conscientious objectors, Englishmen and New Zealanders, to be 'transported' to France, greatly abused, and compelled to carry the wounded.[6]

Not even Simpson has been entirely free from the derogatory under-tow. On the fringes of Gallipoli folklore, expressed privately for the most part, some will still tell you that 'he didn't fancy the soldiering bit', that bad teeth ended his career in the fighting ranks; that the real heroes were the ones who lugged a stretcher—who couldn't put it down and had no free hand to brush the flies away; that the donkey was a lazy dodge; that its master was a deserter from the British army; that Australians shot him because he drew too much fire down Shrapnel Gully; that it was a shame he became the hero he did, and a pity that a better character had not become the legend. Others try to reclaim him from different rumours: 'He wasn't an alcoholic you know?'[7]

The chaff of 1914–15 was scattered widely by the gusts of war, by the heroics of the colonial troops and by the common bond that united men under fire. The assault on Gallipoli marked the beginning of a radical readjustment in the hierarchy of military manhood. The padre's words came true: men bit their tongues over their idle words. Said E.C. Buley: 'Ask any Australian who were the bravest men at Anzac, and you are sure to get the answer, 'The stretcher-bearers''. Buley also said that jokes about the band were no longer popular once the casualty lists for the non-combatants were recognised.[8] As the war progressed, Major Beeston, who deeply resented the bastard-title of Linseed Lancer, discovered that 'the AAMC could hold up their heads with any of the fighting troops'. 'Pray be undeceived', wrote Trooper Bluegum from Anzac Cove, 'Oh, you who think the Army Medical Corps is always comfortably and safely situated at the base—pray be undeceived'.

At Cape Helles a New Zealand officer spoke at an open-air church service in full view of the enemy. A bearer noted in his diary that 'he praised the ambulance men very highly for their hard work done and hoped that all would take a lesson from the sympathy shown to the wounded while in our hands. It was very good of him, as we (were) looked down on while in Zeitoun and other camps, but now opinion has changed in our favour'.[9] A sergeant at Anzac Cove confirmed this view. An observer by profession, C. F. Laseron had been a member of the scientific staff of the Technological Museum in Ultimo before the war. On Gallipoli he observed the stretcher-bearers at work, and it was a graphic revelation of the courage they showed in the face of danger that he chose to record:

> Right up the valley for about a mile and a half we went, past more stretcher-bearers, all taking burdens to the rear. Some of these non-combatants have caught it very hot, and as I could see afterwards, their work was by no means the easiest or the least dangerous. Too much cannot be said of their devotion, for the difficulty and danger of getting wounded to the rear was exceptional; and there is hardly a stretcher-bearer that has not earned in some way or other the highest of honours. One showed me his pocket book with a neat

hole through one corner. The bullet had been deflected by the button of his tunic.[10]

There were some, it seemed, who would never be convinced, like the major who wrote to his mother from France in 1917 that he was filling in for the 'regular pill merchant' who was on a Blighty for fourteen days. He was not happy: he told his mother he would much prefer some real work 'to just loafing in the ambulance'.[11] But the major was in fact an admirer of the stretcher-bearers. It was those members of the ambulance who were not under fire whom he derided. A senior Australian officer from administrative HQ in London who was at Bullecourt during some terrible fighting had to discover this crucial distinction for himself, before he could fully appreciate the men who carried stretchers. He told a fellow officer that he had felt 'quite a hero' walking calmly over those roads, but that when he saw the bearers labouring with equal calm over the same roads, not once but twenty times, he said he knew that he 'was only a damned squib compared with them'.[12]

It was the experience of the first months at Gallipoli that set the mould. Arrangements for the wounded were completely inadequate. The terrain was precipitous and getting a man to the beach was a nightmare for the bearers. As one military historian has put it, 'In subsequent wars the medical authorities made the transporting of the wounded from the firing zone to the base hospital a top priority. At Gallipoli it was hardly a concern at all, let alone a priority, and men were often given specific orders to ignore the wounded'.[13] The first month—Simpson's month—was the worst. The stretcher-bearers were worked to exhaustion. Their diaries and letters record periods of thirty and forty hours without sleep, of torn hands and blistered feet. Their ranks thinned at an alarming rate. The 3rd Field Ambulance, Simpson's unit, took a terrible toll. Fighting men watched from the trenches and sailors from transports close by: 'What was most pathetic to us who could see everything going on ashore', wrote one of these, 'was the shooting down . . . of our AMC men, working in pairs carrying the wounded. Machine guns mowed them down and there they lay on the beach all day'.[14]

'From all hands comes paeans of praise for the ambulance men,' insisted the New Zealand press in August 1915. 'They are no longer looked on as "Cissies", as some colonials ignorant of war used to think, but as dyed in the wool heroes'.[15] A diary entry for 5 May records with some satisfaction that the call for volunteers to carry the wounded across a 'desparately [*sic*] dangerous' gap had never gone unanswered: 'I think the old legend of the uselessness of the Medical Corps has been killed dead—at least our wounded bearers, now numbering about a dozen, have given their blood to clean this slate'.[16]

Bean made a special effort in his dispatches to convey the extremely dangerous nature of the bearers' work. In his dispatch of 12 June, which began with the tale of Simpson, he told of ambulance men ladling out water to the troops amidst heavy shellfire. ('The orderly at the water tins looked up at the sky line, as if to make sure where the visitor had come from, and then went on with his ladling.') Bean had seen them walk coolly through a deadly hail on their way to the wounded; one had even stopped to light a pipe. He cited the casualty figures for various field ambulance units, including Simpson's which had lost five men dead and thirty wounded before the middle of May. Finally Bean made a point of the exceptional circumstances at Anzac Cove where it was not possible for the clearing hospitals to be well outside the range of guns, as they were supposed to be. Everyone was under fire, from the highest ranked officer to the orderlies in charge of ladling out water. To stress his point he reminded readers that Simpson had been killed on the same spot as General Bridges.[17]

Bean elaborated on this theme in his *Story of ANZAC*, a summation of the AIF experience at Gallipoli. He considered the stretcher-bearers' work was probably more dangerous than that of the riflemen, and believed that it was quickly recognised as such. He insisted that stretcher-bearers, in trading safety for independence, epitomised the distinctive qualities of the digger. Their position in the field was extremely vulnerable but subject to minimal regimentation: 'The main inducement which led men to undertake stretcher-bearing was relief from certain hated "fatigues"', Bean wrote. He singled out a routine, familiar to stretcher-bearers, of having to rush to the site of a shell burst and attend the wounded, knowing that the most likely place for the next shell to land was the same spot or nearby. This, he argued, was an important sacrifice in the military scheme of things: 'The system was unorthodox, inasmuch as it involved heavy loss of life . . . But it probably saved a much greater loss, and its effect on the morale of the troops was distinct'.[18]

The point about morale is crucial. A tradition arose which insisted that colonial troops did not desert their wounded, and men going into battle were cheered by this conviction. Among Australian and New Zealand troops there was talk of how the 'Tommies' would ignore the agonising cries of their wounded and leave them to die. There were incidents that quickly worked their way into the soldiers' folklore to confirm this. At Passchendaele, Private Leonard Hart spent a night listening to the screams of men from the York and Lancaster regiments. In the morning he and others crawled out and were 'astonished to find about half a dozen tommies, badly wounded, some insane, others almost dead with starvation and exposure, lying stuck in the mud and too weak to move'. Then they realised that the shell craters all around them held similar horrors.

> We were dumbfounded, but the awful truth remained, these chaps, wounded in the defence of their country had been callously left to die the most awful deaths in the half frozen mud while tens of thousands of able bodied men were camped within five miles of them . . . I have seen some pretty rotten sights during the two and a half years of active service, but I must say that this fairly sickened me. We crawled back to our trenches and inside an hour all our stretcher bearers were working like the heroes that they were, and in full view of the enemy whom, to his credit, did not fire on them.[19]

The legend that quickly built up around the Australian stretcher-bearers both derived from, and contributed to, the heroics of the men who were its subject. The earliest accounts of Simpson's work were, in every case, part of a chorus of praise for the noble work of the Army Medical Corps in general. They stressed collective heroism and cast Simpson as a representative figure:

> It is utterly impossible to express in words the work done by this gallant body of men. Unremitting in their deeds of heroism, self-sacrificing to what appeared almost like madness, ever ready and anxious to rush forward to the aid of the fallen comrade, there they would kneel, under a withering fire, and tend some poor suffering soul, and carry him to a place of safety. Such acts as these were common amongst them and many a DCM was won by them which will never be known of.

This is from the *Daily Malta Chronicle* report of 12 June 1915, the one that culminated in the first published report about Simpson. The

Argus reproduced those words in July, and the *Weekly Press* in New Zealand followed suit in August.[20] Simpson's legend was launched amidst the chorus of praise for the saintly bearers.

These were men who never shirked a call for volunteers, who worked quietly under 'withering fire' whilst others watched and marvelled from dugouts nearby. It was said that they had watched Simpson at the outset of this great tragedy, spellbound in their trenches. The bearers carried twelve and fourteen stone loads, and more, down impossible ravines and gullies, clambered half-dead with exhaustion through the sucking mud of the Western Front, lifting patients over parapets and picking their way as best they could around shell holes. They worked at night, one moment in the full light of flares and shell stars, the next stumbling along in the intensified blackness. Their knuckles chafed and bled in Gallipoli trenches barely the width of a stretcher. In the hot months their lips and eyes were thick with flies. Quite frequently they died while kneeling by a wounded comrade. It was little wonder that soldiers were touched by the sight of the stretcher-bearers at work, and they had good reason to seek character in the men who might save them from death. 'There are two cries that I will always remember', wrote Major Drake-Brockman from Gallipoli, 'and they are "Stretcher-bearer wanted on the right" and "stretcher-bearer wanted on the left" . . . To see them bringing in the wounded and attending to them under the hottest fire was splendid'.[21]

One soldier wrote of fleeing for his life, running like an Olympic competitor past wounded comrades who called, 'Don't leave us mates, boys, etc'. But he thought it would have been 'murder' to have stayed and helped the wounded. Back in the trenches his commanding officer sent a runner to medical headquarters to bring up the stretcher-bearers.[22] Albert Facey's Gallipoli memory was scarred by images of wounded men stranded beyond the trenches. He remembered their calls and his instructions to ignore them. 'I would think for days, I should have helped that poor beggar', he recalled. The same account mentions only two men by name—his brother whom he helped bury, and Simpson, whom he claims he saw at work and believed should have got a VC. Simpson figures in the account as a symbolic compensation for Facey's sense of guilt and helplessness.[23]

Watching men go out under fire for the wounded was a widely shared experience. It is not hard to find memories of the wounded calling for help or for water, or of the cry for stretcher-bearers going down the line; indeed they are common in the diaries, letters and reminiscences of soldiers. It was one of the most powerful and emotive spectacles of the war. Private Robert M. Calder wrote to his father while convalescing on the island of Lemnos. He had landed at Gaba Tepe and was immediately in the thick of it. For two nights he and his comrades could hear the wounded calling through the dark, pleading for their salvation, begging for water. Under cover of darkness the troops crawled out to give them water, but could do no more. Calder then gave half his own water ration to an AMC man who was going out to rescue them.[24] The diary of a Royal Engineer goes into some detail when describing the sight of the saintly bearers responding to the call:

> A long drawn-out cry is passed from lip to lip down [to] the beach . . . Stretch-er Bear-er. It reaches the dressing station and out run four men, one of whom carries a stretcher—doubling along ready to dodge behind a pile of bones should they hear the whistle of a second shell.
> As they run they are guided by shouts of 'Higher up higher up' to where the cry originated. In a few minutes back they come—no thought of dodging this time—as if they had never heard of such a thing as a shell. The man with SB on his arm doesn't get half the appreciation he deserves.[25]

George Davidson, who mailed home flower specimens from Gallipoli, and whose diary is replete with their Latin names, was given to wondering about being fired on when alone: 'you ask yourself how long you may have to live, if you get wounded, before anyone comes along', he wrote.[26] Surrounded by dead comrades, Private Albert Sutton lay wounded for twenty-four hours, his left leg shattered at the knee. The stretcher-bearers came for him 'under a terrific fire all the time', he wrote. 'The stretcher-bearers in my opinion are the bravest men in this war. They are always exposed to fire and never fire a shot. I lift my hat to the chaps who came for me'.[27] Reginald Baker was rescued from Rhododendron Ridge, carried to Anzac Beach and eventually hustled on board a hospital ship by his anxious bearers. He recalled: 'One of the bearers bestowed me a huge wink as they laid me on the deck of the lighter. I don't think I ever felt more thankful to anyone in my life'.[28] A New Zealand surgeon's diary—wordy, witty, and rich with medical detail—speaks of the faces its owner saw coming in on stretchers.

Convention has helped to soften the screams, to romanticise the wounds and to elevate the stretcher-bearers:

> All day long the stretcher bearers toil down the Valley of Death, climb over the steep side of Hell Point, and carry their bloody load into the Collecting Hospital . . . What struck me most was the wonderful look of relief on the patient's faces as they reached the hospital. Their trip down the Valley of Death with sniper's bullets whining over them, and the ever present expectation of a crash of shrapnel, is over. There is the sea; and a mile off is the white hospital ship . . . the worst is over: the man has done his job, got his wound of which he is desperately proud, and is going to have a spell from this hellish place. All this is written large on each man's face. Those that can talk say 'Thank you chums!' to the sweating stretcher bearers.[29]

And sweating they rest, before going out again.

Patients rarely knew the names of the heroes who saved them. From this situation emerged a tale told frequently enough to be conventionalised: stretcher-bearers risk their lives to rescue a wounded man ('two chaps came through the thick of bullets and carried me off'); the man is badly wounded ('they ought not to have come; they risked two good lives to save a doubtful one'); they remain nameless, but their devotion will not be forgotten; their anonymity is experienced as an enduring loss ('I don't know even who they were and can never thank them').[30] Not surprisingly, anonymity was a motif that worked its way into the tales of Simpson through the uncertainty about *his* name, and many drew the conclusion that 'Murphy' or 'Simmy', or whatever, was just a tag, a name for want of a name, a name that signified the unknown stretcher-bearer.

The celebration of the saintly medical corps men took another turn in a poem called 'The Doctor's Disc', in which a dedicated doctor runs out of bandages whilst toiling on the battlefield. Since he is an Anzac, he has no trouble innovating. He begins tearing his clothes off, stopping up wounds with bits of shirt, binding limbs with shreds from his coat, and so on until:

> When he found his bandages done, he
> swallowed down his oathes,
> And kept on tying soldiers up with frag-
> ments of his clothes.[31]

Finally, clad in no more than his boots and the disc on a chain around his neck, he takes up a rifle and charges the Turkish trenches, naturally to find the Turks fleeing before him. The poem is a light 'moment', a bizarre fantasy amongst the otherwise grim and predictable accounts of medical men at work in the field.

The irrepressible Oliver Hogue (Trooper Bluegum) began to write dispatches from his 'Dug-out Delux' towards the end of the first month on Gallipoli, when the wounded had come down to the beach in their thousands, and the stench of unburied bodies was in every nostril. He had arrived on the peninsula on 20 May, the day after Simpson's death, and later wrote a 'first hand' report on the man he never saw. His account dated 24 May celebrated the stretcher-bearers in general:

> The Ambulance men work very hard and when this war is over the part played by the Red Cross brigade will long be remembered. There is a certain section known as 'stretcher-bearers' and these men have played a particularly heroic part. The conveying of the wounded men out of the danger zone is a very precarious business, and one fraught with the greatest danger, but our 'SBs' have done noble work and *we are never likely to forget it.*[32]

He was right; they did not forget it. They distilled these memories into a folkloric brew in which there was an element called Simpson, a mnemonic of flesh and blood, remembered long after other details had faded.

Unarmed, fearless and smiling

The appeal in 1933 for a statue of Simpson at the Shrine of Remembrance was launched with the following words:

> There is something infinitely inspiring in the story of Simpson, the Donkey Man, a private soldier, *unarmed, fearless and smiling*, going to and fro on Gallipoli with his donkey, seeking the wounded and dying, and bearing them to shelter and to succour knowing full well that at any moment such a journey might be his last.[33]

Unarmed, fearless and smiling: it was a careful choice of words, which derived from the established lore of stretcher-bearing, and insisted on the unflinching *passivity* of the stretcher-bearer in the face of wild, indiscriminate and even vindictive aggression. They were brave, they were effective, they boosted morale, and they were celebrated accordingly. Other soldiers soon became aware of the extraordinary constraints imposed on the stretcher-bearer at work, a kind of extra burden that required superhuman composure. The paradox of men tending patients amid the maelstrom impressed Bean: 'The stretcher-bearers working out with the front line in battle—as the Australian stretcher-bearers did from that day (the 25th) to the end of the war—had dressed the wounded until they were all wounded themselves', he wrote in amazed admiration.[34] In the course of their duty stretcher-bearers had to calmly endure aggression without recourse to the warrior's compensating response in kind. The most common methods of self-preservation were denied to the stretcher-bearer. Fighting men knew this and so did the bearers. Consider this thoughtful passage written by a New Zealand corporal amidst fierce fighting on the Western Front:

> I had the cold fear of death on me for the half hour it took to get over the top, shells landing before and behind, and on both sides, and by the time we reached the Regimental Aid Post I was done. Infantry, with a bayonet, and with spirits running high for a charge face barrage fire constantly I know, but it is a vastly different thing with a sling round your neck, supporting a dead weight, and crawling at a snail's pace over shell torn ground. The most common and effective method of escape—falling flat on your face, or tumbling into a shell hole, is denied the stretcher-bearer. His first consideration is the man he has to get in, and nothing but a direct hit will make him drop his burden. I had only one case of cowardice, and he was a boy who should never have been sent out.[35]

The New Zealand bearer who worked with Simpson for five days— the one who did not think to take a photo of him, but later wished he had—was well aware of the obligations that went with the rescue of the wounded under fire. His diary entry for 29 April tells of collecting the wounded all day and night, but more at night because daytime was too deadly. James Jackson wrote of moving in those deadly open spaces 'at full speed and half doubled up', but with a wounded man 'it is very trying for us . . . we can't run and have to take our time'. He believed that the Turks had absolutely no respect for the red cross, a worry which added to his sense of peril.[36] A few days later Jackson's unit acquired several donkeys and he was one of a small group of New Zealand bearers who began to use them to rescue the wounded.

Soldiers knew that aggression in response to aggression could overcome fear. There were those who took comfort in vengeful deeds as their comrades fell around them. (Newspapers said it was a *manly* obligation.) Fighting men knew the stretcher-bearers had no such recourse, and they sensed the ordeal of passivity amid incredible human devastation. Surrounded by raw bone, shredded flesh, depleting numbers, mass graves and spatterings of lime, they knew their own fear could be subdued in a wild charge or a frenzy of killing, that fighting could transform fear into something else; at least for some of them it could. Lack of such an outlet made the bearers extraordinary. Their bravery put a curious twist into the meaning of soldierly manhood: the paradox of going 'unarmed, fearless and smiling' into the fray, made their role more 'masculine' than violent confrontation and killing.

The non-combatant role of the stretcher-bearer, at first belittled for those 'feminine' associations that had produced shame and anger among the ambulance men, was now seen for what it was—a role that called *routinely* for the most extraordinary show of courage. A correspondent for the (Sydney) *Sunday Times* wrote of the Red Cross brassard ('The Band of Mercy') in a way that emphasised the new-found standing of the bearers:

> The Band of Mercy shot straight and surely; and the men went about their fighting relying upon their Spartan kindness, should the worst come to the worst.

The language here is important: the rescue is likened to a bullet or an arrow, the ambulance men are likened to Spartans; 'Mercy' sits comfortably alongside 'shot', and 'kindness' is acceptably 'Spartan'.[37] A poem about Simpson from the 1930s defines this gentle touch as the combination of manliness and saintliness:

> Not in the splendour of command,
>   Nor in the warrior's flame-swept ranks,
> In clamorous charge or glorious stand
>   Where shattered lines held 'perilled flanks—
> But of the host who heard the call,
>   Walked he, the humblest of them all.
>
> By shell-rent paths with bullets scored,
>   In mercy moved he, unafraid;
> By ways where death alone was Lord
>   He brought his broken comrades aid.
> Meekly he went—his only creed
>   The measure of another's need.[38]

Simpson and friends, 1914
A photograph taken whilst Simpson was in training at Blackboy Hill Military Camp near Perth. The second man is Albert Currie, a Boer War veteran who, according to one version of the legend, may have encouraged him to join the Field Ambulance.

To some extent passivity was the lot of all soldiers, for war is often about waiting: 'We have become waiting machines', was one soldier's description of his plight. Because it was a 'protracted defensive struggle', in Gallipoli no less than in France, the sense of passive waiting was almost universal. As Eric Leed has written, no war before or since has more effectively eroded the 'officially sponsored conceptions of the soldierly self as an agent of aggression'.[39] Of all the troops, the stretcher-bearers suffered this erosion more than most, yet this seems to have slipped the notice of historians of the war. Stephen Kern, summarising some of the psychosocial studies of World War I, drew conclusions for soldiers in general, apparently unaware that one group of soldiers suffered the circumstances of passivity to an even greater degree:

> The normal response to mortal danger is active aggression, but the front-line soldiers were forced to be passive. Their humiliating circumstances produced a kind of 'defensive personality' that became a distinctive characteristic of war neurosis. One psychiatrist observed that nervous tension was especially destructive among men who had to remain inactive while being shelled.[40]

The diaries and letters of Australian soldiers in the Great War show that they were aware of the connection between passivity and fear, aggression and 'compensation'. Captain A. G. Carne of the 6th Battalion spoke about these connections in a narrative based upon his diary entries:

> To sit in a trench and wonder when the next shell is coming, and be able to do nothing is very trying; an open charge is much preferred—there you have something to strive for, and can see something gained, and give a knock to the enemy.[41]

These words might have been lip-service to literary conventions of boldness—it is easy for memory to be audacious—but explicit references to the anxiety of watching and waiting were commonplace and authentic. The expected attack, the calm before the storm, was a great strain on many men. Some thought it was worse than all the fighting, clamouring and climbing a soldier could do.[42] And if soldiers recognised the compensation of 'action' as part of their own circumstances, some of them were also moved by the plight of those who had to operate without it. Lieutenant J. T. Hampson wrote to his mother about this from France:

We might be drafted into a Field Ambulance at any time. I would far rather be in a combatant corps, if your time has really come it is a great satisfaction 'potting' a few of them before they get you but the Field Ambulance men are shot down like dogs and not even given a sporting chance.[43]

Harold G. Massey wrote in a similar vein to the *Sydney Morning Herald* in 1916. He was quite explicit about the circumstances that made the stretcher-bearers' activity exceptional:

The stretcher bearers are great. They go up and down all the time in the open, carrying the wounded through a withering shell fire. It's magnificent to see them. They are the real heroes of the affair, *because* they are unarmed and are exposed to everything. With no means of kicking back.[44]

Unsustained by the hot-blooded action exhibited by some men in combat, unable to retaliate, having only the dubious protection afforded by a Red Cross flag or brassard, the saintly bearers calmly risked death to save their comrades. In so doing they built up a tradition of dutiful service that was acknowledged as heroic by the civilian populace and fellow soldiers. The pathos and tragedy of it rose strongly in their hearts, indicating how mythology (in this case the Simpson legend) has its roots in the circumstances of real life. As one journal put it, they were out there 'searching for some mother's boy who might be lying in the scrub bleeding to death'.[45] Many years later when the Australian War Memorial sought an explanation for the celebration of Simpson, one of its conclusions was that the tale showed how 'the most profoundly moving acts of heroism are not those performed in hot blood, but those where a man calmly exposes his own life to danger to save a comrade without the stimulus of active retaliation to offset his fears'. As Dale Collins later wrote in his book about Anzac for children, 'the stretcher-bearers had to be classed as the bravest of the brave'.[46]

At home the legend of the saintly bearers grew from tales told by convalescent soldiers, from correspondents behind the lines and from soldiers' letters, either direct to the press, or passed on by loved ones and friends. The wounded—evacuated, lying-in, accessible, and some of them eager to talk—were an especially important source.[47] Journalists buzzed round them in search of good stories. The amputees, the blind and facially disfigured, the nerve cases, the 'enterics', and those with a mere 'holiday wound' supplied the full gamut of daring, uplifting, humorous, soul stirring, ghastly and tragic escapades. Bean saw the loquacity of convalescents as a potential problem. In a dispatch from Gaba Tepe he expressed his doubts about whether a soldier suffering from shock and nervous strain could be a source of accurate information: 'One must carefully judge his mental condition at the time', he warned.[48]

The tales of and by the wounded were ever present in the wartime press and the propaganda publications. Buley wrote his *Glorious Deeds of the Australasians* from interviews with wounded men in London hospitals. H. C. Cavill wrote *The Imperishable Anzacs* (1916) after being wounded and evacuated from Gallipoli on the first day of the fighting. Trooper Bluegum was an unhappy enteric case who set about his convalescence without delay, turning out two volumes in 1916. And there were many others, for reminiscences were an 'industry' within publishing before the war was out.

Newspapers were full of wounded men, headings and captions were as thick and random and relentless as shrapnel: Blown up by Land Mine. Soldier's Details; Hospital Life in Egypt; A Canterbury Trooper's Experience; Wounded while Bathing; Poison Gas at Ypres; One Armed Cobbers; How They Die; Comforts of the Wounded; Details of Casualties; Three Blind Men; From Trench to Hospital: Delights of Bed and Fresh Food; Buried by a Shell—a Soldier's Letter; What a Nurse Saw; Six Men Passed Out; How I Fought the Turks by a Wounded Australian; The Wandering Wounded; Maimed but Cheerful; Oh, But God They are Brave; Wheelchair Croquet. Convalescents, as subject and source, were drawn on from every possible angle.

Much of this 'wounded journalism' was superficial, rose-coloured and cheery. 'Wounds are nothing to these men—a lost arm or leg is immaterial—but the objective must be reached', wrote an unblemished, two-legged, two-armed Reuters' agent from Alexandria.[49] Occasionally accounts were more balanced. One correspondent told the people of Christchurch, New Zealand, about hospital life in Egypt. He wrote of wounds arriving full of straw and vermin, of putrid field dressings and rough field splints, of the walking wounded asleep in food queues. He followed a patrol nurse as she searched a ward for the next haemorrhage. Torn thighs, exposed arteries, glazed motionless eyes, unrecognisable hands, the quietening as morphine took effect, scissors at work on damp clothing, a knife slicing through a blood-soaked boot. Then came nightfall and, with it, horrible bubbling coughs and savage beast-like screams. A nurse sits in a thicket of traction—ropes and pulleys and little sand-bags, and white bandaged limbs point up into the dark. For a few moments all is quiet.[50]

Accounts of wounds received would frequently become records of rescues effected, of heroic stretcher-bearers working like Trojans till another call took them off or a bullet brought them down. The agonies of No Man's Land were followed by the miracles of deliverance and renewal. 'Maimed but Cheerful' and 'Eager to Return to the Fray' were headlines that seemed to sum this up. Sunday sermons and lesson books in class soon echoed the newspaper accolades for the ambulance men. 'Many of the soldiers letters mention the bravery and the devotion of the stretcher-bearers', said the *Sydney Mail*. 'All the wounded speak in glowing terms of the Red Cross work', sang the *Weekly Press*:

> They say their men were simply wonderful, and every one of them deserved the Victoria Cross. They went about their work absolutely fearlessly, taking the maximum of risks and many a brave man fell as he was attending to a wounded comrade. The fire to which they were subject was not ordinary fire: it was simply appalling and the Red Cross men moved about in the open, never thinking of their own lives in their concern for the wounded.[51]

On the home front the spectacle was presented to children. In the *School Journal* (for New Zealand) and the *School Paper* (for Australian States), it was working on their emotions: 'Wherever the bullets rain the thickest, there they are most needed, and there they will be found, passing from point to point with their stretchers, bandaging the wounded, or holding a refreshing draught of water to the parched lips of a dying soldier'. Teachers could now fit Simpson into a lesson on Kipling's poems. The saintly bearer was like Gunga Din, that other water-carrier who sought out the wounded on the battlefields of the empire: 'E lifted up my 'ead,/An' he plugged me where I bled,/An' 'e gave me 'arf-a-pint o' water green'.[52] Or they might link his story to that of Grace Bussell, the horsewoman who saved many lives after a shipwreck off the West Australian coast. Simpson was now one of the many rescue stories that provided moral lessons and role models for schoolchildren.[53]

Ferocity and tenderness

Empire propaganda told terrible tales of how the Germans and Turks neglected their wounded. Most of the crimes of neglect attributed to the enemy applied equally to the British army and, for a time (at least until September), to the arrangements for colonial troops at Gallipoli.[54] That, however, was hardly the business of empire propaganda which told a simple, one-sided tale: the enemy's wounded were massed and mangled and left to wallow in dirt and droppings and steaming, urinous straw.[55] Tales of enemy attacks on Red Cross tents, hospital ships and barges full of wounded troops abounded. It was said the wounded in the field were also tortured by the bestial foe, and correspondents could work up a special kind of fury over such crimes. As could soldiers, for violent revenge was allegedly most fierce after stories came through of enemy attacks on the saintly bearers.[56] Empathy for the bearers could be worked to a pitch of fury at the enemy: 'The Turks behaved disgracefully firing at the Red Cross at every opportunity'. One Australian said he saw a Turk slash out at a Red Cross soldier with a long knife as he was carrying a wounded New Zealander to a place of safety. 'When I jumped on him with my bayonet he held up his hands, but I could have no mercy for a brute like that, and I thrust my bayonet through him'.[57] A New Zealand surgeon noted in his diary that bearers on Gallipoli got permission to remove the red cross, 'as it has been a good mark for snipers'.[58]

Another Australian who was lying badly wounded in the Casino Hospital at Alexandria told of the treachery of a German officer. The officer, seriously wounded, had been cared for by an Australian ambulanceman who dressed his wounds. According to this account, the gratitude shown by the German was to draw his revolver and shoot the ambulanceman in the back as he walked off to assist his wounded comrade. 'I felt very bad indeed', said the Australian, 'but the sight of such a ghastly outrage put the life into me. I crawled along the ground slowly and summoning all my strength put an end to the life of the German with my bayonet'.[59] If propaganda helped shape public attitudes to the war, this German officer was on the top rung in a hierarchy of low acts, while the saintly bearers became a focal point of sympathy and righteous indignation. Soldiers helped to create this propaganda, but they were also its targets, as were civilians at home. What better proof that the fight was both necessary and just could there be? What better terrain in which to find a legendary stretcher-bearer with the 'hands of a woman'?

The stretcher-bearers were the organised expression of the Australian soldier as both brave and compassionate. They were sanctified by the press. Simpson was their personification; heroic yet tender, 'every man of them was a Simpson at heart', wrote Buley.[60] One of the neglected features of the Anzac legend is the regularity of these references to the soft and caring side of the soldiers. The interpeters of the legend may have overlooked virtues most strongly concentrated in the non-combatants, but the creators of the legend did not. In the legend's early history there are frequent affirmations of the Australian soldier's valour *and* compassion, his humanity and the rough exterior that disguised it. Bean's *Story of Anzac* describes the Australian's 'cynicism' as a mask behind which he coyly secreted his feelings with an 'almost feminine sensitiveness'; the Australian, he added, was 'as sensitive as a girl concerning any display of those feelings which he did profoundly possess'.[61]

There were times after the war when it was said that the Anzacs had been ruthless killers. Their defenders countered in several ways, sometimes with huffing indignation: 'Sir John Monash Describes Stories As So Much Moonshine'; at other times with cheeky sarcasm: 'Oh them terrible, terrible things we done,/An' the 'orrible tales we told'/The Digger drawled, 'an the deeds recalled,/Would make yer blood run cold'. On Anzac Day large congregations sang 'Oh Valiant Hearts' and were reassured that their soldiers had trod in the steps of Jesus Christ, 'following through death the martyr'd Son of God'. And frequently the retort would insist on a softer kind of Anzac, a soldier '*with a touch like a woman's*'. Even Albert Jacka, VC, an extraordinary fighting man, was remembered, on his death in 1932, for a 'curious tenderness and gentleness'.[62]

This sort of talk began during the war, when newspapers were overloaded with the heroic deeds of stretcher-bearers, with tales of their steadiness, unarmed and under enemy fire, and their ubiquitous acts of mercy. The rightness of the cause depended on a balance between the ferocity of the Australian soldier and his compassion. Propagandists wanted to assert the Anzac's savagery 'and yet maintain that he was a civilised and chivalrous character', for they were already battling stories about excessive brutality.[63] The Anzac had to be a soldier who could love as well as fight, who carried in his heart—however well disguised—the civilised values that made the Empire worth fighting for. The *Age* put it neatly in July 1915:

At times the casual observer regards them perhaps as rough and ready, using strong language when excited. But when you see them looking death straight in the eye and never a flinch, when you see a boy dying in mortal agony . . . and he looks at you and smiles; and when you see them tenderly lift a wounded Turk and give him a drink with all the tenderness of a woman, then you understand why you love them.[64]

Herbert Grattan worked this duality into his 'Grieve Not for the Anzacs'. He wrote of 'the dauntless heroes of the gum tree and the fern', of saving the empire, of a 'heritage of glory', of 'cruel wounds' and 'noble deaths', of flinging 'the gage at tyranny', and of Anzacs as 'young Crusaders'. And in the midst of this high diction he found tenderness:

> Rejoice instead that our dear sons were faithful to their trust;
> The bravest men God ever made when filled with fighting lust;
> Yet tender as a woman when the wounded needed aid,
> Our Anzac lads went forth to fight high-souled and unafraid.[65]

One of the correspondents wrote of having watched a party of soldiers come out of a front trench for a rest. He said they were dirty and hungry, burdened with the equipment of their dead mates, and 'fed up' with everything, yet, when one of them caught 'a helpless little bird' they stood about for ten minutes, each offering the other advice as to what might be best for its comfort. The despatch claimed that they 'laughed and chatted like children' as one of them tried 'to give the bird a drink from his lips'.[66] Hardness and softness, fierceness and tenderness, were routinely coupled in the description of the Anzac. The coupling was an important part of the epic formula. To recognise that these qualities went together was just as important as to understand that war was splendid, that it made boys into men, that wounded Anzacs were ever cheerful and that death was never feared when a man's duty was done. The single dispatch or published letter would draw on just one or two of these motifs. This remarkable composition from Malta drew on them all:

> Ah Bob, you don't know how grand our boys are out here. Every Man-Jack of them is a hero. They are there to win . . . Life is only valued according to fighting strength by the lads nowadays. When one of them is hit his last bit of breath is generally used up recounting the particular occasion in which he got in some good

work [ie, killing the enemy] . . . They are not the boys we all knew
in camp. This life has transformed them. Fear is unknown. They
fight like wildcats and yet are as tender as girls. They are heart
and soul in one thing—to win the fight . . . There's no use wasting
sorrow about a soldier's death, Bob. I'm satisfied that it is not a time
for sorrow. It is just the only death that a fellow could wish to die.
I've seen so much of it that I have got to look forward to my turn
with a happy content.[67]

The stretcher-bearers were the purest element in this balance within
the Anzac legend-in-the-making. They were 'so tender and solici-
tous', said one Anzac, 'they might almost have been women, so
gently did they deal with us'. 'They were lions in the fight', said
another, 'but just like women when it came to doing something for
you'.[68] The *Lone Hand* saw it much the same: 'So tender they are
when handling a case; like women. Big men in character, they show
themselves thoroughly in action'.[69] Perhaps the simple tale of
Simpson acquired additional impetus because the Anzacs had won
recognition for extreme ferocity and a dubious reputation as 'white
Ghourkas'.[70]

To see Simpson as the 'true Anzac' is to recognise that the Anzac
legend was about mateship and toughness. Our national hero had
to be found on the battlefield because this wider legend was based
on the performance of Australian fighting men. The hero Simpson
could not have been a nursing sister working tirelessly in a
Red Cross tent on the island of Lemnos or on a hospital ship off
Gallipoli. He was revered because his work represented the feminine civilising mission on a thoroughly male terrain. His appeal
depended on the fusion of the feminine and the masculine in the
form of the heroic stretcher-bearer. The presence of the feminine
in this context enhanced the legend, and with it the cause, for
heroes such as these could fortify the faith.

Chapter Five

The Name of Unsung Heroes

'Here was the world's worst wound. And here with pride
Their name liveth for ever,' the Gateway claims.
Was ever an immolation so belied
As these intolerably nameless names.'

Siegfried Sassoon, 'On Passing the New Menin Gate' (1928)

Bean wrote a great deal about the feats of the stretcher-bearers and other soldiers who risked their lives to bring in the wounded. So did his New Zealand counterpart, Malcolm Ross, and many others. In one of Bean's accounts two unknown men respond to a call for help by strolling casually through heavy fire 'with no arms and accoutrements'. One of them lights his pipe on the way and the two work for ten minutes over a dying soldier. Bean thought these two were as valuable as men on machine-guns. That dispatch reiterated his belief in the morale-boosting powers of such exemplars:

> Their officer was sitting up on the crest—a sure target for every sniper, and I suppose that inspired them to show an equivalent amount of carelessness in the face of danger; but to a mass of men, straight off the ships, thrown right into the middle of that shrapnel, there could have been nothing more comforting than to see the absolute indifference of these men to danger.[1]

When Bean wrote about this officer, the behaviour he was praising was fast becoming a literary convention, part of the language of Australian heroism, an epic formula in which we find daring escapades performed by men who never flinched, who were indifferent to shrapnel, who sauntered through 'storms of metal', who lit their pipes at extraordinary moments, and who sat sedately in the most vulnerable positions; men who liked to gamble with death, or, more likely, to marvel at those who did, to trade folklore about fate and shrapnel.

Despite his complicity, Bean had private doubts about this kind of reporting. Aware of the journalist's role in the making of myths about war, he was unhappy with grandiloquent phrases, efflorescent adjectives and comic-strip nouns, with reports that called Australian soldiers 'titans' or 'demigods' or 'supermen'. His doubts tempered his prose thus making him unpopular with some newspaper editors, but such scruples did not stop him entirely: 'What is a barrage against such troops!', he wrote of the AIF at Pozieres. 'They went through it as you would go through a summer shower . . . '. In his diary Bean could write angrily about other journalists, 'soldiers are not the fictions which war correspondents have made of them, but ordinary human men'. Privately he believed that it was heroic simply to defeat one's own fear and to carry out routine duties in the circumstances of modern war, and that the gross exaggerations of the press corps had obscured this. Yet he went on to edit *The Anzac Book* into a light-hearted, sanitised portrait of the digger and the war experience. (The material he deleted would have painted an entirely different picture of Australian soldiers). In the last analysis Bean remained faithful to the over-riding need to galvanise the public at home, stimulate recruiting and raise the morale of the troops. He contributed to the heroic myth of the Great War, as did so many other Australian writers, by concentrating on the thrill rather than the terror of battle and, in *The Anzac Book*, on the good humour of the diggers. He abhorred the war's carnage but acclaimed the wit and warriorship of his star performers.[2]

Soldiers reacted variously to this sort of reporting; a few with sarcasm and derision, most with relish. In the written record—the diaries almost as much as the letters and the memoirs—the relish most often prevailed. When Private Dick Finch wrote to his wife from Gallipoli in May 1915 he revealed the Australians' sense of national mission and the desire to make a mark:

> We have been here just long enough to be looking for newspapers to come to hand with accounts of our noble deeds. It's a sort of natural conceit; although we have settled it in our minds that we are the best ever we want to see it in black and white from some-

body else—no struggling company of actors ever looked forward more eagerly to the next morning's reviews after a hopeful opening night.[3]

Some of this bombast was designed to put worried relatives and friends at ease, while at other times it helped soldiers to deal with their own fears. Their seemingly inflated tales could also be honest reports of extraordinary heroism in battle. The pro-imperial press sought out these conceits and the honest reports that supported their claims; it fostered them, favoured them, and where necessary invented them.

The language of flagrant daring

The language of flagrant daring was part of that 'spleandour' in the epic formula which asserted that war turned boys into men, killing into sport, and death into sweet sleep. It was common for soldiers to report on the exotic and filthy cities of the Middle East, the terrible day of the landing, the blood and guts, the horrible stench after a massed attack, the weird peace during an armistice to bury the dead, the awful sights, the food, the flies, the lucky escapes, the cries from No Man's Land, the acquired indifference to death, and the evaluation of the Turk as a fighting man. Also common were the accounts of raw courage and sang-froid under fire, and the implication in many of these accounts was clear: wherever you were on the front there was a good chance you would see something similar, some nameless hero risking his life as casually as he might have a cup of tea.

Billy Hutchison landed at Gallipoli on 25 April, brimming with enthusiasm. On 26 April he wrote in his diary of events that made him feel as big as a bull: 'The boys are all in good spirits. We were being shaved by one of the lads acting as Barber and quite indifferent to the hail and bullets flying around our heads'.[4] Two months later, he would die of typhoid fever in a Cairo hospital.

Later in the campaign an infantry private recorded the difficulties of making a stew under fire, having to cut an onion, nip into his dugout as a shell went by, then out again to give the meal a stir, and so on: 'We were laughing all through because it was so comical', he wrote. Another soldier who landed in August told his family how inspired he was by the bravery of the first division men. He confirmed what he had learned from the newspapers:

By golly it is a treat to see the cool way these men who have been here since the first landing go about their work they dont seem to worry a bit about anything bullets and shells might be so much cotton wool for all the notice they take.[5]

Soldiers' letters appearing in the press included accounts of stirring deeds seen from a distance, the most remarkable behaviour silhouetted against a skyline or against a backdrop of mud and blood. The wounded were encouraged to call up memories along similar lines for the correspondents who hankered to hear them. They poured drinking water and dispensed cigarettes, to coax these stirring tales from men who could talk. Trooper Bluegum's prose took flight when he wrote from his dugout overlooking Shell Green:

Some day I'll get a virgin vellum roll, a pen richly chased and jewelled, and in letters of gold I'll try to tell the people of Australia something of the heroism of these stretcher bearers.

This sentence was the finale to a paragraph on the nameless heroes he had watched from afar: a signaller who sauntered out to repair a telephone line, 'established the connection and sauntered back, despite the shrapnel'; a medical officer of the 7th, time and again 'streaking across the danger zone and tending men under fire'.[6]

Editors and correspondents with the pro-imperial press, the censors and sections of the officer class, collaborated in the spread of this kind of talk. There was military advantage to be gained from the promotion of such role models. Strategic thinking in the Great War hinged on the cannon-fodder syndrome. Here was a war in which men were routinely compelled to deny themselves cover and initiative and dumbly pit flesh against steel. The language (and the code) of flagrant daring made the great blood sacrifice easier. The epic formula made sacrifice more willing by setting standards you could die by. Otherwise Bean's high praise for a man who makes himself a 'sure target', an officer, a leader of men, makes little sense. Bean had no time for John Monash on the grounds that he 'took no delight in running bodily risk', yet he approved of General Bridges' habit of taking his meals in the open with shells bursting nearby. The general did not last long but Bean chose to see the inspirational side of his death.[7]

The Sydney *Sun* said soldiers paid no more attention to the shells wailing from Achi Baba than to the buzzing of bumblebees.[8] According to the Melbourne *Age* in July 1915, the defiance of shrapnel had become something of a cult, and even raw newcomers fell quickly under its spell:

After one or two days (if they have fortunately escaped injury) they
cease to think whether they have a fear in their hearts. They will walk
along a parapet or commence an advance much as they might in
peace time . . . Captain Levi, an officer of the Fifth, told his men as
he led them into action he was a fatalist, and he continues to walk
about unhit—one of the very few who have escaped without [*sic*]. He
is a public school boy, and his attitude has been followed by others.
I am told it is a kind of cult now.[9]

The New Zealand stretcher-bearer, James Jackson, saw it as a matter
of familiarisation: 'The old saying "familiarity breeds contempt" is
very true as regards shrapnel', he wrote. 'When we landed the first
two or three days if one landed 200 or 300 yards away we all ducked
and hid ourselves but now we wait until they come close up and then
we hide'.[10]

Bean wrote from Gaba Tepe of the 'contempt for shrapnel'. Men
got used to it and 'simply worked on as if shrapnel was non-existent'.
His mythic patter fell short of words like 'titan' but still included
'huge men', men 'hardened to rough places' and officers who these
men 'wellnigh worshipped'.[11] He had seen men unloading barges
and stores as shells were falling, and 'others bathing or sitting up on
the barges like caretakers (who) would often play up to the spirit of
the thing and neglect even to sit under the protection which the
side of the barge offered'. It was the same at Cape Helles.[12] Bean's
praise for General Birdwood was in a similar vein to his thoughts
about Bridges: the general's rapport with the men was inspired by
his manifest bravery, for Birdwood slept in an exposed tent on the
most dangerous part of the beach. 'Many a man lost his life within
a stone's throw of the place', including Birdwood's aide-de-camp, 'a
gallant, handsome English boy'. At one point Birdwood's cool
humour allowed him to prevail in a ritual test of courage. A shell
burst nearby and a soldier joked: 'You ducked that time general'.
Birdwood replies, 'A sensible thing to do'.[13] In *The Anzac Book* a
soldier who could not discriminate as Birdwood could earned the
scorn of his comrades by ducking every time a shell burst.[14]

At least one newspaper expressed the view that Bean himself was
contemptuous of shrapnel and rifle fire. The *Sunday Times* claimed
he possessed the one crucial qualification for the task of official
historian—'he is completely oblivious of danger'—and there was an
incident to prove it. Allegedly, Bean had watched the fighting for
Gaba Tepe from a dugout near the firing line which he shared with
officers of the Australian general staff. Equipped with just a type-

writer and a periscope he watched and worked as the battle raged. Picture him, typing away, peering through his periscope 'completely oblivious of danger'. The perils of his position are of no concern to him, for only when he has finished his work does he find that of eight or nine occupants of the dugout, he alone has escaped being hit. The report concludes: 'A man like that is not likely to be beaten in getting and transmitting news'.[15] Nor was he attuned to the welfare of his fellow officers, if this report is to be the measure.

The heroic myth-in-the-making brimmed with accounts of exposure to shrapnel, cool rescues under fire and other selfless acts, of charmed lives and sacrificial deaths, of collective behaviour you could not buy in peacetime. Men spoke with authority of extraordinary things that were said to be commonplace among the diggers. And not surprisingly, this is how they spoke about Simpson. Every facet of the Simpson story became a distillation of the routine wonders and miracle heroics that eager press agents acquired near the front or at the hospital centres in Alexandria, Cairo, Valetta and elsewhere. One of the early Simpson poems is a good example:

> Gleaning and binding the broken sheaves,
>> Where the piled gun-harvest lay,
> Flouting the threat of the whining shell and
>> the drone of the ricochet,
> Swift to the jest and the back-flung word,
>> tireless, well content,
> Coatless and careless and long of limb, the
>> man with the donkey went.[16]

War writing and reporting celebrated the whistlers and the casual pipe-smokers, the sure target silhouettes, the flouters and jesters, those coatless and careless heroes. Simpson was all these things, except a pipe-smoker. (He preferred Wills' Woodbines.) His actions were projected against the wider convention of flagrant daring which was quickly into print on the home front. He too was contemptuous of shrapnel and snipers according to the *Sydney Mail* in November 1915: 'He scorned the danger and always kept going, whistling and singing—a universal favourite'. His trips, under heavy fire, were made in the most 'leisurely manner'. His return, every time, was something of a miracle.[17] Sydney de Loghe, whose first and last day of fighting on the peninsula was 25 April, claimed Simpson was known to all: 'They said no fire disturbed him'.[18]

Ashmead Bartlett told his readers of Simpson working on amidst 'the most furious shrapnel fire [that] swept every crevice incessantly'.[19] And Bean claimed that 'Simpson had escaped death so many times he was completely fatalistic; the deadly sniping down the valley and the most furious shrapnel fire never stopped him'.[20]

In his *Child's History of Anzac* Buley described the work of an unnamed water-carrier in terms that could have come from the tales of Simpson. You read it expecting to come across him and the donkey. But Buley is talking about someone else and Simpson's story arrives a page later, quite separately, relatively brief, and surprisingly free from hyperbole, possibly because the author has already used all the appropriate phrases so close by. We learn that the water-carrier took his precious cargo to his mates; that he had to cross an open space where he was a target for snipers; that he did this again and again; that he seemed to bear a charmed life; that nothing could make him move any quicker, or make him stop ('He walked at a steady, even pace through this danger zone, without showing any sign of fear'); and that many men watched him walking among the bullets, spoke of him and remembered him. Of Simpson we learn that he was a *typical* stretcher-bearer—no risk was too great for him; that the soldiers lost count of the numbers he rescued; that he was a great favourite who 'thought nothing of going into the open under fire for a wounded man'; and that he was able to go into the thickest shrapnel and come out unharmed. Then he is killed. 'Simpson is mourned to this day by the comrades he tended with so much care and devotion.'[21]

A similar ploy is evident in another book written for a youthful audience, Joseph Bowes' *The Young Anzacs*. Here we find the principal motifs from the Simpson legend absorbed into the life of an ambulanceman called Tim Hogan. The book tells the story of several young, strapping, country lads from Queensland, among them Tim, an expatriate Irishman and a bush worker when the war broke out. After the ritual eulogy to the courage of the non-combatants and to Tim's 'charmed life' in the thickest of gunfire, Tim finds himself behind enemy lines with a badly wounded Australian officer to rescue: 'Arrah, captain, darlin'!' he says assuringly, 'shure'n ye're worth ten dead Chineymen yet!' Then he scouts about in the dark and literally bumps into a donkey: 'His joy knew no bounds, but at the same time his grip [on the animal] strengthened, for here was a deliverance!' The captain praises him with the words, 'Bless you my noble boy!', but Tim is quick to deflect

'Donkey Man of Gallipoli'
The War Memorial note on this photograph reads: 'Men who served with Kirkpatrick in the 3rd Field Ambulance have declared that this is not a photograph of him'. The War Memorial was right.

the praise, 'Bless the donkey, captain. He's the boy wot's goin' ta do the trick . . . A treasure he is, the darlin''. They set off and some hours later they are almost home:

> The sun had now risen. Nearing their haven were two men and a donkey. From early dawn they had progressed towards their goal, guided in part by the rifle fire which indicated the position of the Anzacs. The tortuous route had not been without its vicissitudes. Again and again they were on the brink of discovery, but they had evaded the enemy . . . 'Be jabers, captain, dear, we're home or nixt door to it [says Tim]. See! there's the beach below, an' the boys! An' by the piper, there's the beautiful ships, an' the rowin' boats bringin' in more men!'

At this point Tim is shot. He drops in a heap beside the donkey and the roles of the two men are reversed. The captain somehow lifts Tim across the donkey's withers in front of him and then, 'driving his heels into its sides, sends it helter-skelter down the ridge towards Anzac beach'. The donkey is shot from under them, but Tim and the captain live to fight another day. Bowes summed up the adventure with words befitting the epic formula: 'All Tim had done had been wrought in the spirit of one who should say, "I'm a lucky dog to be in this!"'[22]

In October 1915 the *Bulletin* carried a parable of flagrant daring in the form of a dramatised dispatch. Simpson has what appears to be a minor role, figuring as a casualty at the outset. As shrapnel wreaks havoc on the mule convoys carrying water to the troops, a sergeant-major reports to the colonel:

> 'Have to report mule convoy shelled up the Gully, sir. Private Simpson and Lance corporal Farquhar killed; Sergeant Jones wounded, back in hospital. All B Company . . . '
> 'The devil,' said the Colonel.
> 'Also two mules shot, and two others bad enough to be shot right away. Water-cart back in camp, damaged. New cask and repairs wanted'.

The colonel is compelled to order a stop to the daytime convoys. Soldiers on the heights above are parched. For a while the 'sorely-tried convoys' attempt the rugged gully at night, but it is 'as dark as a nigger's pocket' and too difficult. The drivers curse their way up and they curse their way down. They 'almost went down on their knees to the powers begging permission to risk the job in the daytime', and so permission is granted. All goes well for a day or two with 'a Sabbatical calm' settling on the gully, much to everyone's surprise, but the calm is shattered when a mule convoy is subjected to withering shrapnel and machine-gun fire. Three men and their mules take cover. They can chance the last quarter of a mile or wait till dark. No question. 'The meeting signified that it'd sooner chance the job now than skin its shins among the boulders in the dark'. They choose bullets rather than boulders and take off. The sound of an express train roars down the gully. 'Shrapnel, blast thim,' says the Irish Sergeant Mullaney. Several mules are laid waste and Private McFadyen pitches forward in a heap, stone dead. The third man answers only to the name of 'Colossi'. 'Run for it Colossi, run for it I tell ye!' shrieks Mullaney, but a sniper's bullet cuts off his sentence. He reels like a drunkard, gasps and falls backward. Another shrapnel shell roars down the gully. Colossi works feverishly to get the stupefied mules running. The shell bursts high above and Colossi, mounted on one of the mules, charges through a 'leaden hail storm' towards the beach:

> Five minutes later the camp fatigues saw a riotous mule team careering like scalded cats out of the gully, with a black-haired lunatic on top of the cart, singing weird songs in a foreign tongue. Colossi had come home.

The finale is comic yet heroic. The dead are back in the gully. It is Colossi's rousing performance we are left with. Simpson's part, fittingly, comes early in this account of water-carriers with no time to waste, men who prefer the full light of day. As testimony to the growth of the legend, his name needs no explanation. Mullaney, McFadyen and Colossi follow in his footsteps. The legend was by then attached to a name (a life) that had been eclipsed early in the campaign, a foundation for the evolving convention of flagrant daring.[23]

Simpson's grave provided another opportunity to spread the talk of inspirational deeds. In a dispatch published in the *Argus*, highly coloured if not a total invention, a battle-scarred Australian general, not surprisingly unnamed, inspects a row of white crosses at Gallipoli. A sergeant carries the Roll of Honour with its details of the dead. Bullets are kicking up dust around them, but the general shows no concern, he is too engrossed in the business at hand. (The casual indifference to danger survives, passed down from the dead to the living.) As the two men move from grave to grave the sergeant reads aloud. There was a dead man whose bush skills had been of inestimable value (he had a wife and five children in Gippsland), another whose confidence had been contagious (a schoolteacher, he was there on 25 April), one who had fought on though riddled with bullets (a rabbit-trapper from Queanbeyan), another who had insisted on working the most dangerous ground, and yet another who was always 'ready to lead any adventure'. Simpson's grave was next. The sergeant read out the now- familiar tale, telling of conspicuous bravery and the *spectacle* of his many rescues under fire with the help of the donkey: 'Everyone here in the early days knew Simpson. He was a wonder'. For a time the general could not speak. Then he said, 'What brave fellows they all are . . . For them the war has finished. Their joys and troubles are ended. Australia should be proud of them—and she is'.[24]

After the war the talk of daring deeds remained central to the content and meaning of the folklore about Simpson. Jim Stubbs remembered him 'slouching along with his donkey, and his last remarks were, "There's no Turk on here who can kill me"'.[25] A West Australian officer reminisced on Simpson's 'competent, casual nonchalance' in the performance of his self-imposed task: 'It was one of the most inspiring sights of those early Gallipoli days . . . Soldiers watched him spellbound from the trenches'. Another West Australian said, 'He was the type of man who made the AIF famous'.[26] His contempt for shrapnel was celebrated in a 1934 poem where men are again joking with one another about the 'ducking' game. The two stanzas silently tell us that Simpson is about to die because they conform to earlier accounts of his death that make note of a fine morning, an early start, the man too eager to wait for his breakfast, then an exchange in which he says he will get it later:

> Then as I stood before my dugout yawning,
> I saw Murph and his donk come up the track.
> I called out, "Hey, Murph, bonzer morning."
> "We'll have your breakfast here when you come back."
> "Y' lazy cloons," (he always would chi-ack)
> "I'll have my dinner then, Y're gettin' slack."
>
> Murph and his Duffy trudged on up the track.
> His little donkey, with its Red Cross sign,
> I watched him lay a hand upon its back, . . .
> Then suddenly I heard a shrapnel whine.
> Murph saw me duck (and only just in time).
> Then he called back, "y' said the mornin's fine?"[27]

Not surprisingly one of the few stories about the childhood of John Simpson Kirkpatrick is a tale in which he exhibits the most casual indifference to his safety. The boy was working on Fred Patterson's little boat, taking milk and stores to the ships anchored on the River Tyne which ran through South Shields to the sea. The wind was blowing hard and as they approached a ship called the *Bride*—it was laden with grass—young Kirkpatrick fell overboard. In the 1920s Fred Patterson told the *South Shields Gazette* of how he had pulled Kirkpatrick back into the boat with great difficulty, whereupon the first words the boy spoke were, 'Look at my tabs'.

> He was holding a penny packet of Woodbines [said Fred Patterson]. They were soaked with river water. I said "never mind your tabs man, it's your life you've got to think about."[28]

The boy had not a thought for his life. The story in isolation is plainly trivial but the way it conforms to the established legend of Simpson and the diggers made it meaningful.

Simpson's many brushes with death and his apparent immunity became an important part of the legend. It was said his treks up and down Shrapnel Gully were spellbinding, presumably because he ran such risks and had so many narrow escapes.[29] Other soldiers figured in the tales as an audience witnessing a great spectacle that was also something of a mystery. Was it pure chance that allowed him to make so many trips, to rescue so many men, or was there some design to his fate? Some men reckoned he had a charmed life such was his freedom of movement, which suggests that Simpson was absorbed into a wider set of superstitions common to the Great War.

As Paul Fussell has observed, one of the paradoxes of modern war is the way in which it gives rise to very 'un-modern superstitions, talismans, wonders, miracles, relics, legends and rumours'. Fussell wrote of the 'prodigious renewal of oral tradition, the ancient mother of myths and legends'.[30]

Soldiers were fascinated by anyone who was pre-eminently mobile, and the coatless and careless diggers were no exception. Their own limited mobility was the basis of their fascination. 'Immobility made movement a magical, fantastic possibility to be specified in dreams, legends and myth', wrote the historian Eric Leed in his study of the European war. It produced legends like George Mitchell in France, and anti-heroes like the mythical spy-officer who was said to move freely through the English lines.[31] It also contributed to the Simpson legend as part of a Gallipoli folklore that was rich with charmed lives, ruminations about fate and faith, and omens good and bad. The *Bulletin*'s Red Page passed on the following piece of trench wisdom in August 1915:

> If it whistles like a cricket with a bad cold it will pass harmlessly overhead. If it sounds like far distant cheering such as Hooray-ay-ay, duck for cover as your chance of Kingdom Come are good.[32]

The *Age* recounted a story told by a convalescent of how one charmed fellow carried a dixie of hot tea to his mates through a bullet-whipped zone, saying 'I'm not going to spill this for anyone', whereupon he turned to the Turkish trenches and shouted, 'And you d——fools are not going to make me run'.[33] He didn't spill a drop of blood or a drop of tea. The 'invulnerable' Colonel McKay 'just stood up in the middle of that storm of shot and shell as if only grasshoppers were flying past him . . . Bullets plucked his clothing right and left but none touched his skin'.[34] Oliver Hogue thought such things 'savoured of the supernatural'.[35]

A lance corporal wrote to his sister of his surprise at how some soldiers were hit immediately they landed, while others survived for months without a scratch, himself included.[36] A New Zealand infantryman noted superstitions all around him. A mathematician in peacetime, he carried a violin through the entire Gallipoli campaign, filled his diaries with literary and classical allusions and wrote down the chords of soldiers' impromptu songs. He also noted how the men of his platoon spoke of bullets marked with your number and of shells marked with your name.[37] Many soldiers became convinced of this, having seen men walking through shellfire unscathed, without quickening their pace or turning a hair, and others running frantically, only to be smashed by a direct hit.[38] The 'charmed lives' could rub shoulders with death and get away in one piece. Bean noted one soldier who, in a matter of moments, got a bullet through the top of his hat that parted his hair, and another that ripped his left sleeve. Three more hit his ammunition pouches, another struck his entrenching tool, and two went through his left leg, leaving him only slightly wounded.[39]

The stretcher-bearers were also the subject of much philosophical speculation. The press printed accounts of stretcher-bearing parties walking through a tornado of shot and shell, where a minute before there was carnage and a minute later the same again. 'But some kind of fate spared them from disaster', the *Weekly*

Press concluded. 'Scarcely had the toilers of mercy passed on their way safely than the traffic was resumed, but the first man coming each way was wounded'.[40] One stretcher-bearer told of the great experiences at the landing, of the dreadful loss of life, and of carrying the wounded all day and most of the night on his birthday. He was astonished at the vagaries of shrapnel; he had seen miraculous escapes from death. His account was full of the wonders of it all as he reckoned that every soldier and ambulance boy who got through the war unscathed must have a charmed life. He felt as if he had one too.[41]

A surgeon with the New Zealand Medical Corps pondered another mystery of survival as he looked out to sea:

> May 14. I have been watching the Red Cross launch towing two boats of wounded off to the hospital ship. At least 8 shells fell within a few feet of her. We are so high up that we could give no help if she was hit. It was a horrible quarter of an hour. I would rather be hit anyday myself than see a boat of wounded under fire. I humbly believe that God does look after our wounded on their trip to the ship. The only time I saw the launch hit, one of her crew and not any of her wounded, was hit.[42]

At times, the troops thought the donkeys were charmed. Soldiers followed their lead, sticking close to the ones that seemed immune; some chose to stand among tethered donkeys during a barrage of shells.[43] There were tales about Simpson in which he too moved under the protective spell of his four-legged partners, but mostly the charm was attached to the man himself:

> At times they [the man and the donkey] held trenches of men spellbound, just to see them at their work. Their quarry lay motionless in an open patch, in easy range of a dozen Turkish rifles. Patiently the little donkey waited under cover while the man crawled through the thick scrub until he got to within striking distance. Then a lightning dash, and he had the wounded man on his back, and was making for cover again. In those fierce seconds he always seemed to bear a charmed life.[44]

It became a convention that Simpson bore a charmed life, part of the legend to be handed down.[45] Early in 1916 an officer with the Indian Field Ambulance commented on his death in a way that confirmed the speculation that had come to surround him: 'The mystery was cleared by Jack Simpson proving mortal like all the rest of us'.[46]

A flesh and blood allusion

Simpson was extraordinary and typical; a hero in an army full of heroes, men with 'a reputation for daredevil bravery in the mass'.[47] At one level the uncertainty about his real name was a puzzle about individual identity, but at another it was a necessary confusion grounded in his humble and representative status. There was incessant talk about giving them all a VC or a DCM. When the *Daily Malta Chronicle* announced Simpson's exploits to the outside world it was in the context of the stretcher-bearers in general: 'Such acts as these were common amongst them, and many a DCM was won by them that will never be known of'.[48] Many men shared in an undecorated heroism, an omission much lamented by soldiers at the time and down the years. A soldier recuperating in England wrote to Simpson's mother expressing these sentiments: 'I often think about Jack especially when I tell people about your son saving me and losing his own life after doing such good work, and if anybody was worthy of a VC it was Jack'.[49]

It was no simple coincidence that such things were said frequently, for soldiers were reacting to one of the most powerful spectacles of war, to an emotional motif central to the emerging Anzac legend: the collective heroism and sacrifice of the bearers, and of all soldiers who took risks rescuing their comrades. Major General Brand wanted to immortalise all the AIF stretcher-bearers, because 'when a man continually entered a bullet-swept zone to succour a wounded comrade he displayed the highest form of bravery'. Brand remembered Simpson as someone who would not heed the warnings of his comrades, and who 'gambled with death'. General Sir Harry Chauvel was another who gave voice to this idea. He thought Simpson's daily service was typical of three notable features of the Australian soldier—'initiative, self-sacrifice and solicitude for his wounded comrades'.[50]

Simpson became the name of many unsung heroes, the embodiment of all those officially unrecognised acts of valour, the story that regularly led to some broad claim to collective heroism. As legend he was a generalisation in the form of the particular. He was just one of thousands who earned a VC but never got one. A poem in the *Boy's Own Annual* celebrated this facet of the legend in 1916:

> No medals blazed on Murphy's breast,
> No stripes adorned his sleeve,
> Yet Fame upon his place of rest
> Her laurel wreath shall leave.[51]

As the returned soldiers' newspaper *Duckboard* put it during the memorial appeal of 1933, it was hard to believe that recognition had taken so long, 'but it is probably true that there were so many spectacular deeds of bravery at Anzac that it has become difficult to discriminate amongst them'.[52]

The official record underpinned this belief because it had little to say about Simpson and did not really distinguish him from thousands of others. The War Diary of the 3rd Field Ambulance, for instance, mentioned his initiative and hard work, noted that he went missing on 25 April, recorded his death and reported that he had been mentioned in dispatches. There were four brief mentions in all.[53]

Official policy also reinforced the sense of unrewarded heroism during Simpson's time on the peninsula. A Routine Order made soon after the landing on 25 April 1915 stated that no decorations were to be given to stretcher-bearers for acts of valour.[54] Buley told a fast-growing readership about this late in 1915, in his *Glorious Deeds of the Australasians*:

> After the first few days on Gallipoli, its officers recognised the impossibility of officially recognizing deeds of bravery, and practically no awards have been made since the end of April.[55]

The tales of Simpson rarely offered a reason for his failure to be decorated. What mattered was that the absence of the decoration became a vital part of the legend. 'If ever a man deserves a VC', said the Reverend George Green in 1933, 'it was Simpson'.[56] When the statue at the Shrine of Remembrance was unveiled in 1936 the *Bulletin* joined the lament. Never a journal to hold back on explanations, it proposed the idea that the wrong people often got medals for the wrong reasons, while Simpson had been forgotten by the powers-that-be. Some time after the war there had been a collection organised in Sydney to raise funds for Simpson's mother (who was never far from the legend), 'but no person in authority thought to bespeak even a posthumous OBE for her son'.[57]

Few of the many soldiers who have talked about Simpson ever saw the man John Simpson Kirkpatrick; fewer still had known him. His legend was fostered by soldiers who had observed many men performing many tasks, and from the sense of collective and unsung heroism they had shared or marvelled at. It became the concentrated form of these observations. The Simpson legend was an essence, a conventionalised discourse on brave deeds. It was a symbolic response, a motif for a collective performance. Simpson, Simmo, Simmy, Kirkpatrick, Murphy, Murph, Duffy, Tipperary, Scotty, Latimer—whatever he was called—was many men. He was a flesh and blood allusion for a plurality of faceless heroes. He was an extract, the active principle still present when the multitudes of unsung heroes had disappeared in the smoke of No Man's Land, or retreated honourably to the vegetable gardens of post-war suburbia, or taken up dusty selections in the Mallee or the Wimmera. His legend evolved out of the language of flagrant daring in which the Anzac legend itself was grounded, and from the painful emphasis within that legend on *unsung* heroism.

It has been said that soldiers found it easy to talk about Simpson because it led away from their own awful experiences, but the opposite is also true: when they spoke of him they were talking about themselves. Simpson talk was a feint which led, circuitously, back to the speaker. Just as the Menin Gate monument to the missing presumed dead was addressed to a psychological need to know what had happened, a need evident in the words of Lord Plumer at the unveiling, 'He is not missing, he is here!', so the Simpson legend satisfied a similar need to give unnamed heroes a name, to recognise that which could never be recognised individually.[58] Simpson was a 'disguise' in which this palpable need was frequently dealt with and expressed. His legend entailed a displacement of emotion and meaning from one thing to another.[59] As Buley said of the stretcher-bearers, soldiers will tell you that 'everyman of them was a Simpson at heart'.[60]

The pro-imperial press conveyed the pain of living with the anonymous deeds and unsung marvels of Australian manhood, of knowing that so much was given freely, yet so little could be recognised and rewarded. Such loss was a great burden for those who wished to pay homage, to decorate every hero, yet so much was missing—the men, the names, the stories. The Australian

Another Donkey Man

correspondent writing for the *Egyptian Mail* in 1917 pinpointed this sense of loss when he spoke about the mourners of the dead, saying, 'No chronicles have told them the details of what was done at Anzac. Only a few names and the echo of some isolated feats have reached them'. But these names afforded great compensation—they were 'witness to the courage displayed by all our troops'.[61] Similarly, a headline in the Sydney *Sunday Times* emphasised not so much the return of the wounded as what might be recovered through them:

> Eyes That See Nameless Things Tell
> Unwritten Stories of the Battlefields Horrors.[62]

The wounded would speak and perhaps some of the lost marvels would be reclaimed. Other papers used similar language and evinced the same hopes. Collectively they expressed this sense of loss; not just the loss of men, though that was part of it, but the loss of what they had done. The ultimate paradox resided in the knowledge that so much of it you would never know. Consider this for a photograph: an Australian soldier, a horseman, sits astride his bay horse on the beach at Anzac. There are dugouts in the background and several onlookers, three of them Indians. The headline, 'A Daring Unknown Australian' is complemented by the caption as follows:

> Twice a day this member of the Australian forces at Gallipoli rode through a hail of bullets for about a mile carrying despatches from the headquarters of the Division at Anzac. He used to cling to the off-side of his mount, and although he had several horses shot under him, he himself escaped unhurt.[63]

Here we have everything but the name. The title acknowledges the loss, but also the partial reclamation.

Another case, that of Private Bobby Burns, is recounted in language which focuses on imminent loss and a sense that much that is worthy of honour is sinking out of sight: 'From the scores of unnamed heroes of those days *one rescues with gladness* the name of Private Burns, whose story is told in the words of another Private'. And so Bobby Burns' story is told and it is a story of selfless heroism in the rescue of two badly wounded soldiers, concluding that 'if anyone deserves a VC Bobby Burns does'. He will not get a VC, that goes without saying, but his gallant deed has been rescued from the scores of unnamed heroes, and in the course of the rescue this small but gratifying compensation is acknowledged.[64] To borrow a line from Byron: 'These are deeds which should not pass away,/And names that must not wither'.[65]

Some two decades later, when the statue of Simpson and the Donkey was to be unveiled near the Shrine of Remembrance, a poem appeared in the Melbourne *Argus*. It spoke of a legend that was a compensation for thousands of men who were not rescued as Bobby Burns had been, men whose deeds would never be remembered as they ought to be—reverently and individually.

The Man with the Donkey
by Christina McAskell

Type of all those who serve their fellow's need
And die unknown,
Stand here, beside your little patient steed
On his memorial stone.
Not called by your own name
But by a chance name such as comrades give,
Here stand for all the unnamed, forgot by fame,
Who in the course of duty went and came
By death-swept paths, that wounded men might live.

Stand here, to keep alive in memory
The evil times gone past
On far Gallipoli and those drear days
When, though earth shrivelled in destruction's flame,
You followed cheerfully your appointed ways
And, walking long unscathed amid the blaze
Others to save, saved not yourself at last.
Until the dream behind such deeds we see,
Until our deeds to that high dream we frame,
By this green hill abide, our watchman be![66]

The memorial was to symbolise all those who were unknown, unnamed, forgot, to stand for all 'the unnamed, forgot by fame'. If the legend has a core that explains its longevity in Australian folklore, it is the pain of bearing witness, the cruel sense of loss, and the search for symbolic compensation. The tale has been shared by soldiers and civilians alike. The legend spoke to its inheritors of a nation searching for emotional reparation.

John Simpson Kirkpatrick in Shrapnel Gully

Simpson was the name of unsung heroes. His name stood for them, his typicality singled him out. Yet it was this same typicality that raised a modicum of resistance to his legend: some soldiers said his typicality was precisely the reason why he should not be honoured or commemorated. Their position was ultra-democratic in that they insisted that none should be elevated or singled out above the collective sacrifice. This was a point of view with a following among front-line soldiers, and it was put emphatically by men who said they had nothing against Simpson, it was just that many others had been as brave as he, at Gallipoli and elsewhere. They wanted to speak of the unnamed rather than give the un-named a name. Even in their resistance they confirmed the social function of the legend.[67]

The braggart Simpson

Not every soldier could come to terms with the standards set by the language of flagrant daring (signifying the likes of Simpson), with the contempt for shrapnel or the acquiescence to fate. Those who ducked might have to live with the shame of it. One soldier denigrated his warrant officer whom he called Billy the Bastard, claiming that he ran for his 'funk-hole' whenever shells came over.[68] There were men who called bullets 'canaries' and wandered amongst them as calmly as if they were strolling in a garden.[69] There were others who froze in their foxholes and prayed for a clean shot to finish it.[70] One of these was so frightened he swallowed his false teeth. 'Let these things be called by their proper names', growled A. C. Aitken, his violin case by his side.[71] He was sick and tired of the bravado, the romanticising terminology and other ridiculous tripe served up by the press, like the *Sunday Times* headline 'Test Match Bomb Team Catches Live Grenades'.[72] Another soldier wrote to the *Sydney Mail* about bursting shells, candidly admitting he could never view this occurrence with unconcern. 'I envy those chaps who declare that they became so accustomed to shells dropping about that they took very little notice of them. They always made me nervy, and I had some wonderfully narrow escapes'.[73]

As a confession this was a curious mixture. The unnamed soldier 'candidly' declared his envy, as well as his fear and his wonder at his own narrow escapes. Daring behaviour was a performance that provoked a variety of responses. Envy, for example, was not too far removed from resentment; and resentment when bitter could grow into hatred. How many soldiers resented the deadly standards that this convention set for them? Bean and others spoke only of the inspiration drawn from daring exploits; they said nothing of fear or envy and where it might lead.

Yet we have to confront this possibility in order to explain what is, at first sighting, the most bizarre account of Simpson ever to appear in print. It is a poem that was published in the *Bulletin* late in June 1915. 'Was It Simpson?' was written by David McKee Wright under the pen-name Curse O' Moses. It is hardly likely that Wright knew about *the* Simpson because the legend was not yet in circulation in Australia. Wright was fond of plucking common names out of the press and using them repeatedly in his poems. Yet the 'Simpson' he wrote of is an embodiment of flagrant daring, much as the real Simpson would soon be, with one notable difference— this Simpson might be a traitor:

> He looked like Simpson, though the rags he wore
>   Were Oriental in their make and dirt.
> Smith eyed him through the smoke the war-wind
>   bore.
>   Careless he walked as though no shell could hurt,
> Or bullet pierce a man so fine and brave—
> He looked like Simpson by his walk and shave.
>
> Twice in the scrub along the dire-scourged hill
>   Smith saw him as he swaggered to and fro;
> Three times above the trenches, careless still,
>   As if he owned the fight and all the show.
> Surely it must be Simpson! None but he
> Would make himself a mark for all to see.
>
> Smith clenched his teeth. If Simpson were turned
>   Turk,
>   Here was the chance that he had sought so long;
> Here he was free his vengeful wrath to work
>   And settle scores for years of shame and wrong.
> Smith watched. If it were Simpson it was plain
> The braggart would reveal himself again.

He does reveal himself again. In fact he laughs as the bullets whistle round, and Smith thinks he knows that laugh. The battle rages and

Smith, with the question of identity still unclear—now it's 'the Turk that looked like Simpson'—goes after him with the bayonet.[74] He leads 500 men into battle 'foremost in the furious race/To see if that tall Turk had Simpson's face'. The Turk (or Simpson) turns and flees, with Smith in hot pursuit:

> Achilles chasing Hector's horse hair plume
> > Was not a circumstance to that mad race.
> The whole peninsula must give them room,
> > So fierce and frantic did they make the pace;
> For whether he was Simpson or his double,
> The front man understood that Smith meant trouble.

Smith chases this fellow to the 'verge of European soil'. Simpson, or the Turk, plunges into the sea, with Smith quick to follow, realising his quarry 'could do the crawl':

> Smith wildly followed, daunted not at all.
> > Suspicion in his soul had larger play.
> Simpson or Turk, this man could do the crawl
> > That Simpson learned from Smith at Watson's Bay.
> Reckless of floating mines they crossed the flood,
> And landed angry in the Mysian mud.

The chase goes on and the poem comes to an end with Simpson (or the Turk) rushing onward towards Australia, and Smith hot on his heels.[75]

Any attempt to fit this bizarre and puzzling poem into a history of the legend is at best tentative. But it may have a place as a response to the language and practice of flagrant daring; that is, to the behaviour that the legendary Simpson would soon signify or embody. If this be the case then the poem can be seen to operate at two levels. The first is a fairly straightforward account of a betrayal, with its origins back in Australia. Smith revelled in his chance to 'settle scores for years of shame and wrong'. His desire to kill this man clearly arises from the possibility that he is not a Turk, but an Australian, a former acquaintance. The desire for revenge is facilitated by the confusion around the man's identity, by the possibility that he is both 'Turk' and Simpson, that he is a renegade. 'If Simpson were turned Turk,/Here was the chance that he had sought so long . . . ' The poem makes sense as a personal vendetta culminating in a bizarre chase, and had it been submitted a few months later the *Bulletin* may not have published it.[76]

The second level of the poem entails the confrontation between Smith and Simpson as a symbol of flagrant daring. The opening stanzas make great play of Simpson's apparent courage: 'Careless he walked as though no shell could hurt,/Or bullet pierce a man so fine and brave'. But the admiration quickly turns sour. The Turk (or Simpson) swaggers, he behaves as if he 'owns the fight and all the show', he is a braggart. And lastly, it appears he is not so brave after all—when confronted by Smith's bayonet he flees. This braggart who has taken on the appearance of a Turk is chased off Gallipoli by an Australian soldier. We can read his behaviour (his flagrant daring) as being the nub of his treachery and the poem as a wishful fantasy. At this level it is flagrant daring that is alien, that could well have a longer history (explaining the 'years of shame and wrong'), that is found to be somewhat hollow when confronted, and that must be chased from the battlefield. How many soldiers must have wished it so?

'Was It Simpson?' followed a number of Wright's earlier poems, parodies in which the Trojan War is reduced to a sort of punch-up, with larrikin episodes replacing fine Homeric accounts of exemplary manly deeds. These poems engaged in a curious debunking of the mythic type and were deliberately at variance with the fashionable use of the ancient past by McCrae, Lindsay, Sidney Long and others. All were written before the Anzac landing. Wright celebrated the landing, and his other poems about Gallipoli in 1915 were notable for their serious-minded adoption of the epic formula. 'Was It Simpson?' is therefore an aberration, the last gasp of Wright's facetious series, and a momentary recognition of the bizarre workings of flagrant daring.

Chapter Six

All Creatures Great and Small

No road too rough for the tiny hoofs
and never too long the day . . .
And the richest prize in the world to him
was a wisp of ration hay
Thro' stony creek and unyielding scrub,
in thirst and in heat and in cold,
He picked his way with unerring feet
and a spirit serene and bold,
And ever the wounded men gave thanks
for the two great hearts of gold!
And I think that angels walked beside
as they marched in their lowly state;
Day in day out where the red death smote,
they carried their precious freight—
And the sunshine's glow is in hearts today
that else had been desolate.

T. H. 'Crosscut' Wilson, 'Simpson's Donkey', 1916

When the prophet Zechariah foretold the coming of a messiah 'lowly, and riding upon an ass', he was employing a symbol that his audience would immediately understand. For here was a king not driving a chariot like other kings, not encased in armour, not demanding tributes, not thrusting men out of his way and leading about guards, but instead riding an ass to indicate the peaceful nature of his advent. Centuries before Israel's patriarchal age the ass or donkey had been domesticated and mythologised, figuring as a draught animal and a beast of burden and having myriad associations with the demons and gods of 'idolatrous' cults and clans. The Christian scriptures indicate that the kings of Israel rode a descendant of the legendary white *onager*, an ass of far greater stature and speed, and finer colour, than the common strains.

With the introduction of the horse from the northern parts of Asia, however, the association with the high and mighty was completely broken, and after the time of Solomon the ass was banished from the royal stables. There could thus be no ambiguity in Zechariah's chosen symbol which has, in any case, always been rendered as a common ass. It identified the messiah with the lowly, and it emphasised his essential peaceableness. To drive home these contrasts (high–low, war–peace and, by implication, oppressor–oppressed) the prophet also foretold a reckoning with the weapons of war. 'And I will cut off the chariot from Ephraim, and the horse from Jerusalem, and the battle bow shall be cut off: and he shall speak peace unto the heathen: and his dominion shall be from sea even to sea, and from the river even to the ends of the earth.'[1]

In the New Testament neither the chariot, nor the horse, nor the battle bow is cut off—Britishers in 1914 could still believe this task had been left to them—but the prophecy of the triumphal entry is fulfilled on Palm Sunday with the multitude spreading their garments as straw for the ass to walk upon and the enemies of peace and righteousness becoming 'sore displeased'.[2] Apart from the imagery of the crucifixion, the triumphal entry of Jesus into Jerusalem was perhaps the most familiar of Christian images to filter through to the present era, the association of the ass with meekness and peace was near universal in Christian cultures of 1914. The ass has in fact signified many other things in the proverbs and fables that have fed European literature—cleverness, lust, cuckoldry, conceit, stubbornness—but the triumphal entry has been the enduring image in our culture, its meaning numerously woven into the fabric of our history.[3]

When the Great War began the urge to find a higher justification for the sacrifice was widespread and inevitably it was found in Christian purpose. 'From pulpit, platform, editor's desk and chapter house a single message came forth: God called on Australians to accept suffering and sacrifice to defeat the evil ambitions of Germany and to bring forth a higher civilisation in Australia'. People were constantly being reassured that God was on the Empire's side and that Christ, were he an Australian, would be a digger. The belief in Christ's martyrdom and resurrection was thus projected on to the nation in the form of a powerful civic religion, what might be called, borrowing from George Mosse, a 'cult of the fallen soldier'. Against this background it was inevitable that the tale of the man with the donkey at Gallipoli, of his good deeds and his death, would appeal to the propagandists and to many in their audience. The figure of the lowly Simpson would merge with figurations of Christ (the crucifixion as well as the triumphal entry) and with other heroes of the New Testament, notably the Good Samaritan.[4]

If these religious associations enriched the Simpson image for people on the home front, they were of far less significance for soldiers at Gallipoli where the donkey's utility mattered most, followed closely by its endearing qualities as a pet and mascot. In each of these respects its place in military culture was secured within months of the landing. The donkey became a focus of considerable affection; its part in the leisure time of soldiers was possibly as important as its role in the ambulance units.

Pets and mascots

As the Anzacs prepared for war in Egypt, a London correspondent declared that 'one could almost stack a menagerie with the numerous animals that are treasured as mascots by the New Zealanders and Australians'. The *Sydney Mail* commented that this was a 'humorous exaggeration', implying it was not entirely wrong.[5] Soldiers readily took animals to war. Individuals might have their own talismans or keepsakes—a lock from a sweetheart's hair, a souvenir ribbon, gum tips or pepper-tree leaves tucked away in a diary, a photograph secreted in a locket—but most units also took something they could share, often a pet of some kind. The *Sydney Mail* observed:

> Every ship that leaves the Commonwealth with troops on board carries a miscellaneous collection of Australian animals and birds as mascots of the different troops.[6]

When the Gilgrandra men marched to Sydney in 1915 to enlist, they were feted in townships all along the way. They were given food, speeches and song; the young women dealt out rounds of 'patriotic kisses'. They were also given a horse and dray, a kangaroo, a cockatoo, a fox cub and a cattle pup.[7] Cats, possums, wallabies, kangaroos, dogs (bulldogs, sheepdogs and other breeds), monkeys, birds, pigs, donkeys, white rabbits and possibly other animals too; all made the trip to Gallipoli or Europe. The 'regimental pet' of the 7th Army Services Corps at Gallipoli—a miniature donkey dressed in pyjamas and hat—was photographed with its handlers on board an outgoing troopship, indicating that at least one donkey mascot was taken off the peninsula by the Australians.[8] Another donkey mascot was known to drink tea from a mug. There was a bulldog called Cupid, a pig called Dennis, a sheepdog called Rags, and two monkeys, Alice and Jack.[9] There were also unnamed creatures with anonymous masters, their existence captured by the unseen camera, and unforgettable by virtue of their presence in an alien world: a koala in an Alexandrian hospital, a wallaby in a troop camp by the pyramids, a bulldog in a crowd of Egyptians, donkeys at desert 'polo'.[10]

A mascot had no official status, though in the English army it was traditional for units to have them. The King's Own Yorkshire Light Infantry in India had a donkey mascot called Tirah. In the AIF an animal usually became a mascot when a soldier took a pet along and his unit adopted it as their own. The mascot's function was to bring luck, to rally spirits and to provide fun. Pets were contrary to routine orders, but as mascots they were a collective indulgence that officers could understand and frequently permitted. Soldiers were disappointed if they had to give them up. In 1917 a fox terrier was destroyed after it had been smuggled aboard a New Zealand troopship at Capetown en route to Europe. The infantryman who reported this event was particularly unhappy about the inconsistency of the rules regarding animals and other indulgences, for

> it was a different thing altogether when the nurses brought a mouse kitten on board and three of our officers brought monkeys. We are not even allowed fresh water to wash in, and yet they are given fresh water to wash the monkeys and cats with. You must agree with me dear when I say it is a rotten system.[11]

Perhaps pets, like cameras, became more of a bother as the war went on. In 1914 Simpson took a possum to Egypt and no officer complained. The possum was apparently a source of great amusement and distraction on board ship, as were other animals. When Major Beeston of the 4th Field Ambulance lost his dog (Paddy) overboard it was quickly retrieved by the soldiers. Beeston arrived on deck to

'Mascots on an Australian Transport'

'Every ship that leaves the Commonwealth with troops on board carries a miscellaneous collection of Australian animals and birds as mascots of the different troops.' The mascot's function was to bring luck, rally spirits and provide fun. Here soldiers on board ship are in the company of, from left to right, a bulldog, a possum, a cat and a bird (type unknown), another dog (possibly a Jack Russell) and a kangaroo.

find 'Colonel Monash . . . running up and down the deck with the dog so that he would not catch cold'. Later the dog got lost at Port Said. Monash gave Beeston permission to go searching for him and he was found at the abattoirs; the two returned to the cheers of Beeston's men. Paddy went on to Gallipoli and was killed on Anzac beach where he got 'a soldier's burial'.[12]

The soldiers' pets were a good talking point and a great diversion, a focus of affection that had few other outlets in an otherwise unsentimental military culture. As John Keegan has pointed out in writing about the Somme, men 'seemed to find in caring for animals an outlet for the gentler emotions to which they could give no expression among their fellows'.[13]

Donkeys were also a source of amusement during long periods between battles. They were relatively few in number, good-natured and rarely a threat to life or limb. Bean contrasted donkeys with mules, noting that the latter could do more work, but that 'the donkeys are the favourite with the men on account of their temper'.[14] They generally did the lighter work: carting water, meals or biscuits, or testing for poisoned water; they frequently featured in the leisure time of soldiers, who fed them biscuits when they could; and some were pets or mascots. After Private Wilfred Doe, his foot badly infected, was carried to the beach on one of them, he wrote home that the donkey was not much bigger than a goat and that he should have been carrying it. His feet touched the ground. 'You would have laughed to see me,' he told his family.[15] Soldiers referred to them as the 'little donkeys', 'wee donkeys', 'tiny donkeys' and 'donkey pets', and had individual names for many of them. A New Zealander recalled in the 1950s that his unit quickly made pets of the donkeys it acquired on the way to Gallipoli.[16] His diary entry for 23 April 1915 describes how 'two little donkeys' were brought alongside his ship in a rowing boat:

> They looked such dear little things with shaggy hair all over. All the men hoped that they would be brought on board so that they could make pets of them. Eventually they were hoisted up by the winch and landed safely on deck. They are for water testing. A donkey will never eat bad or poisoned water. So these poor little donkeys will always have a go at it before the horses and us.[17]

The surgeon, Lieutenant-Colonel Percival Fenwick of the New Zealand Medical Corps, said his bearers had been given some 'tiny

Sick and moulting for want of a proper diet
This 'native bear' was shared among soldiers and nurses at a hospital in Egypt. Their kindness and affection could not make up for a lack of gum leaves.

A weird presence in an alien world

Many Australian units took kangaroos to Egypt. This one was photographed in the lines of the 9th and 10th infantry battalions in December 1914.

donkeys [which] are now wearing red cross brassards round their foreheads'.[18] Padre C. J. Bush-King, one of the Church of England contingent with the first New Zealanders sent to Egypt, claimed he had found time to worry about Simpson's donkey in the course of a day's work. 'I used to help him lift off the wounded into the No.2 Dugout [Dressing] Station', he wrote.

> While helping him one day, I said: "Your donk hasn't got a Red Cross. Wait." I went into the dressing dugout, took a piece of white cloth; went to the Naval Landing dugout and with permission used the red paint and brush, made a rough cross, and, taking it to Simpson, I tied it on the donk's nose.[19]

In the *Sydney Mail* in 1916 soldiers argued about who had made the brassard for Simpson's donkey, but Bush-King did not get a mention.[20]

Trooper Bluegum also knew of several little donkeys. There were two at Shell Green whilst he was there in August 1915. He wrote about them in one of his dispatches to the *Sydney Morning Herald*: 'They divide their time between the 2nd Light Horse Brigade and the 3rd Infantry Brigade, and the boys give them biscuits'.[21] When he wrote to his supposed fiancée there was a third donkey, a foal that he referred to as Little Shrapnel, 'born over a month ago and just the cutest little thing you ever saw. They are regular pets of the brigade and come up for biscuits every day'. There was also more information about the 'Ma Donk' which had been slightly wounded a month after the foal was born, 'but she never seemed to trouble about it'. [22]

Dinkum Oil was a handwritten Gallipoli newsheet which, on 4 July, reported the birth of an infant donkey to 'Mrs. Murphy'.[23] *The Anzac Book* recounted the death of Jenny the donkey foal, but revealed a lot more in the process. To modern ears this passage might sound sarcastic, but the tone is more likely the result of an all too sincere sentimentality derived from the Victorian emotional indulgence in death-bed scenes:

> Her congenial company and high spirits, her affectionate ways and equable temperament, were the factors which gained for her the obvious rank of 'Camp Pet'. Her friendly regular visits will be missed, and the picture of her patrician head and dark-brown shaggy winter's coat. Her refined voice was music compared with the common 'hee-haw' which characterises her kind, or the peremptory

foghorn of the sergeant-major. But now she is no more. Our sorrow is immeasurable. The mother never left the babe whilst it suffered excruciating agony through a deadly shrapnel pellet. Skilful, indefatigable attention, innumerable applications of the 'invincible iodine' proved futile. Jenny Senior is grief stricken, and now lies upon the neat little grave in which her infant was placed by the big Australian playmates who now mourn their irreparable loss.[24]

When Private Fred Knight wrote to his mother in September 1915 he apologised for not having much to chat about, for he had devoted a good deal of his letter to talking about the soldiers' pets:

> The arrival of some domestic animals has given the depot [B Depot, Anzac Beach] a more cheerful appearance. We now have an Irish Terrier and a bewildered fox terrier pup. We are daily visited by 2 donkeys and a foal about 6 weeks old. Unfortunately the foal and puppy don't exactly hit it off.[25]

Soldiers wrote to children about the donkeys too. Lance Corporal Alf Weymouth's letter home was addressed to his sister, May, but it contained a message for 'little Marjorie and Reg'. He sent them kisses in return for the ones they had sent him and he told them there was 'a little, black baby donkey that wanders about our camp, with its mother'.

> It is only as large as a big dog, and not old enough to work like the other donkeys that carry the soldiers' dinner, and letters, up the hill to them. It is just big enough for Reg to ride, but he will have to come and get it if he wants it.[26]

Alf drew a rough picture of a little donkey and then went on to write about other things—the coming harvest at home, about May's forced change of address, the nerve-racking shells and a 'first class plum pudding' made with the help of some maize supplied by the Indians.

Later recollections confirm that donkeys had a place in the spare time and recreation of soldiers on Gallipoli. A report in *Standeasy*, 'Mystery of Murphy', recalled how the donkeys had provided entertainment in the evenings for New Zealand and Australian troops who enjoyed watching 'their biological occasions'.[27] Others reported times when the donkeys figured in lighter moments on the peninsula. A New Zealand stretcher-bearer, James Gardner Jackson, told the Australian War Memorial that he did not know what eventually became of 'the donks', but he could remember an amusing incident sometime after August. He had been sent on an errand to Anzac Cove, and

> on my way back I noticed quite a big crowd of Aussies in Rest Gully. There was some barracking and cheering and I thought that there must be a big two up ring to attract a crowd of about 150 men. I went up to have a look and here were two donkeys with boxing gloves on their front feet, standing on their hind legs and going for it hammer and tongs. The MC struck an old biscuit tin for time, and the two donks came down on all fours and walked to their corners where the [*sic*] sat down on a box arrangement. When time was up the gong went again and up they went and sparred for another round which was the last. I don't know who was responsible for the exhibition, but he had certainly trained them well. Perhaps, who knows, these might have been two of the original donks. You will probably run up against some of the early Aussies who will remember these boxing donks. At the time it was one of the most amusing incidents that I had seen on Gallipoli.[28]

There was more to the donkeys than carting for and amusing the troops. Many soldiers thought they were charmed in some way. Tom Gorman recalled the donkey foal that was born about 1 May:

> I saw it myself and thousands of other men must remember the little black donkey with a purple tie tied around its neck. It used to graze in Rest Gully about July 1915, before the Suvla Bay stunt—and what miraculous escapes from shrapnel![29]

The foal was a pleasing diversion and the miraculous escapes were something to ponder. Like many soldiers Gorman played with the idea that the donkeys had lives to spare. As Eric Leed has shown, superstitions, along with absurd omens and fetishes, were employed to give some control, however spurious, over the circumstances that dominated all soldiers: to hold a particular object, to whistle so many bars of a tune, to occupy a lucky corner or adopt a certain position, any one of these tricks might help a man through.[30] For some, the 'little donkeys' at Gallipoli seemed to fill the bill. There were stories about the animals' indifference to shellfire, their survival amidst scenes of carnage, and about men sticking close to the donkeys to save their own lives. Take the entry for 1 May 1915 from the diary of Private Victor Laidlaw:

A number of donkeys have been grazing nearby and shells have
been bursting all around them, it is marvellous how none of them
have been killed. We are getting better food on active service than
we ever were in camps.[31]

Two days later Laidlaw noted that the snipers were killing mules in
great numbers, but that the donkeys were still safe.

Trooper Bluegum had also seen the charm at work, and he had
seen it wear off as well. But did it wear off? It was as though the
charm had finally shifted from the animals to the men:

Morning and evening the Turks shelled our lines and Shell Green
was plastered with pellets and splinters. Yet by some miraculous
chance the donkeys escaped harm. Men were struck down on either
side but for a couple of months the lucky animals escaped scatheless.
The soldiers swore by the donkeys luck, and when the shells burst
stood by the animals rather than fly for shelter. At last the luck
turned. A high explosive burst over 30 men, scattered everywhere,
wounded both donkeys and never touched a single man. We buried
one of the donkeys next day. The other, wounded and lonely,
wanders disconsolate over Anzac.[32]

In one of his 'love letters' the story omits the bloody conclusion,
Hogue evidently having decided to spare his correspondent the
twist of the charm, or the twist of fate:

They meander about the Green [he told her], and the shells seem
to burst all round without touching them. They certainly seem
immune from shell fire, and the boys reckon if they follow the
donkeys' lead they will never get shot.[33]

The Anzac Book also pondered the mystery, further referring to Jenny
the donkey foal, as 'a delightful diversion, with her frolics and
gambols'. She was such fun that she was more than a 'mere mystic
mascot for the humouring of an especially created superstition':

Though of short duration, her life appeared a charmed one while it
lasted. Her freedom of action being the envy of every soldier on the
beach. Her disregard for the enemy's bullets and shells commanded
our unbounded admiration. But whether her immunity for six
months was due to the kindness of the Turks or their bad shooting,
or her own good judgement, who can say?[34]

In Simpson's case there is considerable irony in the fact that a charmed life could be attributed to one who survived less than four weeks. In some versions of the tale this good fortune derived from a particular combination of man and donkey. It is claimed, for instance, that soldiers took their cue from Murphy's shrapnel wisdom:

> It was a queer sort of beast that donkey—a regular bantam in size, except for his ears, which were unusually long, and generally carried at half cock. When his ears went to full-cock, the boys knew it was time to look for cover, for it was a sure sign that a big shell was on its way.[35]

Another account attributed Simpson's survival in Shrapnel Gully to the use of two other animals. When Private Fraser told the story he said that Simpson was working so hard that he had to use several 'relief' donkeys in place of Duffy No. 1 and Duffy No. 2, his favourites. Eventually all of the reliefs got shot, either by sniper or machine-gun fire, while the Duffys escaped time after time:

> Their lives, as well as that of Simpson, seemed to be charmed. They had to traverse very dangerous ground, and were almost constantly under fire; but so long as "we three" remained together they remained unscathed.

It was the partnership between Simpson and the two Duffys, 'we three', that seemed to activate the charm. Sure enough, it is when the partnership is broken that Simpson is in peril and finally killed:

> Then one day a stray shrapnel bullet got Duffy No.1 in the rump. Simpson was sorely distressed. He tried to relieve the poor animal, then he succeeded in getting him down to the beach where the surgeon performed an operation and removed the missile. But the accident meant Duffy No.1 had to go into hospital for a day or two, and during the time he was off duty almost every substitute that took his place was killed. In one day two donkeys and six men were picked off by a sniper on Simpson's Shrapnel Gully round; but he went on as if it were all in the day's work.

According to Fraser, Duffy No. 1 recovered and went back to work, but Duffy No. 2 was later killed by a stray bullet. Simpson was greatly saddened. He went on working with Duffy No. 1, but, the partnership broken, Simpson was dead within a fortnight.[36]

In the beginning

Donkeys worked with the stretcher-bearers at Gallipoli from the beginning of the campaign. They were preferred to mules, which soldiers did not seem to like very much at all. Hardier, stronger and bigger than donkeys, the mules were better carriers and more easily maintained than horses. They did a large proportion of the heavy work: carting, traversing and relocating. On the beach—where it seemed the whole army and its stores had been washed ashore in a gale—they dragged ambulance wagons to and fro, and hauled steel, piping, guns, shovels and picks and other equipment, even water tanks, from the barges. 'Here we are . . . 100,000 of us, and nearly as many horses and mules, and every inch within easy range of the enemies' guns', wrote a soldier who was somewhat prone to exaggeration.[37] In the hills mules could take a 12-pound gun or a box of bombs almost anywhere. Photographs show them, single file, forty and fifty at a time, wending their way up the steep gullies that ran from Anzac beach.[38]

They needed little attention, lived on next to nothing and were as agile as cats.[39] They were also stubborn, cantankerous, and dangerous with their back feet. 'The beach is a mass of men, mules and munitions', wrote Lieutenant Colonel Fenwick. 'The mules are more deadly than the shrapnel.' Even in death they were considered a curse. An attack on a casualty clearing station reported 56 mules and one man dead;[40] there were bits of 'half cooked' mule all over the place and hundreds of carcasses were towed off shore and sunk.[41] At various times the carcasses threatened to spoil the bathing, one of the few luxuries the soldiers could enjoy on a regular basis. Soldiers called them 'brutes' and 'cows' and were glad that the Indians were largely responsible for their care—a lowly responsibility, caring for a mule.[42]

The official record suggests that Simpson began working with donkeys on 26 April and other soldiers were doing the same soon after. Within a short time some were trained to carry a man up to the operating table and then to reverse out of the tent on the command 'back-pedal'; it was a novel method of ambulance transport and the evidence suggests that medical corps men were grateful for the help. The donkeys were good in a crisis;[43] they were in demand; and any stray was a prize to be snapped up, something you put your mark on, then swore you bought it in Lemnos.[44] Various units reported on the donkeys' utility:

> We picked up some little donkeys yesterday [said one New Zealander], and the [*sic*] came in handy for taking down chaps who had been wounded in the feet. We have annexed them now and I took the exalted position of muleteer last night.[45]

Elsewhere an officer, a man of some literary sensibility, talked about the heavy casualties suffered by 'our donkeys'. He thought their hides not thick enough—certainly not as thick as 'the shagreen skin of the wild ass of the "Peau de Chagrin" of Balzac', but 'as water carriers they were, while they lived, invaluable'.[46] When the Australian 4th Field Ambulance was relocating in August a great deal of equipment had to be moved; donkeys were ideal for the purpose, according to Major Beeston:

> I pointed out a drove of ten of these little animals, which appeared handy and without an owner, and suggested to the men that they would look well with our brand on. It took very little time to round them up, cut a cross in the hair on their backs and place a brassard round their ears. They were then our property.[47]

How these donkeys got to Gallipoli and how Simpson came to be working with some of them is not clear, though many soldiers expressed views about the matter and some claimed a part in the tale. To elaborate on their claims is to illustrate another instance of the circuits of Simpson talk at work, the official and popular levels of the legend interacting. In late 1916 General Birdwood wrote to *Coo-ee* to thank the editor for sending him a copy. He was pleased to see that Simpson's donkey, 'whom we knew on the Peninsula as "Murphy"', had got a mention. Birdwood said Simpson's donkey was one of a batch that he had bought on the island of Imbros. The purchase, he recalled, was made the day before the landing in April, when he was worrying about the problem of transporting water to the troops in forward positions. 'I therefore obtained about 100 small donkeys to carry tins of water, which I am glad to say they did with great success.'[48] Later Birdwood told C. E. W. Bean the same story, adding that it was a Colonel Maxwell who actually made the purchase on his behalf, that Maxwell also bought about 300 mules with refugee drivers from Alexandria, and that the donkeys each had a little saddle that would support two water-filled kerosine tins.[49]

Another version went around some years later, its currency as much testimony to the liveliness of Simpson folklore as evidence about the donkey's past. The claims began when a correspondent told the Perth *Sunday Times* that the donkey was from the 16th

Battalion and had belonged to a Colonel Pope.[50] The following week a man called Tom Gorman responded with new details, supported by photographs. He ran the Railway Refreshment Rooms at Perth Central and had been quartermaster to the 16th Battalion in 1915. It was he who convinced Colonel Pope that the battalion needed a couple of donkeys; he bought them on Lemnos and the donkeys were on board when the transports sailed for Gallipoli. The photos were good ones. One of them shows the lieutenant quartermaster standing with his purchase outside a butchery. Several pig carcasses are hanging in the background against an old stone wall, suggesting that he may have got his donkeys in the nick of time. A second photo shows Pope and Gorman supervising the lightering of the donkeys in Mudros Harbour. In the foreground there is another soldier taking a snap of his own. A third photo shows a donkey in a sling, its legs thrashing wildly, as it is lifted on to a troop-carrier.

Gorman, like many soldiers, had a sizeable collection of photos and documents from his war years which he had kept to himself. He was, he said, 'moved to publicity only because of a feeling that the interest evinced in the brave Simpson and his faithful accomplice warranted the lifting of what in the minds of so many people was a mystery'.[51] Unfortunately he said nothing about how this particular beast of burden had met up with Simpson, and offered no evidence that one of his purchases was *the* donkey. Other papers around the country picked up the story. The Sydney *Telegraph* ran it the following day, while back in Perth it continued to grow.[52] The *Sunday Times* said the story had 'awakened memories in many diggers'. It cited only one, Henry Thorne, who had been a private in the 16th Battalion. He said the donkeys had been transported on the troopship *Haidar Pasha* and were to be used to carry machine-gun gear and ammunition. They had long hair and were alive with lice and it was his job to clip them when they came on board, but there was not enough time. When the orders to disembark were given he abandoned one donkey only half clipped, and as the rowing boats pulled away a naval officer sang out, 'Who do these donkeys belong to?' Thorne said no one replied because no one wanted them.

> We pulled away without them, and looking back I saw them pushed overboard into the water and they must have swum ashore. Anyhow that is the conclusion that most of us that survived came to when we recognised them later on . . . It goes to show once again the truth of

that old saying 'It's an ill wind that blows nobody any good'. What we considered as almost a calamity to have two donkeys thrust upon us, turned out a blessing for quite a number of wounded diggers who otherwise might never have got down from Pope's Hill and other very awkward spots.[53]

The New Zealanders also figure in this part of the legend. J. G. Jackson told a tale similar to the accounts of Gorman and Thorne. At least two donkeys were on the New Zealand troopship, the SS *Goslar*, which was as lice-ridden as the donkeys. They were to test drinking water, since it was thought that donkeys would not drink impure or poisoned water. The stretcher-bearer had photos too. In 1953 he supplied the Australian War Memorial with a print that showed a donkey in a sling being transferred by crane from one ship to another. A second photo showed a game of cards on deck 'with one of the donkeys in the background looking on'.[54] Jackson said the New Zealanders had about 12 or 14 donkeys in all, and many more mules. He took issue with a 1915 newspaper report that claimed Simpson's donkey was a very tiny one that had been somehow smuggled ashore. Jackson would have none of that:

> It certainly was not a very small donkey but was of normal size. I think that Simpson, being a true 'Aussie', just 'borrowed' it from those that were landed openly. In any case I just can't imagine a naval officer of the type that was at the landing allowing any smuggling of such a thing as a donkey in a lifeboat.[55]

The most remarkable account of how Simpson's donkey got to Gallipoli was told by Padre Bush-King. The padre said that while the troops were still in Egypt, a plan was hatched to capitalise on the superstitions of the Moslem Turks. The landings were to be made in the dark, and here was the advantage:

> The Eastern peoples, as many coloured races, are brave in daylight, but afraid in the dark. Acting on this idea some donkeys, old and decrepit, and about to be sent to the zoological park as food for flesh eating animals, were collected, put on board ship with faggots and lanterns. On reaching the landing place the faggots were loaded on the back of the donkeys, lanterns were fastened round the necks on some; quietly taken ashore the candles were lit, and the donkeys turned loose. In the loom of starlight these looked weird to the Turks. They shouted, cried to Allah, fired rifles, and in the greater excitement, the donkeys ran fast in all directions even

towards the Turks. The lights stirred up greater fear; nothing known to the Turks could account for them. Spontaneous fear started them on the run. The Australians landed from barges in the more shallow waters at dawn on that fateful day. The Auckland Regiment, the first unit of New Zealanders to land were ashore by 10 a.m. . . . By daylight many donkeys were killed, others caught and used. One was used by Simpson to pick up severely wounded from a dangerous part of Shrapnel Gully named Bloody Angle.[56]

No one else ever told such a wondrous story about the landing, but Padre Bush-King told it many times. He liked to reminisce about those glorious days. He told his friends about his first-hand acquaintance with the famous Simpson whom he classed with the immortals of the European races. The padre had firm opinions on blood and breeding.

There were other views on the origins of the donkeys at Gallipoli. Some said most units had purchased at least two or three either in Egypt or in Lemnos—perhaps to test for poisoned water, perhaps to carry guns and ammunition into the hills, or to cart biscuits to the troops. One suggestion was that the donkeys were there to lighten the load for the long march on Constantinople. Much later General Sir Harry Chauvel confessed that he did not really know, but that 'officially' Simpson had acquired the donkey and paid for it out of his own pocket.[57] In one account Simpson seizes his donkey from the Turks.[58] In *The Anzac Book* it is a whole family of donkeys—Murphy of Red Cross Fame, Jenny Senior, and a foal, little Jenny—that wanders into camp, 'refugees for so long as the objectionable Hun element obtained in their native country'.[59] In several versions the devoted relationship begins with the donkeys running wild on the beach, the day of the landing. 'There on the body-littered beach, fate decreed that the English born stretcher-bearer and a frightened New Zealand owned donkey should meet.'[60] Fate would appear to have been working overtime, forging bonds between man and beast, uniting nations in battle, making history.

In some of the tales, fate has a history of its own which begins back in South Shields when Jack was just a boy. Fate is a sub-plot about his love of animals which takes young Jack, step by step, towards the encounter that will become the picturesque and pathetic legend. Thus, childhood becomes a preparation for a later, greater life. In keeping with an old-fashioned biographical convention, some tellers of the tale would marshal evidence to prove

**A donkey foal under the affectionate gaze of
Brigadier-General Ryrie and Colonel Cox**

*Several donkeys were foaled on Gallipoli while Australian troops were there. They were
incorporated into the legend. The bagging on the donkey mare's neck covers a bullet
wound that was inflicted on the night before this photograph was taken.*

that childhood traits were a precursor to adult greatness. There was his dog Lil, about which he wrote home while in Australia. (His mother didn't have the heart to tell him that Lil was dead.)[61] There was the old grey horse called Andy which worked the milk rounds with him. Best of all there was Brown's Fair, which came to town each year and employed Jack to take children on penny rides along the beach on the backs of placid donkeys. This was where it all began, with Jack, still in his school years, eagerly awaiting the arrival of Mr Brown and his team of donkeys. Though donkeys were a common sight on English beaches and there was nothing unusual about Simpson's exposure to them, such facts did not impair the legend. When the Reverend Benson was in South Shields doing his research, he walked down to the beach to take it all in:

> Looking over the beach that Summer day I thought long, deep thoughts of a laddie who liked to be with donkeys and learned to know and handle them in preparation for a destiny that he could not see.[62]

The war, enlistment, training camp and drill did not prevent Simpson from indulging his love of animals. One of his mates remembered how 'soon after he entered camp he disclosed a passion for animals, which gave a clue to the peculiar form which his heroism was to take near the end of his short career'. His life was always being re-read in the light of the legend. It was said that he always had some dog following him around. Then he captured the possum, so the story goes, and kept it in his slouch hat, tied to his belt, or else 'in the bosom of his shirt'. It went everywhere with him, Egypt included. It was forever going missing on board ship whereupon Simpson would rampage about shouting 'Where's my possum?' It fascinated the Egyptians and attracted the girls in the cafés of Cairo who would pat it as it peeked out of his shirt. When the possum went missing there was a great search, with soldiers— men who knew how much Simpson loved his possum—scouring the city, but to no avail. The 3rd Field Ambulance sailed for Lemnos on the *Malda* without Simpson's possum.[63]

He did not mourn for long. In one branch of the legend Simpson quickly found another animal friend while still in Egypt: a 'little donkey', which he managed to smuggle on board ship and which soon 'followed him around like a dog'. On the day of departure, so this tale goes, Simpson appeared at the gangway leading his new pet, but an officer turned the donkey away and Simpson sulked off, refusing to go on board alone. Later he came back with a large sack slung over his shoulder and marched up the gangway unchallenged. The story is preposterous, but instructively typical, no more unlikely than the legions of laughing wounded who constituted the Anzac legend. Thus,

> it is said that this is the way Murphy started for Anzac. If true, it would be quite characteristic of the man; indeed of all the men of the First Australian and New Zealand Army Corps. They were not easily beaten.[64]

On Gallipoli, Simpson and his donkey struck up a special relationship. 'A remarkable comradeship and abiding trust grew up between them,' claimed Sydney's *Sunday Times* in September 1915.[65] 'The donkey, christened Duffy, followed Simpson about as a dog would,' wrote Tom Walsh, the man who had interviewed Padre Bush-King and published his story about the superstitious Turks.[66] Benson felt that the special bond came from Simpson's 'sure touch' which in turn was derived from his boyhood experience at Mr Brown's Fair.[67]

The tales are replete with instances of Simpson's devotion. He bivouacs with the Indian Mule Corps because it alone can ensure forage for the donkey. He is in trouble for stealing forage from other units.[68] He goes to his own unit only for shoes, or a haircut, or a yarn with his old mates. He takes care near the firing line, leaving his charge behind cover, before dashing into the open to rescue the wounded. He reprimands another soldier for riding Murphy up Shrapnel Gully, pointing out that 'the only spell that poor donkey gets is when he comes back from the beach'.[69] Another tale, with many variations, tells of how he rescues one of his donkeys when it is wounded. A stray bullet hits 'Queen Elizabeth' in the leg and Simpson is forced to leave her for the sake of a wounded soldier. But he comes back with a couple of his comrades and together they half carry, half drag the donkey down to the beach for medical attention. Always a willing worker, 'in a few days it was back on ambulance duty, though limping'.[70] It is hardly surprising that the donkeys liked Simpson and showed a clear preference for working with him. Other stretcher-bearers tried to take them out but they wouldn't budge. According to some accounts, they would go only for Simpson.[71]

In the end

According to most accounts of Simpson's death, the donkey he was using at the time was unscathed. In some versions it stands close by the body of its master; in others it continues on its way, carrying a wounded passenger to the dressing station; and in one version, told many times, it then leads a group of soldiers back to Simpson's body. In Bush-King's account, it is he who follows the donkey back up the gully. It had come into the dressing station with

> a wounded man unconscious and sagging over its neck, but no Simpson. Turning the donkey round I slapped its rump; it started off from when he came. I followed. Moving slowly, the donk browsed on what rough feed he could, and went along the only track made familiar by use. When he came to the most dangerous place, Simpson's body lay there with a wound in the head. I did not examine the body for further wounds; he was dead. Some Australian troops came by and took charge of the body.[72]

The last of Simpson's donkeys is usually called Murphy, and most of the accounts have it that Murphy was adopted by one unit or another and looked after until the evacuation. The fate of the donkey figures prominently in the legendary tales of Simpson for several reasons. First, it was a part of the Simpson epic. The legend had become a distillation of the heroic experience shared by numerous 'donkey men'. Secondly, it was part of a wider allegory for the bearers and the diggers in general; placid and dutiful, it added to the melodrama of their ordeal. Thirdly, the Christian connotations were significant for, as *Duckboard* put it, Christ had ridden upon 'a progenitor of Simpson's assistant'.[73] And finally there was the donkey's place among the mascots: it was one of the many furry diversions that soldiers took to heart. When soldiers dress a donkey in pyjamas and a hat, the creature is something more than a beast of burden.

It has been said that Simpson was first noticed because he was different, and that he was different because he worked with a donkey: 'We did not know much about him as he kept to his own mob and it was not till we saw him with the donkey that we got to know him better'.[74] In some accounts it is the size of the donkey that catches the eye. The tales frequently describe it as 'no bigger than a Newfoundland dog', a comparison which may have come from one of the Newfoundlanders who were on the peninsula or perhaps from literature, for it was Robert Louis Stevenson who described his donkey, Modestine, in this way, in his *Travels with a Donkey in the Cévennes*.[75]

Some soldiers were inclined to elaborate on the size of the animal: 'It was a curious, almost grotesque spectacle to see the sturdy little dark-brown donkeys—neither was much over 30 inches high—picking their way slowly down the rough bush tracks'.[76] No doubt the grotesque or the picturesque quality made a memorable spectacle, but there was more to the donkey's contribution to the legend. Murphy became a pet and the pet lived on, a part of the community, a focus of fun and affection. The tales of Simpson lived on with it, and with the other donkeys too. Their numbers dwindled as months went by, but some survived the entire campaign. Any one of them might trigger the legend, excite or even enrich it. As one officer put it, the donkeys were 'a peg for many a pious tale'.[77]

Various accounts suggest that Murphy stayed on, after Simpson's death, as part of the menagerie at Gallipoli. Sergeant McPhee's diary entry for 19 May recorded that some of the 4th Field stretcher-bearers took charge of 'Murphy and Duffy' soon after Simpson fell dead.[78] A major with the Indian Mountain Artillery wrote of how the men of the Kohat Battery 'treasured [Simpson's] last donkey and evacuated it safely . . . with a view to presenting it to Australia with a short history of Simpson', but according to this source the donkey was stolen from mule lines at Mudros.[79] The *Sydney Morning Herald* reported in September 1915 that 'Murphy is still plodding along, the idol of the soldiers'.[80] When Andy Carnahan wrote home to New Zealand in the same month, he told his family the Simpson story and concluded with its aftermath: 'The little donkey is still with us, with his red cross brassard tied across his head. The Australians are going to take him home he certainly deserves a good pension'.[81]

In January 1916 Bean confirmed the legendary quality of the donkey's standing. He was searching for Simpson's donkey with a view to bringing it home, an idea that had come, he said, from soldiers who were worried about its likely fate during the evacuation and who held firm views about what should be done. Some said it should be presented to the King; others thought it deserved a good retirement back home in Australia. From France Bean sent out a circular requesting information and received numerous replies. One letter said the donkey was shipped off the peninsula but was lost in Port Said, where Colonel Beeston had lost and found his dog

A regimental pet in pyjamas and hat

This donkey pet is seen here on board ship after being evacuated from Gallipoli. Whether or not it was the famous 'Murphy', we cannot know. As one officer put it, 'the donkeys were a peg for many a pious tale'.

Paddy some eight months earlier. Soldiers had searched hard but to no avail.

Another reply assured Bean that Murphy was living happily behind the lines in Abbeville in France; a transportation unit had left him with one of the Advanced Horse Depots there. There was a reply that claimed that the Indian Field Ambulance had evacuated the donkey which was now in the hands of the 3rd Field Ambulance. Another letter said the 7th Indian Mountain Artillery had taken the donkey along with their mules, 'as they thought a great deal of him'; Murphy was probably now with the 7th in Mesopotamia. One response suggested that the No. 2 Australian General Hospital 'would be able to furnish some information as to the present whereabouts' of Murphy, and concluded that 'it would be interesting to know how Murphy is being looked after'.

Two replies to Bean's circular provided comparatively detailed accounts of Murphy's evacuation and subsequent disappearance. One was from Lieutenant Colonel Falla of 4th Brigade headquarters, New Zealand Field Ambulance. Falla explained how he had joined the S.S. *City of Edinburgh* at Mudros on 27 December. On board were two donkeys, one of which was said to be the famous Murphy, though he could not confirm the identification. Both donkeys were landed safely on the wharf at Alexandria on New Year's Day and left in the charge of an Australian sergeant who had arrived with the *Edinburgh*. Falla added that he had heard the Australians had stolen the donkey from the lines of the 26th Mountain Battery, but he confessed that the whole story was hearsay and he could confirm none of it:

> I regret that I cannot say what credence can be attached to the story that 'Murphy' was on the 'City of Edinburgh', as I do not think any of those on board were at all certain of their facts, there being such constant changes of personnel and animals on this ship in her capacity as a dump ship.

The last letter was from T. J. Carey Evans, surgeon to the Indian Field Ambulance. After Gallipoli he was based at Suez and from there he wrote to Bean, enclosing a photograph of 'Murphy'. He was confident that Bean would be pleased to hear that Murphy had been safely evacuated from Anzac and had arrived at Mudros with the 26th Mountain Battery, but

> the night they landed at Mudros Murphy disappeared, and though all the villages near were searched by the Indian drivers no trace of

him was found. My belief is that he was taken from the lines by Australians as he had on him two huge labels, on which were printed, "Murphy, V.C. Please look after him." I hope it is so and that he is now in their possession. I was afraid that he would not be evacuated and that I would have to shoot him or leave him to the Turks—but my men begged of me to get him away and I am glad to say I managed it. I should be thankful if you could cause enquiries to be made as to what happened to him and where he is now.

On 21 March 1916 Bean sent this extract from Carey Evans' letter to General White, commenting that he and General Birdwood might be interested, and there, it seems, he let the matter rest. He thought there was a good chance Murphy was in Abbeville and hoped that Birdwood and White might be in a position to pick up the trail. He too wanted to take the donkey home to Australia, but he was a very busy man. The search for Murphy seems to have ended with Bean's last lines to General White: 'If you should ever happen to hear news of Murphy's fate I should be thankful if you would let me know sometime when you see me'.[82]

Murphy's whereabouts continued to figure in the speculations surrounding the legend, one of the folkloric threads that has spooled out across the years. Some reports had him living with Jenny and Little Jenny on the deserted battlefields around Anzac Cove. In 1916 a returned soldiers' publication called the *Anzac Memorial* said the intention had been to evacuate the donkey but that 'nothing was decided upon and the movement was allowed to drop'. A year later the *Anzac Bulletin* expressed the view that Murphy had been looked after until the evacuation and then shipped back to Egypt, but it offered no further information.[83] Others had their own conclusion to this version of the tale. One returned soldier informed the *Argus* during the fund-raising campaign for a Simpson memorial in 1933 that he had been told 'that the two donkeys were evacuated with the troops and taken to Egypt, with the intention of getting them to Australia, but I assume they finished their days carrying some fat Arab about the desert'.[84]

The idea that the Indians took the donkey(s) back to India was another strand; and there was also a tale, told much later, about how most of the donkeys were shot before the evacuation, but one unit, believing it had the original Murphy, had arranged to get it off the peninsula on a barge: 'The donkey was put in a sack and loaded immediately the barge came in, without any regard to the many tons

of material to be put on board later. Presumably the flattened
donkey was cast overboard alongside the transport to which the
stores were transferred'.[85]

The truth in these stories, if there is any, cannot be determined
and it is not of real concern here. The donkey disappeared and, as
these stories indicate, the puzzle became part of the folklore that
sustained the legend after the war was over. The liveliness of the
legend was underpinned by a curiosity to know where the donkeys
came from and what their fate was, by that narrative inclination to
give the tale a beginning and an end. For the soldiers it was important to know these things, because the donkey had acquired a
special place in military culture. It was one of the pets, part of the
menagerie at Gallipoli, a focus of affection that had figured in their
recreation as well as their salvation. We arrive at this conclusion by
seeing men at Gallipoli not as soldiers but as human beings and by
grasping the *social* (rather than purely *military*) nature of their
circumstances.

What remains is to account for Bean's attempt to find Murphy
and return him to Australia. His efforts were quite probably inspired, not by narrative convention or sentimentality, but by politics
in the form of the recruitment crisis on the home front. Prime
Minister Hughes was trying to entice home Albert Jacka VC for
recruiting purposes, but Jacka would not have it.[86] While Jacka
fought on in France, Murphy was to be shipped home along with
numerous other trophies of war, 'with a view to stimulating recruiting'.[87] The trophies, which also included captures from France,
had been shipped to England and got stuck there as a result of more
pressing military and naval priorities. Through 1916 and 1917
Australia's representative on the War Office Committee of the
National War Museum in England was arguing for their hasty
return, 'in order that any practical value . . . [they] might now hold
should be used to further the Recruiting Campaign'. While the
Committee tried to find a spare ship, Bean tried to find Murphy. But
there was no ship to be had, and no Murphy to be had either. The
imperial patriots in Australia had to make do without the envisaged
travelling exhibition of jackets, bullet-riddled helmets, the inevitable fez, buttons, guns, bombs and bayonets, without Albert
Jacka VC, and also without the donkey. The politics of recruitment
are present, even in failure.

Chapter Seven

Photographic Mysteries

There is a great deal in what you say about there being no
need to advertise the fact that Moore-Jones's picture does
not show Simpson. The trouble is, however, that those
interested in Moore-Jones's picture have claimed that it is
'a perfect portrait'.

J. L. Treloar to J. G. Jackson, 3 November 1937, AWM 93, 417/20/35

The founding fathers of the Australian War Memorial were akin to
the martyrologists of the early Christian church. They were men
who believed that the written record was incomplete without those
shrines, relics and icons that preserved the sacred in a martyr's faith.
They shared with St John of Damascus the idea that just as 'we listen
with our bodily ears . . . to understand spiritual things, so through
corporeal vision we come to the spiritual'. The written word and the
icon were two different means of knowing one and the same truth.
Inspired in this way, they compiled their own *Acta Sanctorum*,
and they enshrined their relics and icons—including a massive
collection of photographs—with the aim of building a national
tradition around the achievements of the Anzacs in war.[1]

The photographs had a special place among the icons for they
had an authenticity no painting could match. Each one was appreci-
ated as a 'trace, something directly stencilled off the real, like a
footprint or a death mask'. The popularity of photographs sprang
from the simple notion that the photo cannot lie and the belief that
no other form of representation can convey the real—the clear
standard of goodness and morality in the martyr's face—as it can.

The founding fathers were eager to acquire a photograph of Simpson. They wanted an image that would suggest courage and stoicism as well as obedience to the call of King and Country. There was just one problem—no one had the last word on what he looked like, and opinions were numerous. The confusion around Simpson's identity was the final proof, if any was needed, of his mythic status. It was part of the folklore and ongoing discussion about his life, his deeds in war, how he spoke and dressed, his real name, his personality and his origins. For those who talked about Simpson in schools or pubs or RSL clubs, this kind of uncertainty was grist to the mill, the stuff of folklore, but for the keepers of the official legend, the conservative version, it was a vexing problem that threatened to disrupt and deflate their Simpson.

The pursuit of an image

The uncertainty about Simpson's appearance was evident from the early days of the legend and it was still a problem in 1918 when the official medical historian, A. G. Butler, was doing groundwork for his history of the Australian medical services in the war. Butler wanted an attested picture of Simpson and, although he had a copy of the 'photo portrait' from the *Sydney Mail* of 29 September 1915, he insisted on finding someone who could confirm the identity of the central character. So he wrote to the 3rd Field Ambulance, which was in France, and not long after got a reply which provided a brief account of the man and his deeds but did not address the request for an authentication of the *Mail* photo. In the margin he scribbled a brief note: 'No photographs'.[2]

This sorry situation had not changed by March 1920, when the Australian War Memorial was still hunting for a genuine photo portrait.[3] The Memorial was not yet open to the public, but its small staff had already gathered an impressive collection of relics and trophies: everything from a stuffed dog (mascot of the 13th Battalion) and Bean's typewriter to German tanks, and a huge collection of war photographs—about 20 000 negatives by 1921.[4] Yet there was not one authenticated picture of Simpson among them. A preliminary exhibition of selected photographs from the Memorial collection was held in 1920, at the Fine Art Society's galleries off Collins Street, Melbourne. Simpson was not among the 27 photos chosen for the Gallipoli series.[5]

Another exhibition followed in 1921, while the Memorial was busy preparing for its official opening. The photographs would be displayed in two large halls next to the Aquarium in Melbourne's Exhibition Building, the Memorial's temporary home. The photos were a kind of forerunning advertisement. The daily papers were peppered with reminders of the 'unique display' that would soon be open to the public. The number of photographs on exhibit was greater this time and came from all major theatres of the war. The work of the official photographers and snaps from soldiers' collections would be featured. They would include 'battle scenes in natural colour, done by a secret process', and the public was assured it was 'not proposed to include photographs revealing the gruesome side of war'. Reproductions could be ordered in three standard sizes and viewers were encouraged to decorate their homes with enlargements. There would be a Digger's Orchestra at the opening each evening and parents were advised that their children could see the performing seals at the Aquarium after they had seen the display.[6]

The exhibition ran for more than a month with great success. Some 40 000 people had seen it when the organisers announced that the season would be extended to run over Show Week until 24 September. By that time it was estimated that some 60 000 would have filed past the display. There had been thousands of orders for photos and the Memorial's darkroom staff were busy for several weeks after the event.[7] However, there was not one image of Simpson. The organisers had tried hard to find a photo of him, and had come close, but the problem was authentication.

One of the organisers was Captain W. D. Joynt, VC, a man who would later carry a photograph of Simpson in his wallet, but as yet his wallet was bare. It was during the exhibition that Major R. G. Casey sent in his Gallipoli snaps, apparently in response to a request from the Memorial for photos, and negatives if possible. 'I have tried hard to locate the negatives of the photographs I took at Gallipoli, but so far have only been able to put my hand on three', wrote Casey to Major J. L. Treloar, the Memorial's Director. But he had at least found three, and seven prints as well, which he hoped would be useful. He enclosed them with his letter, and extended permission to publish. Major Treloar replied with thanks, and a query:

There is one [photo] which is particularly important and that is the one of the donkey used by Simpson in connection with the rescue of the wounded. I am sure, of course, that you are certain that the donkey in the photograph has been correctly identified. Could you tell me, however, if either of the two men with it is Simpson? We have made repeated efforts to secure a photograph of him, without success. He will always stand out as one of the picturesque characters of the Australian Forces at Anzac, and for this reason we would be particularly glad to secure a photograph of him.

Casey could not remember; he was not even sure if he had taken the photograph. And the exchange did not make it clear why the donkey's identity was less of a problem than Simpson's, or whether Treloar was joking. But that is typical of the Simpson trail in the Memorial archive—there are gaps and silences that we cannot tread. Casey referred the major to Colonel Martyn, who apparently took lots of good pictures while he was on Gallipoli and may have taken this one. There would have been time, even then, to get it into the exhibition. Captain Joynt was eager to have it if some confirmation could be found, but Colonel Martyn was no help and once again Simpson proved elusive.[8]

Then came a breakthrough. In June 1922 ex-private Ralph Clark sent the Memorial a photograph of 'Murphy and his Donk'. It seemed bona fide for Clark had been on Gallipoli with the 2nd Field Ambulance and, best of all, it was a marvellous picture, though a bit grainy—a head-on shot, stationary (no blur), the small peak on Murphy's 'cheese-maker' hat threw no shadow, his facial features were clear, the wounded man was sitting upright and looked relaxed after his rescue; the donkey stood patiently against a scenic perspective, the sea in the background. Major Treloar was pleased. He wrote to Clark expressing appreciation and seeking his permission to sell copies of the photograph to the public. Clark was only too happy to add, 'in a small way', to the Memorial's collection and its success.[9]

Clark's photograph arrived too late to be included in Bean's *Story of Anzac* since volume one, on the early part of the Gallipoli campaign, was published in 1921. Simpson got a paragraph but no picture. But the photo was not too late for volume twelve of the official history, *The Photographic Record of the War*, which was coming together under the editorship of Bean, and Henry Gullett.[10] This volume was published in 1923 with Clark's photo on page sixty-nine. For the first time the 'official' Simpson was available to the public. Readers could gaze at that photo, contemplate his passive, determined face, and perhaps find some visual truth to confirm whatever else they knew.

The photograph sent by Ralph Clark

This was the first photograph to be endorsed by the War Memorial as a bona fide image of John Simpson Kirkpatrick. It was acquired in June 1922, in time to be published in volume twelve of the official history, The Photographic Record of the War.

There were just two problems: first, the grainy quality suggested it was not a direct print from the original negative; second, some returned men doubted its authenticity.[11] They said it didn't look much like Simpson to them. Again the major and his followers had doubts, but they could not settle the matter for they had lost touch with Mr Clark and no one with conclusive evidence, one way or the other, came forward.[12] Simpson had so many names and personae. It was decided that Clark's photo was the best bet as his story seemed solid enough to Bean and Treloar. But there was more to it: the Memorial was reluctant to interfere with the legend; the public was buying copies of Ralph Clark's photo; Volume XII stimulated sales, and now newspapers would use the picture when Anzac Day came around, or when the official history was in the news, or at other times when Simpson was needed. The Memorial failed to do the obvious thing—to send a copy of the photo to Simpson's mother. She was alive and well in South Shields, Durham.[13]

Mrs Kirkpatrick had not been completely ignored. She had been in touch with Colonel Butler, who was still writing his official history of the Australian army medical services in the Great War and who was ill and somewhat alienated from Bean and Treloar who thought he was not up to the job. At Butler's request she had sent him two photos of her beloved son, the 'light of my life', but they were a disappointment—one was a studio photo taken before the boy left England, and the other had no donkey in it. Butler wanted Simpson the stretcher-bearer, preferably with his donkey. The word went out, replies came in. One of them enclosed three photos, all of the same man, apparently taken by Major Beeston of the 4th Field Ambulance. They included a man with a donkey on Anzac beach, the two figures standing beside a mountain of biscuit tins. The broad brim of his hat shaded his face, making identification difficult, but Beeston had apparently said this was Simpson, so Butler opted to accept the relayed word of the distinguished Gallipoli surgeon, author of *Five Months at Anzac*, yet another memoir that made special mention of brave Simpson. It must have been hard to resist—it was on Anzac beach and it had a donkey in it, saddled and carrying a pack. Call it the Anzac beach photograph. It was published in Butler's official history in April 1930 and drew no controversy from the press.[14] It was absorbed into the Memorial's collection as the second official photograph of Simpson.

But the man in Beeston's snap was not the man in Ralph Clark's photograph.

In 1933 the public mind was once again focused on Simpson by the call for a commemorative statue at the Shrine of Remembrance, nearing completion in the King's Domain, Melbourne. The *Argus* ran a competition for the best design, and the call was championed by the Red Cross Society of Victoria which headed a fund-raising campaign. Clark's photo appeared widely in the press, including newspapers in Perth. There was some feeling there that the monument should be in Perth, from whence Simpson had embarked for Egypt, but that was secondary to the question of authenticity. Simpson had comrades in Perth still loyal to his memory, men who insisted they had been close to him. They were convinced Clark's photo was a 'ring-in'. To make matters worse, a second edition of Volume XII (*The Photographic Record*) had recently been published without any changes. Andy Davidson, 'a close friend of Kirkpatrick', wrote to Major Treloar to complain. Captain C. Longmore ('Non-Com' of the *Western Mail*) sent Bean a piece he wrote for the *West Australian*. His lead paragraph described Simpson as 'a humble private soldier to whom no decoration was ever awarded' and went on:

> In the circumstances it is important to draw attention to the fact, vouched for by men in this State who served on Anzac with Kirk-patrick, that the photograph published in the 'Argus' [i.e., Clark's photograph] and taken from the original in the Australian War Museum, is not the Man himself. One of the few authentic photo-graphs in existence of him and his donkey is published on this page.[15]

It was a poor photograph, very poor. It showed a man walking beside a donkey, a casualty was on the donkey's back with an arm around the man's shoulder. The man's Red Cross brassard was clearly visible on his arm, but the face was blurred because it was an action shot taken at a distance. It was hardly a triumph of portraiture, with none of the charm of Clark's photo. And to the extent that a face could be made out it did not seem to be the same face.

The Memorial confirmed the bona fides of the Perth men, establishing that they were in the same unit as Simpson and had served on Gallipoli with him. They were 3rd Field Ambulance men. It took note of their strong protestations. Major Treloar thought it significant that, every year on the Sunday nearest the anniversary of Simpson's death, these men would meet and drink a toast to their dead comrade's memory. He was further influenced by news of

The Anzac Beach photograph
This photograph was apparently taken by the surgeon, Major Beeston, of the 4th Field Ambulance. It became the second official photograph of Simpson.

The Post Office on Anzac Beach

Censorship regulations covering troops in Egypt and Gallipoli stated that parcels must be censored before despatch, and troops were forbidden to post letters or parcels at civil post offices while on active service in order to ensure that soldiers' mail passed through field censorship.

their long struggle to have another picture of Kirkpatrick removed from the Soldier's Institute in Perth because it was not Kirkpatrick either. In its place Murphy's comrades had mounted a composite photo consisting of a face taken from a training camp snapshot and superimposed on the body walking down Shrapnel Gully, so the viewer sees a smiling countenance at right angles to the direction in which the body and the donkey are travelling. For the Memorial this was further proof of dedication and familiarity. This must be Simpson. In the midst of the controversy Major Treloar made it clear that Clark's photo was no longer acceptable and the Anzac beach photo—the one Butler had used—would now be in the revised edition of *The Photographic Record*.[16] Perhaps its greatest virtue was the indistinct features of a heavily shaded face.

A few days later there was a most disconcerting and untimely development. The Melbourne *Sun* ran an article challenging the Anzac beach photo in Butler's medical history. Mr Les Johnson, a Flinders Lane fruit-barrow man, had been reading the *Sun* while sitting beside his barrow on the previous Friday when he had come across the Anzac beach photograph. To complicate matters the newspaper claimed Simpson's mother had authenticated the photo and it would probably become *the* official photo of Simpson at the Memorial. Johnson was aghast, and for good reason:

> That is not Murph., as we used to call Simmo, that is me . . . His mother is wrong and for the sake of accuracy I don't want my photograph to go down in history as Murph's. Poor old Murph was killed the day after he had his hair cut—May 18 or 19, I think—and I had been clipping him. Shot through the back as he came down the gully. I took his donk afterwards and used to work his and mine in relays and that photograph, I'll bet a £1000 to a gooseberry, was taken by Colonel Beeston as I brought Captain Welch's pack back. Look, there's the old Turkish saddle I put on the donk to hang the pack to. It is Murph's donk all right, but the picture was taken three weeks or a month after Murph had been killed.[17]

The *Sun* concluded that Johnson must have known Simpson well for he too was a field ambulance man (4th Field Ambulance), and he had cut Simpson's hair.

When the third edition of Volume XII appeared, in 1934, there was a change. The Anzac beach photo was gone. In its place was the fuzzy Shrapnel Gully photo, the original action shot that had been sent from Western Australia. The studio photo supplied by

The composite Shrapnel Gully photograph

The only photograph showing Simpson at work in Shrapnel Gully was a poor one, in which the facial features were badly blurred. Members of the Soldiers' Institute in Perth had this composite image made, with Simpson's face from a training camp snapshot superimposed on the Gully photograph.

Simpson's mother—a very boyish portrait—was inset in the top right-hand corner. Bean and Treloar, and perhaps Gullett too, must have breathed a sigh of relief when no one challenged these two Simpsons. They were now aware that the legend was full of un-certainty, with many faces and many names. They were committed to choosing the most likely Simpson on the available information, but suspected that the legend was still capable of producing another face or returning to an earlier one. Given this uncertainty the power of the legend resides in the Memorial's persistence with official photos, its refusal to drop them altogether, and its naive hope that the current solution could be the final one.

Horace Millichamp Moore-Jones and the Adelaide Art Dispute

Sure enough another face did appear, this time in watercolour. It was a painting of Simpson and his Donkey in action, bringing a wounded man out of battle. It bore a striking resemblance to the subject in Clark's deposed photo. The painting was the work of a New Zealand soldier-artist, Sapper Horace Millichamp Moore-Jones who had gone to Gallipoli with the British section of the New Zealand Expeditionary Force. In 1937 the original watercolour was purchased in London by the Agent-General for South Australia, C. F. G. McCann, who deemed it fitting that the original should reside in Australia. News of the purchase reached New Zealand, specifically the manager of the Auckland Commercial Travellers' Club, who was most disturbed to hear about this original when the original, in his opinion, was hanging outside his office in the club foyer. He immediately cabled the Adelaide *Advertiser* to say there must be some mistake.[18] Another controversy was under way, this time with a trans-Tasman dimension.

The South Australian government was embarrassed. The painting had cost £75, though some reports were saying it was £500, and there was considerable public interest in the controversy because thousands of people were familiar with the image and many more were familiar with the legend. They were acquainted with this particular image because a copy of the painting—a photolitho-graphic print—had been selling in Australia and New Zealand for nearly twenty years, and, like Will Longstaff's 'Menin Gate at

Midnight', had sold in great numbers as a reproduction at the close of the war. It had been reproduced in the newspapers, and at least once had appeared as a full-page colour lift-out.[19] The London publisher W. J. Bryce had acquired the rights of reproduction in 1918, after Moore-Jones had been repatriated to New Zealand in bad health. Thus when the South Australian Treasurer cabled London in 1937 to insist that the bona fides of the purchased painting be established, the Agent-General was relieved to find that W. J. Bryce was still alive, for he was hoping Bryce would have all the answers.

Bryce, not surprisingly, was most helpful for it was in his commercial interest to be so. The print had been sold as a copy of the *original* and occasional orders were still coming in. His written statement claimed that Moore-Jones had done the painting on his return to New Zealand in 1916 and then shipped it to London for reproduction. The Agent-General reported that Bryce went further in conversation, claiming that he had known the artist very well, that Moore-Jones was 'quite sure that Simpson stood for him on one occasion to make the original sketch', that he was not by nature a copyist and that any other version of the same subject would have been quite different, all of which was exactly what the Agent-General wanted to hear.[20]

As the cables moved between Adelaide and London a public debate was also under way in the newspapers: a friend of Moore-Jones said the artist had exhibited his Simpson painting in England during the war, by command of HM King George V. He said Moore-Jones had been offered £200 while in England for the rights of reproduction to the painting but had rejected this offer on the grounds 'that the subject was too sacred to be commercialised'. It was not possible there was another copy because Moore-Jones never made copies, 'such a thing was repulsive to his artistic sensibilities'.[21] Another man, a 'close associate', said he had shared a tent with the sapper on the island of Ispathio, after he was invalided off Gallipoli. He was with his friend until his departure for England on the *Mauretania*. He could remember the work of art taking shape: 'I have vivid recollections of his adding finishing touches to a watercolour sketch of "Simpson and his Donkey"'. He remembered the artist saying his plan was to sell the picture after exhibiting it in England. The inference was clear: the original was in London. It had been sold, and years after sold again—to the South Australian government.[22]

**'Heroes of the Red Cross. Private John Simpson, D.C.M.,
& His Donkey at Anzac'**

*The print was first produced in 1918 and was still available for purchase in 1937.
Moore-Jones painted several versions of this subject. One of these was purchased by
the South Australian Government in 1937, leading to controversies about the
painting's originality and whether or not it featured John Simpson Kirkpatrick.*

A few days later the Dunedin *Star* said it was all a lot of quibbling and it was an artist's privilege to paint the same subject over and over again. The old masters certainly did it, why not Moore-Jones?[23] The same day the *Herald* in Auckland reported that a close friend and fellow artist was with Moore-Jones (in New Zealand) when he did two versions of 'The Man with the Donkey'. The one now at the Commercial Travellers' Club was finished first. The second was sent to England for reproduction by a London publishing company. 'I was frequently with Sapper Moore-Jones while he was doing these pictures . . . ', said the close friend. 'The painting sent to England was much smaller . . . There were some slight differences in the two paintings, the wounded soldier's head in one case.'[24]

There were other contributions too: the commissionaire at the Adelaide Stock Exchange had something to say, so did a barman from an inner city hotel. They added nothing to the plot, but a Melbourne businessman, Mr F. B. Cox, managing director of Australian Reinforced Concrete, was able to add yet another 'original': he told the Melbourne *Age* that he purchased his painting 'about 15 years ago from a collection that had been offered to the federal government'. It was signed by the artist and surely it must be the original, he said naively, if Moore-Jones had offered it to the government.[25]

These contributions were all made in the space of two weeks in September 1937. The press was calling it 'the Adelaide Art Dispute', an embarrassed government was seeking further documentation, 'friends' were speaking out and the issue was getting very heated when there came a voice from Canberra. It was Major Treloar's voice. The major said that originality was not the issue. Was it Simpson? That was the issue. The major's opinion was that it was not Simpson. He had had occasion some years before to compare one of the Moore-Jones' prints with that troublesome photo sent to the Memorial by Private Ralph Clark in 1922. The comparison of the painting with the photograph revealed that the former was un-questionably based on the latter. And the Memorial, by now, was reasonably certain Simpson did not appear in the latter.[26]

Then, predictably, there was another development. An Adelaide man came forward with a photograph identical to Clark's. The Adelaide *Advertiser* was pleased to report that Mr F. W. R. Lill was actually present on Gallipoli when Corporal Lee Thomas of the 10th Battalion took the photo of Simpson and his donkey. Corporal Thomas had given Lill a copy which he had since treasured.[27] It was

Simpson alright, he insisted. Another Gallipoli veteran confirmed this when he scanned Mr Lill's photograph at the *Advertiser* headquarters in North Terrace, Adelaide, saying it was undoubtedly a genuine portrait of Simpson whom he had known on Gallipoli. He added the now-familiar version of the naming puzzle—the donkey's name was Murphy, he said, while Kirkpatrick was called Simpson. A Melbourne man also claimed it was Simpson, saying he had been there when the donkey man was killed soon after Albert Jacka got his VC, and others of the 7th Battalion would confirm this.[28]

The clash of voices went on. Private S. C. Frost came forward to say that Simpson had rescued him on 3 May 1915, then brought him down Shrapnel Gully 'after a hop over Dead Man's Ridge'. He remembered riding down with his arm around Simpson's neck. He thought the Clark/Lill photo, which he had seen in the *Advertiser*, was definitely not Simpson who wore infantry breeches, no putties, khaki coat (nearly always undone), and a Balaklava cap under a digger's slouch hat. (He was not the first soldier to be quite particular about what Simpson wore.) Then the Sydney *Telegraph* intervened. It had published the Clark/Lill photo on 14 September (1937). On the fifteenth it reported that two readers had identified this 'Simpson' as Fred Morrison of Sydney. But Fred Morrison, who was with the 7th Army Service Corps on Gallipoli, said no. Fred Morrison was sure he had never been photographed with a donkey:

> The man in the picture is very much like me in looks, but it is not me. The only 'joker' we knew with a donkey on Gallipoli was a chap by the name of Murphy—'Spud' Murphy. I never knew any one by the name of Simpson who carried in wounded with the aid of a donkey.[29]

There was more to come. Bean told the *Telegraph* that Moore-Jones had known Simpson personally and, 'although the first picture of Simpson published in the official war history was incorrect, it is unlikely that Moore-Jones would have made the same mistake'. But Treloar said Moore-Jones had painted the wrong man because of this mistake: the artist had painted Simpson *from* the photograph in the official history, from the Ralph Clark photo in volume twelve.[30] Simpson's mother then entered the controversy. She upset both Bean and Treloar, saying she had seen a reproduction of the original Moore-Jones painting and approved it. Bean was astonished. He said she could not have seen a picture like the one now owned by the South Australian government because 'the man in the

SA picture was not her son'. Moreover Bean insisted that Moore-Jones knew Simpson so he could not have painted the unidentified man in the South Australian picture. Bean now thought that picture must be the work of another artist, but two weeks later he would change his mind.[31]

It was a terrible muddle with little possibility of any truth being found in it, as was emphasised when Mr Lill announced that he had not been on Gallipoli at all, though he had lost good friends there, and Corporal Lee Thomas had in fact given him the photo when he returned home, invalided, to South Australia. The *Advertiser* had got it wrong. Treloar had to correct the *Telegraph* because he had not claimed, so he said, that Moore-Jones had used the photograph in the official history. And Bean was upset because he had been reported as saying that the *new* photo in the official history had been approved by Simpson's wife, when poor Simpson never had a wife.

The South Australian purchase arrived in Port Adelaide on the SS *Orford* in mid-December 1937. The *Advertiser* stated that Simpson's sister had apparently endorsed the painting, before it left England, as a 'very striking resemblance'.[32] The mother had endorsed it too. Why then did the War Memorial continue to emphatically reject it? Why did Bean and Treloar not swing back and once again endorse the painting and the Clark photo on which it was clearly based? They had swung before. If there is an answer, it must be unravelled from another skein, one that knots into the Simpson legend on the periphery—a peripheral legend in its own right. Smaller and more parochial, it has been feeding into and feeding off the Simpson legend for three quarters of a century. It is the legend of Horace Millichamp Moore-Jones.

Moore-Jones was forty-seven when war broke out. He was an artist with many years of painting and portraiture behind him, mostly in Australia, a little in New Zealand. His family had migrated from England to New Zealand in 1885 when he was seventeen. He soon left what he called the 'confined cultural climate' of New Zealand and went to Sydney with his wife, the noted sculptress Anne Dobson. Little is known of his time in Sydney except that, after the death of Dobson, he married again and also became a member of the council of the Royal Art Society. About 1911 Moore-Jones headed for the art world of London, leaving his wife and three children in Australia. He enrolled in the Slade School and worked for a time under Frank Brangwyn, Philip Lazlow, Quiller Orchardson and

**Horace Millichamp Moore-Jones,
New Zealand artist and soldier, 1868–1922**

Orpen. He became a staff artist with 'Pearson's Magazine' and was a book illustrator of growing reputation when the war began. He enlisted with a New Zealand corps raised in England and was on Gallipoli as a sapper from April to November 1915. It was an unusual corps, its members well over average age, well travelled and better educated than most.[33]

Moore-Jones lost his rifle during the landing but he kept his pencils and sketch paper. He drew the landscape confronting the colonial troops, an activity that proved to be useful and soon became official. He was assigned to make sketches of enemy-held territory and this he did under reportedly hazardous conditions, sometimes in a kite balloon anchored to a balloon ship.[34] The maps available had proved to be inaccurate, and sketching was a way of improvising charts for the soldiers and the Fleet. Moore-Jones was wounded in the right hand in November 1915 and, suffering from strain and privation, he was invalided to one of the Mediterranean islands where, after a short rest, he was sent on to the Birmingham Military Hospital in England. It is said that he did quite a bit of painting there. He turned his Gallipoli sketches into panoramic watercolours. In April 1916 these were exhibited at New Zealand House in The Strand, after which Moore-Jones was commanded to present himself and his work at Buckingham Palace. The painter became something of a celebrity. The London and regional press notices were very favourable.

There was another exhibition and then a set of ten reproductions was published for the artist by Hugh Rees Ltd, each set enveloped in a long canvas holdall with a 28-page prospectus. The prospectus carried endorsements from General Sir Ian Hamilton, Lieutenant General Sir William Birdwood, and Lieutenant General Sir Alexander Godley who headed the New Zealand Expeditionary Force at Gallipoli. Godley said he was first acquainted with these sketches in the trenches, 'coming by chance one day upon the artist while he was busily engaged upon one of them'. Birdwood said he knew many of the pictures were done 'while shells were whistling overhead, and they portray very faithfully the country in which we were operating'.[35] Sketching in the midst of shellfire was another brand of flagrant daring.

The reproductions sold for £5 5s and were available from any bookseller or art dealer in the British Empire, according to Hugh Rees. They sold widely, going through several editions. It was a high point in Moore-Jones' life.[36] There were offers to buy the paintings in England but Moore-Jones refused these as he was already negotiating to sell them to the New Zealand government. He intended to take them home, and he did. The Medical Board classed him unfit for battle duty and he was repatriated on the *Arawa* late in 1916. The 'Gallipoli Sketches' (that is, the water-colours) were exhibited in Auckland to much acclaim, but the New Zealand government declined to buy them, leaving Moore-Jones bitterly disappointed. A lecture tour in 1917 raised much-needed funds for the newly formed Returned Servicemans Association (RSA). Moore-Jones toured the South Island giving 'descriptive lectures on Gallipoli' with the help of lantern slides. The tour resulted in a comfortable credit balance that relieved some of the RSA's financial anxieties. It was praised for other reasons too. According to one contemporary report, the lecture was

> quite free from the ridiculous tripe served up by the Press from time to time to take the place of news. For instance, we were not told that the Turks ran away whenever they saw a bayonet, and we did not see an illustration of an Australian throwing Turks out of a trench with a bayonet as if they were sacks of hay, such as we have been told by the Press took place, but which is a lie. The lecturer gave the Turks a very good hearing and the audience appreciated his remarks much better than if he had indulged in a lot of ridiculous balder-dash such as we have had to read ever since the war started.[37]

When the tour was over Moore-Jones returned to his painting in Auckland. There were occasions in 1918 when he exhibited his Gallipoli watercolours in smaller centres of the North Island. One of these was the city of Hamilton, south of Auckland, where he received a flow of commissions for facsimiles. He set up a studio there and was soon persuaded to teach at Hamilton High School where he became the school's first art master. He travelled from Auckland by road each week, staying sometimes at the Hamilton Hotel. During that year Moore-Jones offered the Gallipoli Sketches to the Auckland Art Gallery which valued them at £500, a figure he rejected.[38] He let the matter rest and went on with his teaching and commissions in Hamilton, but made it known the government had failed him. Others shared his view. It is an opinion that remains current in New Zealand.[39] In 1920 Moore-Jones went to Canberra to sell his paintings. Cabinet was advised by a committee which approved of the paintings and the government bought them for £1500, though Bean was not impressed and thought the 're-

productions quite sufficient [*sic*] our purposes, unless originals
going cheap, maximum five pounds each'.[40] It appears from the
correspondence that Bean's views came too late to influence the
Cabinet decision.

There was no painting of a man with a donkey among the 90
sketches sold to Canberra. We know Moore-Jones had a roving
commission while on Gallipoli (as did Simpson), but there is
nothing to suggest he ever saw or sketched a man with a donkey.
Moore-Jones did not exhibit such a picture in London in 1916. He
probably did not paint this subject on Ispathio and he certainly did
not intend to sell such a painting while in England. A 'Simpson'
picture was not among the ten reproductions marketed by Hugh
Rees Ltd. Had there been such a picture it surely would have been
included. Nor did the lantern slides on his NZ lecture tour include
any such image. On the contrary, when Moore-Jones embarked on
his lecture tour he *spoke* of Simpson, drawing what was described as
a 'word-picture' for his audience, precisely because he knew the
story but knew not how to represent it visually. At one of these
lectures someone actually asked him if he had a painting of the hero
Simpson and he replied, unhappily, no.[41]

What did all this mean for the South Australian government in
1937? Did it mean that Moore-Jones had misled Bryce at the outset?
Surely not, for it seems the artist made no pretence, in New Zealand
anyway, of Simpson being known to him. How was it that Simpson's
sister confirmed it as 'bearing a striking resemblance' and that his
mother agreed? Where did the Clark photo fit into the mystery and
why was Bean claiming Moore-Jones had known Simpson? The
worst thing about the Moore-Jones saga at this point is the time of
his death. He died in the Hamilton Hotel fire of 1922, the same year
that Clark gave his photo to the Australian War Memorial. Newspaper reports said Moore-Jones twice went back into the inferno to
save women and children, he was unrecognisable when they found
him, and he died of burns in the Waikato hospital the next day. He
had always preferred painting to writing. He left not a word to clarify
the painting mystery. Popular memory records a latter life of some
distinction: Moore-Jones volunteered and went to Gallipoli in
middle age; he drew his maps, operating as an independent unit,
often under fire; his work was applauded abroad but unsung at
home; and he died, as Simpson had died, rescuing others.

Major Treloar took another long look at the photolithographic
print during the 1937 controversy. The Memorial copy was accom-

panied by a little booklet featuring the print on the cover, in miniature, and a brief text:

> The artist, Sapper Horace Moore-Jones was aided in his work by having a personal knowledge of the man Simpson, and from photographs taken on Gallipoli by friends.
>
> Acknowledged as a perfect portrait of the Gallipoli hero, Private "Simpson," D.C.M., and his donkey "Murphy."[42]

Treloar had also read this in 1933 when Simpson's comrades in Perth had made such a fuss about the Clark photo and he was convinced then that Moore-Jones' painting was a copy of that photo. In 1937 his opinion was not changed and he reflected on his earlier silence: 'At the time it appeared unnecessary to comment on this fact'.[43] The legend could curb tongues as well as set them going.

That was hardly the end of the controversy: in 1937 matters were a little more out of hand than in 1933. It seemed the South Australian government was making a sad error—an official purchase based on mistaken identity, seventy-five pounds worth of mistaken identity—and silence, this time, in the glare of publicity, was hardly going to protect the Memorial or the legend. Treloar mailed the Hill & Plummer booklet to Andy Davidson in Perth, as Davidson had acquired the unofficial mantle of chief authenticator of Simpson photos for the Memorial. He asked Davidson to comment on the miniature on the booklet cover. He also wrote to the director of the Adelaide Art Gallery, going over the events of 1933 and setting out his own doubts about the painting. He was reluctant to undertake any debunking that would impinge on the Simpson legend, but now felt drawn in because others would not let the picture pass as an 'artist's impression'.[44] Davidson had already seen the print and so recognised the miniature immediately. He wrote to say this was not Simpson and then wrote again, on the same day, deflecting the exchange on to the matter of the Anzac beach photo: Davidson claimed that the man who had posed on Anzac beach was an 'imposter', in the sense that he had taken over Simpson's donkey on 20 May but had not been equal to the task. Under heavy fire in Shrapnel Gully, he (Davidson) and a small group of bearers had found the donkey wandering about unattended with a patient on its back.

> The person who had taken Simpson's job on was hiding in a dugout. I pulled him out by the throat and kicked him. He was never seen again with the donkey, and no other person carried on. This has

never been told outside our small circle, but can be proved today, even in law.

No name was attached to the imposter Davidson spoke of, and the War Memorial did not let the story become part of the public muddle that now centred on the Moore-Jones painting.[45] Moreover it was the Clark photo that continued to stir the legend and its keepers, for Treloar had also received a long and revealing letter from New Zealand. It was a 22-page letter, handwritten over several evenings, late in September. The author was James G. Jackson, a carpenter from Dunedin, who said he had been following the Moore-Jones controversy in the newspapers and was writing to share the truth, being '*the only person living who can give you all the details*'.[46]

The mystery solved?

Treloar read the letter with fascination. Jackson had been a stretcher-bearer in the war. He had landed with the New Zealanders on 25 April, seen out the entire campaign on Gallipoli with a bible in one pocket and a camera in the other, and then gone on to France where he won the Croix de Guerre. He had worked with Simpson in Shrapnel Gully for five days and thought the donkey a good idea. He too got hold of a donkey and three other New Zealanders obtained one as well. He got to know Simpson and remembered him as 'a jovial, hail fellow well met, cheery chap with always a joke for the wounded and a "Hullo Dig", or the particular saying that was in fashion in those days, for everyone he met'. Jackson told the major he would like to say he took a photo of Simpson but he did not. In fact he had taken a photo of someone else. His contingent had been moved, quite early in the campaign, from Shrapnel Gully to Walker's Ridge, where the donkeys were used only on the lower slopes coming down to the beach.

> We never took the donks up Walker's Ridge. At that time it took a stretcher squad all its time to bring a man down safely. It would have been madness to have taken a donk up there. They were used from the bottom of Walker's Ridge to Anzac Cove. As I was returning from the Cove one day I met another of our men with a wounded Aussie on board. We stopped and exchanged greetings and I said "Just stand there Dick and I'll take a snap of you." Well the photo

was taken and we carried on. The locality was practically half way between Walker's and Anzac Cove perhaps a little bit more.

Then follows several pages of detail about the roll of film he sent home and the mistakes made by someone who labelled the prints, possibly his brother John who had been evacuated from Gallipoli in July 1915. When James Jackson finally returned home to Dunedin in 1919, he found the photograph of his friend Dick, whose full name was Dick Henderson, had been mistakenly labelled 'Murphy and his Donk'. He also heard about the Moore-Jones lecture tour which had included Dunedin. A third brother, George, who had not been abroad, had attended Moore-Jones' illustrated talk:

> He told me [Jackson wrote to Treloar] that someone had asked him, Sapper Moore-Jones, if he had a painting of the Australian who had carried the wounded men down on a donkey (Blame Capt. Bean for such widespread knowledge of the Aussies). Moore-Jones said that he had not but if he only had a photo he would be able to paint one. My brother who was at the lecture immediately thought of the photo at home "Murphy and his donk" and next day took it into Moore Jones who according to my brother was very pleased to get what he was told was an authentic photo of Simpson. At this point I would question Cpt. Bean's statement that Moore-Jones knew Simpson personally. He would have immediately recognised that it was not Simpson in the photograph.

Jackson thought there was a certain resemblance between Simpson and Dick Henderson but he had no doubt Moore-Jones would have picked them apart when handed the photograph, had he known Simpson.

Major Treloar read on. He was moving fast down page nine when the revelations took another tangent. About six years previously Jackson had been sent to a Dunedin office to fix some windows, and while there he noticed a copy of the *Peninsula Press*, framed and hanging on a wall. The man occupying the office, a man by the name of J. S. Skinner, wanted to know if he had ever seen one of these before: 'I said "Yes I had" and he asked me where. I told him on the post in the middle of Anzac Cove'. The two Anzacs yarned for a while whereupon Skinner offered to show Jackson some photos.

> He went to a drawer and produced an envelope with about 20 photos in it. I looked through them and said "They're very interest-

ing Mr. Skinner. Where did you get them?" He told me that a young chap Jackson who had come home on the same boat as him had given them to him. I said "That is a coincidence because I took every one of those photos."

Jackson went on to tell Treloar that he proved his point the next day when he took his album along and showed an embarrassed Mr. Skinner the same photos as those he had in the envelope in his desk drawer. It seemed Jackson's brother had given copies to Skinner on his return. And one more thing: among Skinner's photographs was the now-famous image we have been calling the Clark photo—the photo of Dick Henderson and his donkey on the track below Walker's Ridge ('Just stand there Dick and I'll take a snap of you'). Skinner told Jackson that this was the Australian Simpson and he had given a copy to Sapper Moore-Jones when he toured Dunedin in 1917. He had done the same thing as brother George. He had attended the lecture, he had listened to Moore-Jones' word-picture of Simpson, and he had heard the artist say he could do a painting if only he had a photograph. So he gave him one, which must have confirmed the donkey man's identity for Moore-Jones. James Jackson saw it as follows:

> Sapper Moore-Jones received two identical photos from different sources and both the givers unknown to one another and both convinced that the photos were of Simpson he would have no doubt whatever that it was a genuine likeness and the painting would be a sincere work on his part.

What remained of the letter, and there was quite a bit, was not so vital to the puzzle. Jackson told Treloar that Dick Henderson was still alive and teaching school somewhere in New Zealand. He included with his letter an enlargement of the photo in question, taken from his negative—the original negative that he said he had shot on Gallipoli. It was indeed the photo we have been calling the Clark photo, which Treloar had first seen in 1922. Jackson said he would have liked to frame it for the War Memorial but feared the glass would be broken in the mail. He asked the major to compare his photo with the Moore-Jones painting. In many respects the detail had been copied, right down to the knots on the donkey's lead rope. And he explained his long silence on the matter in moral terms that had a familiar ring: he had been aware of Moore-Jones error for many years but felt no good purpose would be served by exposing it.

What good would come out of it. In the first place the whole value of the lesson learnt by thousands of children from the noble example of Simpson would have been lost. The value of that painting in Auckland would have depreciated to the matter of a few pounds. The illustration in the official history of the war would have been regarded as a fake . . . What harm? The doubt that would have been born in everyone's mind regarding other official photographs. And, sir, I am still of the same opinion.[47]

The desire for legitimacy rather than authenticity had prevailed. The letter mentioned another man, a former soldier with a photographic collection, a chemist in Auckland who Jackson said was seeking publicity; Jackson made it clear he did not like publicity seekers, which was possibly another reason he had kept quiet. His long account then came to a close on the topic of what had happened to the donkeys: he didn't know, though he'd seen them keeping soldiers amused while on the peninsula.

Major Treloar accepted the account given by James Jackson. He had expert advice on the enlarged print Jackson had sent. He acknowledged its fine quality and was able to agree that it was from the original negative, and far superior to the prints that had come from other sources. They must have been made from copy negatives. Treloar sent Jackson a cigarette box made with teak from the deck of HMAS *Sydney*, 'a memento of the ship which protected the first Australian and New Zealand convoy from the attentions of the "Emden".' He said if Jackson was a non-smoker the box could no doubt be put to other uses.[48]

The South Australian Premier settled for the painting bought in London by his agent-general. If there was doubt about the identity of the man calmly leading his donkey and his wounded comrade out of the watercolour firing zone, there was none about the spirit of the work. For some years it hung in the premier's office, and was eventually donated to the Commonwealth government in 1958.[49] The controversy flared again in newsprint only once. It was during the lead-up to Anzac Day in 1950, as the Simpson icon was ritually appearing in the press along with a smattering of folklore in the letter's columns, and as soldiers, now from two world wars, began to reminisce. April was the month for Simpson talk.

The controversy flared in two places: first in New Zealand, then, by reflex, in South Australia. In New Zealand it was Dick Henderson who spoke out: he had been nearly blind since early in the 1930s, having been badly gassed at Passchendaele in 1916, and a long losing battle with fading sight had eventually forced him out of teaching. Dick Henderson said he had watched the legend grow but had preferred to say nothing. It never really went away. He had not seen the Moore-Jones print on a classroom wall for a long time, but there were others about. And there was *Stand Easy*, the New Zealand RSA bulletin, which kept the legend alive. Now he was getting old and wanted to set the record straight. Perhaps his timing was also influenced by news of another claimant to the Simpson mantle— William James Henry of Te Kauwhata had died that year; some said that he was the 'real Murphy of Gallipoli'.[50] Whatever the immediate background, Henderson confirmed Jackson's story, for only in minor details did their respective accounts differ, though one of these differences has folkloric significance. Henderson told journalists he took over Simpson's donkey after Simpson had been killed. He had carried on where the legendary man had left off.

Soon after the Henderson revelation James Jackson was 'flushed out' by a newspaper man. He said Henderson was using a different donkey, one of a team that had been working below Walker's Ridge while Simpson was still alive in Shrapnel Gully. In the first instance Henderson was in line with Simpson and carried on 'in his foot-steps', so to speak; in the second, Henderson was part of a legend that New Zealanders built for themselves, a legend that ran parallel to the Australian legend, in no way derivative. Thus another of Henderson's comrades chose to sing his praises by disagreeing with him. 'Henderson definitely began the work with the donkey', he said, 'Simpson took over later'.[51]

When these opinions appeared in the press the legend awoke with a start. Adelaide responded to Dick Henderson's claim within a few days. Two returned servicemen, Stan Little and Beverley S. May, declared that they had a copy of this same photo, printed in reverse, with the words 'Simpson, AMC' inscribed at the base. They were Gallipoli veterans and had acquired their copies whilst on Gallipoli. Lots of copies were made; they were circulating in the Middle East and on the peninsula in 1915. It was Simpson all right, they were pretty sure about that. But they had no evidence apart from the name roughly inscribed on the photo. And they clearly knew nothing of the original, which was the other way around. Whoever inscribed the copy from which these two copies were taken knew nothing of the original photograph and the circumstances Jackson had described.

The cry of the newspapers—Wrong Man in Famous Picture—did not alarm Major Treloar. He knew that. He had known it for years and, like Jackson, he had preferred to say nothing. A legend, undisputed, was more important than the facts. It concerned a higher kind of truth. But the news from Adelaide was new in other ways. The Adelaide men were claiming lots of copies of this photograph were made. They said the photo—we will drop Clark and call it the Jackson photo from now on—was circulating on Gallipoli and in the Middle East in 1915. That seemed extraordinary. Stan Little told the Adelaide *News*

> he had always prized his enlargement of Simpson and his donkey because he had been one of the wounded troops carried to safety on the donkey's back. He had been wounded on May 8 when guarding an outpost less than 50 yards from enemy lines . . . He was then in 13 Platoon, D Coy, 10th Battalion. His mate, Billy Clark [another Clark], with whom he had enlisted at Mount Gambier, had given him the negative of the snap. He knew that he [Little] would be going to hospital and would be able to get the film developed.

Beverley S. May followed up with a letter to the *News* which appeared on Anzac Day:

> I think Stan Little is correct in his statement that Simpson the Australian, and not his successor, a New Zealander, was im-mortalised in the painting "Murphy and his Donkey" by Sapper H. Moore Jones, of Auckland. I think mine and Mr. Little's negatives of the published picture are the only ones in existence. I had six dozen postcard-size prints developed, and gave one to each of the sisters at the Gallipoli hospital. They were delighted to receive them. On my return I was practical and surgical hairdresser at Keswick Military Hospital from April 1916 to June 1942.[52]

Six dozen postcard-size prints for six dozen sisters! Perhaps Sister Davies got one? Perhaps one of these photos was her way into the legend, prior to writing home to her mother—that long letter about the love of the men for one another and the work of gentle Simpson?[53] Here was a photograph with a visible history. Evidence about its taking and its making was already available. Now something more was known about its circulation and presumably its appeal. It was not like most amateur photos: discarded snaps at the back of a drawer, frozen moments from the pages of an old album. For the most part their history eludes us. This one is special because of its subject, but it is also special because its history is recoverable.

The photograph had been circulating on Gallipoli in 1915. Jackson, Clark, Corporal Lee Thomas, Stan Little and Beverley S. May, all acquired either a negative or a copy negative or a print while on the peninsula. Those who got hold of the photograph seemed to treasure it. There are several accounts of soldiers having more than one copy made and giving a second to someone else. May subsequently told the War Memorial that copies were circulating in the Middle East as a kind of postcard. So were many other photographs hungrily bought up by the competing press and publishing agencies. But the photograph of the man with the donkey had a special appeal. May said: 'There were lots of photos taken as different patients were brought in on the donkey, but this one seems the favourite'.[54] What did the six dozen nurses do with their postcard size prints? Were any of those prints copied and put into circulation? We can only surmise.

Beverley S. May returned home in 1916 and continued to circulate copies of the photograph in the course of looking after the hairdressing needs of returned soldiers at Keswick. 'I have had different customers from Victoria and WA and I have given them a photo as a memento and they were very pleased to get one of "Simpson and the donkey".' This circuit of the legend had become as elaborate as that associated with Jackson's photograph in New Zealand. It can be summarised as follows: somehow Private Billy Clark had acquired a negative of the photograph showing Dick Henderson and his donkey, that is, the Jackson photograph. Billy Clark gave the negative to his friend Stan Little because Little had been wounded and so could get it copied and printed when he was evacuated. The words 'Simpson AMC' were inscribed on the negative at the time of exposure, something we know was technically possible, or else on a print subsequently.[55] Stan Little was a cautious man and he valued greatly his photo of Simpson, so he had two negatives made from the photo he had been given, one of which he gave to Beverley S. May, presumably because he wanted the image to survive. As May put it:

> He had two negatives taken off the same photo in case he never came out, and he gave me one and now he has lost his negative. He wanted some photos taken off but the photographer died and the negative cannot be traced. Very bad for him.

Stan Little was doing his own circulating too, but met with bad luck. May, on the other hand, proceeded to distribute prints with care-free abandon but was careful with his negative. He told the War Memorial: 'I could hand to you the negative but I do not want to lose it as I prize it same as anyone else would'.[56] Whether any of the recipients did the same we do not know, but it was a lively circuit within the legend and may have set in motion other circuits that have left no 'footnotable' traces.

The stories told by Stan Little and Beverley S. May in 1950 made an impact at the War Memorial. Major Treloar got back on to the Simpson trail. Late in the 1930s he had wanted to sort out the confusions once and for all, but he and his staff were preoccupied with many things, including the Memorial's move to Canberra, the approach of war, and then the war itself, which produced more epics, new theatres of heroism, new legends and new images for the Memorial to document and commemorate. Simpson had to wait until Little and May spoke out. Treloar then 'determined to put together for the sake of historical accuracy an authentic account of the man and of the various photographs alleged to be of him'.[57] What intrigued him most was the fact that the Jackson photograph had been in circulation on Gallipoli and in the Middle East in 1915. A full-scale investigation was ordered. All the available evidence on Simpson, and images allegedly of him, were to be gathered and analysed. In particular the Memorial was anxious to establish how the Clark photo, which we now call the Jackson photo, got into circulation in the first place. Why did this photo circulate in the way it did and what was its appeal?

Old files were ransacked, letters were copied and catalogued anew, newspaper clippings files were checked, and lists were made of all the photographs and paintings of a man with a donkey that had accumulated in the Memorial's archive. More letters went out; more replies came in. The end result was a twenty-four-page summary which was a helpful document, but patchy. It overlooked many pieces of the puzzle, did not add significantly to the sum of the material gathered and persisted in trying to reconcile the mass of contradictory evidence about Simpson. It failed to treat the legend as legend. Equally disappointing was that some of the material gathered was again dispersed.[58] But in one respect the project carried the search for Simpson forward. A press clipping came to hand. It was the *Sydney Mail* photograph of 29 September 1915—the one Butler had tried to check in 1918. And what was it but a full-page reproduction of the Jackson photo! The caption was a gem, indicating how emphatically and quickly the legend had circulated:

'Murphy'

Who has not heard of "Murphy"? He will never be forgotten by scores of Australians who took part in the early fighting near Gaba Tepe. "Murphy" is a very small donkey who was smuggled ashore and was taken charge of by a brave Australian named Simpson. Backward and forward they went together, up hills and down valleys. Simpson giving first aid to any seriously wounded man he came across, and then placing him on "Murphy" for conveyance to the beach. They did magnificent work but alas! One day a bullet struck Simpson while he was bringing a wounded man out of the fire zone, and he "passed out" having proved himself a hero. "Murphy" is still plodding along, the idol of all the soldiers.

How did a copy of Jackson's photo get to the *Sydney Mail* for publication in September 1915? Major Treloar did not live to find the answer for he died in January 1952, but after his death the puzzle was picked up by the new director, John McGrath. This time the War Memorial was able to track R. J. Clark through Army Base Records and the Repatriation Commission. A letter to Clark set out the long history and the long search, but Clark never replied. Perhaps the embarrassment was too great.

James Jackson on the other hand was as talkative as ever. Sixteen years after his exchange with Treloar he now had a letter from McGrath, puzzling over the *Sydney Mail* reproduction. McGrath told him that no one at the *Mail* could help as no records of the period in question were available.[59] He enclosed a print supplied by Beverley S. May and told him about the latest Adelaide connection. He guessed that Jackson's brother (brother Jack) might have sent it to the *Mail*, or perhaps someone who got a copy from brother Jack. But he did not hold much hope of getting to the truth at this late date.

James Jackson replied at length. It was another extraordinary document—chatty, informative reminiscences, not at all defensive in tone or style, but polite and respectful. The letter was eighteen pages long. Jackson wrote about other photographs he had taken. He thought his brother might have sent *the* photo in question to the *Otago Witness*, an illustrated weekly in Dunedin, and perhaps the *Mail* picked it up from there. But he had been to the library and

THE SYDNEY MAIL

Wednesday, September 29, 1915.

"Murphy." Who has not heard of "Murphy"? He will never be forgotten by scores of the Australians who took part in the early fighting near Gaba Tepe. "Murphy" is a very small donkey, who was smuggled ashore, and was taken charge of by a brave Australian named Simpson. Backward and forward they went together, up hills and down valleys, Simpson giving first aid to any seriously wounded man he came across, and then placing him on "Murphy" for conveyance to the beach. They did magnificent work, but, alas! one day a bullet struck Simpson while he was bringing a wounded man out of the fire zone, and he "passed out," having proved himself a hero. "Murphy" is still plodding along, the idol of all the soldiers.

'Murphy'

The mystery confronting Major Treloar at the War Memorial was how a copy of this photograph reached the Sydney Mail *in time for publication in September 1915. Who sent it, and why?*

checked the *Witness* for the appropriate months in 1915 and found nothing. Jackson was nonplussed. He was certain that the photograph must have come from his film, but how? Perhaps McGrath could try the records of the *Sydney Mail*. The letter digressed at times. Jackson reminisced on his acquaintance with Simpson, on Bean's role in creating the legend and on the donkeys ('they were quickly made pets'). Then he got back to McGrath's account of the other claimants. Jackson thought R. J. Clark's photo had to be a reproduction from a newspaper. He recommended the use of a 'high powered microscope'. He made it clear that Stan Little could not have ridden down with Henderson and his donkey on 8 May because he (Jackson) and Henderson were at Cape Helles, on the tip of the peninsula, at that time. And their donkeys had not gone with them. He thought Mr May sounded a little too positive and again recommended the use of the microscope to put May's photo to the test.

He recalled two rolls of film. One he had sent to Cairo to be developed. He had sent it with a medical student who was returning to finish his studies. (A desperate shortage of doctors had resulted in the repatriation of a number of volunteers, medical students-cum-soldiers, who were shipped home in 1915 to complete their degrees.) But the film went astray and he never saw it again. Someone sold it to the Rotary Press of Paris which printed postcards from it. The photo of Dick Henderson and his donkey was not on this film, he was sure of it, because he sent a second film 'directly' home to New Zealand and this film, which was not indexed in any way, was developed and printed there.

The now-famous photo was on that film. James Jackson saw the print in the album, and the negative, when he returned home with his Croix de Guerre in 1919. His father had mounted a print of each negative from the film on pieces of cardboard so that son James would have them complete when he got home. On the cardboard back of Dick Henderson and his donkey he had written the following inscription:

"Murphy Patterson"
VC Anzac.
Received his Vic Cross on 1st June and killed on June 8

Brother Jack might also have written some of the inscriptions, because there was some familiarity with events and places in the Middle East, but as with 'Murphy Patterson' the details were not always exact. Or perhaps they did it together, father and son at the kitchen table poring over the photos, talking of the war and wondering what James might be doing at that very moment? It was a long time ago. The father was dead and James Jackson had not seen his brother in years. He agreed with McGrath that the puzzle seemed insoluble.[60]

What he and McGrath could not possibly know was that the puzzle was harder still. Jackson's photograph had first appeared in the Australian press some two months before the *Sydney Mail* picture. It can be found in the *Sydney Morning Herald* on 26 July 1915, three months after the Gallipoli campaign began, a mere two months after Simpson was killed and before his legend was in general circulation. Its appearance marked the beginning of the visual life of the legend, for this photograph was the first, and it would appear again and again for decades. The question now is how did Jackson's photo fall into the hands of the *Herald* so quickly?

James Jackson kept a diary. It is now in the Hocken Library at the University of Otago, in Dunedin. His negatives are there too, and a few precious letters, all formerly held by his daughter Betty. The diary provides several clues, but no complete answer. Jackson's 1937 letter said he was sure he took the photo early in the campaign. There is no doubt about that now. The 1953 letter says he had his own donkey with him when he encountered Dick Henderson and took the photo. The diary limits the possibilities considerably because it makes clear he got his donkey on the night of 3 May—'we picked up some little donkeys yesterday . . . and I took the exalted position of muleteer last night'—and was shipped to Cape Helles, without the donkey, on 5 May.[61] Jackson's section obtained several donkeys at the same time so it is almost certain that is when Dick Henderson started his donkey work as well. Jackson did not return to Anzac Cove until the 20 May. He was sure, in 1937, that he took the photo whilst Simpson was still alive. So he must have taken the photo between 3 and 5 May. (Because Simpson was dead on the 19th.) This would be consistent with the novelty of the donkeys and the donkey work and thus the pause for a photo, and it would allow an outer limit of nearly three months for the photo to find its way to Sydney and to be published—plenty of time.

In 1937 Jackson said he had sent that roll of film directly to New Zealand. If the word 'directly' was a reference to the route, then the most direct way was with an injured soldier who was to be repatriated home, but no one leaving Gallipoli could know they were going home because in May 1915 that decision was made in Egypt. On the other hand, 'directly' could have been a reference to the censors, meaning carried by someone with the express intention of avoiding them, thus travelling without unnecessary stops or interference. This is a plausible meaning, but it does not hold here because Jackson would presumably have indicated his use of a courier. He explained how the first film had gone to Cairo with a medical student. The other film went 'directly', presumably from the post office on Anzac beach, addressed to his family in Dunedin. If this film had gone with another soldier, it would have been obvious that that soldier was the key to the puzzle. But no soldier was mentioned. The word 'directly' was not a substitute for a name, it was a reference to another method.

Had McGrath gone back to R. J. Clark's 1922 letter he would have sensed a further complication, for in that letter Clark gave the War Memorial permission to duplicate and sell his snapshot. But he also revealed that he had mailed the negative home to Australia, which is plausible enough for soldiers did sometimes have negatives made from prints, or from other negatives (as was the case with Stan Little), and they frequently held on to select prints but not to negatives, because you cannot look at negatives—all sentimentality being lost in their foggy darkness. The crucial passage in Clark's letter began with his big lie and ended with a familiar snippet from the legend, but in between he may have written down the final step in the solution to the mystery:

> This picture I took myself, in May '15, it was snapped on the rise between the foot of Shrapnel Gully and Anzac Cove. *The negative was one of a parcel I sent to Australia from Rasel-tin Hospital Alexandria, and which never reached its destination.* In regard to 'Murphy' you may or may not know that he had two donkeys, Duffy No.1 & Duffy No.2. The photograph I took was of No. 1.[62]

The 'Rasel-Tin' revelation might have been another one of Clark's fibs but, even if it was true, Ras-El-Tin (the correct spelling) did not open until 5 July 1915, Clark did not arrive in Alexandria until 22 July when he was admitted to the Greek Hospital with a badly poisoned leg, and some time after that he was transferred to Ras-El-Tin. Clark's time there would have been too late for his negative to get to the *Sydney Morning Herald*. Indeed, it would have been too late had he posted it the day he arrived in Alexandria.[63]

A solution to the photographic mystery must be sought else-where. It must be deduced from elusive little clues: in the process of going 'directly' by mail to New Zealand, a package from Gallipoli could easily have been interfered with, particularly in the Middle East where wartime opportunism of every imaginable kind was booming, including a thriving trade in photographs. (In 1915, for instance, stolen Red Cross supplies were being sold to soldiers in the bazaars of Alexandria and Cairo.) Annexing a film and recycling it was not an uncommon event. Jackson's other film, notably, had been lost in the film pots of Egypt and turned to commercial gain.

Bean's diary contains a confirming detail, one of those 'tiny immensities' that the historian of a mystery longs to find: the entry for 29 September 1915 reveals his anger and frustration over a group of officers who are smuggling film to the London press for handsome fees, and it intimates that this practice is unofficially sanctioned by the War Office. Bean said these officers were smug-gling film past the censors, but quite possibly it was the censors who provided the opportunity to get at Jackson's pictures for they could have opened his package at some stage of its journey out of the Middle East. Censorship regulations covering troops in Egypt and Gallipoli stated that 'parcels must be censored before despatch' and troops were forbidden to post letters or parcels at civil post offices while on active service in order to 'ensure that soldiers' mail passed through the field censorship'. On the Gallipoli peninsula the option of a civil post office was not available, so we can be more certain that Jackson's parcel went through the hands of the censors.[64]

Next there is the relationship between the *Sydney Morning Herald* and the *Sydney Mail* to consider: both were Fairfax papers. The former used to report on pictures in forthcoming issues of the latter. The Jackson photo was used by one, then the other; it just flowed on, routinely, from the *Herald* to the *Mail*. But with one important difference: in the first instance, it was published as an unidentified photo and captioned merely as 'A Novel way of carrying the Wounded'. In the second instance, we see a full-page picture entitled 'Murphy' with that long and romantic caption beneath. The build-up of Simpson talk in the press explains the identification of 'Murphy' in the second instance. What the un-identified photo in the first instance suggests is that whoever sent it to the *Herald* knew nothing about it. Jackson had specifically stated that he did not write any details on the film or send any information with it. And his family believed they had a picture of 'Murphy Patterson . . . VC'. It is a big presumption but, presuming the film (and not the negatives) got home to New Zealand quickly and there was time to develop it, then choose and send off the picture to the *Herald* for publication on 26 July, we can be almost certain it would have gone captioned with significance; and the press, eager for a Simpson, would have snapped up the caption along with the picture. But it did not. There was no caption to snap up. James Jackson did not send the photo to the *Herald* for all he had was an undeveloped film. Nor did any of the Jacksons back home. Someone in between intervened, took the print or a copy negative from a censor's desk or from a darkroom bench, and sold copies to an agent or perhaps sent the photo direct to the *Herald*.

It is possible that the procedure was not financially motivated—that some field censors were expropriating good propaganda photos for the press, as part of their war effort. The Censor's Department had, after all, become an instrument of the recruitment campaign and its agents called on to provide 'spirit-stirring stories, fresh and unconventional'. The negative's epic possibilities were visible to anyone in a position to hold it up to the light. What seems certain is that whoever interfered with James Jackson's film felt obliged to send on the negatives, and that Jackson never realised it was cut negatives that arrived in New Zealand and not the original roll of film. So it was no ordinary thief who got off with the film. Military censors were in the best position to do this, and they were the most likely to repackage the contents and send them on. The solution to the photographic mystery may thus reside in the epic qualities of the photograph itself.

Chapter Eight

The Ritual Centre

We few, we happy few, we band of brothers;
For he today that sheds his blood with me
Shall be my brother; be he ne'er so vile,
This day shall gentle his condition.
And gentlemen in England, now abed,
Shall think themselves accursed they were not here;
And hold their manhoods cheap whiles any speaks
That fought with us upon Saint Crispin's day.

William Shakespeare, *Henry V*, act 4, scene 3, 60-67

In October 1933, as Melbourne's Shrine of Remembrance neared completion and the unemployed toiled at the landscape around it, a letter appeared in the *Argus*, signed 'Quinn's Post'. The *nom de plume* suggested a Gallipoli veteran. The letter claimed that Simpson was 'the embodiment of true sacrifice' and called for a memorial to him by the Shrine:

> In the years to come it is to be assumed that statues of generals will surround the Shrine. Why should they, and they alone, be so honoured? Books galore are being written extolling their virtues; honours were showered upon them during their lifetime. I venture to say that a monument to Simpson and his donkey, with the help-less form of a badly wounded soldier on Murphy's back, would possess greater appeal to the rank and file of the AIF than any other example of the sculptor's art . . . The ass is already immortal, for the Salvager of Souls used him. Let us again use the ass as symbolical along with Simpson of the salvaging of human wreckage in war.[1]

The levelling theme was celebrated by others, as was the Christian humility of the simple tale, while a flow of opinions once again worked Simpson into the ranks of those celebrated by the Anzac legend:

> This man was symbolic of a type peculiarly Australian. His casual acquisition of a donkey, his enterprise . . . , the cheery fatalism with which he faced death again and again in the service of his comrades—all were manifestations of that mingled nonchalance and sublimity which so often raised the Australian civilian-soldier to the heights of glorious achievement.[2]

In 1933, however, the idea of a 'glorious achievement' was no longer unchallenged. The call for a monument to Simpson came at a time when the celebrants of the Great War were losing their grip on its meaning. In the daily press the language of remembrance was not what it had been. There was less talk of imperishable glory and daring deeds; there was more talk of hollow slogans, war-shattered nerves and broken bodies. Some people had been weighing the loss and the legacy. DCMs stood in dole queues and VCs were on the wallaby.[3] Moves towards rearmament were now challenged by a growing revulsion against all forms of militarism.

Conservatives warned against defence apathy and the fashion to describe war as evil. They railed against squalid books that cast soldiers as 'beastly and neurotic', and against school teachers who talked of war as though it were a tragic mistake. (Bean wrote in 1946 that a book such as *Anzac to Amiens* would not have been popularly received by school teachers if it had been published a decade earlier.)[4] They reasserted the 'undying inspiration' of Gallipoli, insisting that Anzac Day did not glorify war and should not produce cynicism. But cynicism was not hard to find, and Anzac Day committees were now careful to remove the more obvious trappings of militarism from their parades, while the battalion histories published in this period were alternately sensitive to, or angry with, the spread of anti-war sentiment. The men of 1914-18 were dying off, people were forgetting and distorting, modernity was irreverent. War had lost its glow of romance.[5]

Even the Shrine had its critics. Some said there should be no memorials to the war anywhere, and proposed that where there were guns there should be wattle trees and where there were statues there should be elms. Others picked at 'militaristic' details in the new pantheon. There were objections to Kipling's Ode which was to be chiselled on to an inner wall and which spoke glowingly of 'merciless riders'. There was debate about the need for a shrine guard with fixed bayonets. There was unease with the idea of an equestrian statue of General Monash, for this might suggest 'destruction'. One critic had nothing in particular to complain about, but found the whole thing 'awesomely impersonal'. Responding to a chastened world and a jaded popular memory of war, several others were impressed by the idea that a statue of Simpson would help to humanise the Shrine.

The Victorian Premier, Sir Stanley Argyle, welcomed the proposal for a memorial to Simpson with a defensive flourish. 'There is no glorification of war in it', he said. 'It is rather the story of the reaction of a humble and noble soul to the worst influences which could assail civilisation'. A correspondent in the *Argus* spoke of the Shrine's stately grandeur, but felt that it was the 'homely figures of the plain man and his little grey donkey' that would illustrate the spirit of heroism that underlay the Shrine's conception. Another advocate, a woman who had been a fierce conscriptionist in 1916, thought Simpson might appeal to the critics on their own terms: 'However much we may be opposed to war, none of us can fail to wish to instil admiration of unselfish bravery into the minds of our children and our children's children'.[6]

Philadelphia's crusade

The call from Quinn's Post was immediately taken up. The Victorian RSL, the Returned Army Nurses, the British ex-Service Legion, several churches, the Red Cross, the premier, sections of the Scottish community,[7] several generals and others commended the idea. The Red Cross took charge of fund raising, and the *Argus* publicised the fund daily. A special, one-shilling fund was promoted to give the mothers of Victoria a chance to contribute, the assumption being that so many had lost a breadwinner that a modest, fixed sum was appropriate. The Red Cross took the view that Simpson perfectly embodied the high ideals of its organisation. Lady Irvine, President of the Victorian Division (and the wife of a fierce conscriptionist), wrote:

> There is something inevitably inspiring in the story of this man, that plain private soldier, unarmed, fearless and smiling, going to and fro

with his donkey, seeking the wounded and dying, and bearing them to shelter and succour, knowing full well that at any moment such a journey may be his last.[8]

A special meeting of the Victorian Red Cross Council on 19 October 1933 set up a sub-committee to oversee the appeal. It was headed by the Secretary-General of the organisation's Victorian Division, Miss Philadelphia Robertson, OBE, who remained at the centre of things from beginning to end.[9] Her committee's principal task in the early stages was to liaise with A. C. C. Holtz from the *Argus* and to oversee the incoming donations. Two months later, when the appeal came to an end, it began to organise for a monument, but hopes for a life-sized statue were dashed by the small amount subscribed. Money had flowed in steadily, but the donations were mostly small and the flow became a trickle. By late November it was clear the fund was falling well below target. Robertson called on generals to back the fund and circularised country newspapers around Victoria, but to no avail.

The *Argus* decided to close the appeal on 9 December, when the fund was somewhere near £350, well short of the £1000 needed for a life-size representation. The *Argus* editor, Roy Curthoys, had already given up hope of any kind of statue and was thinking that it might just be possible to 'erect within the Shrine a plaque in bas relief, which will be a *not unworthy* monument to Simpson'.[10] Holtz wrote vaguely of 'the monument—whatever it might be', and mentioned the possibility of a plaque in high relief on the wall of the Shrine, or a granite column, though he believed that there was still hope for a statue of 'fair proportions, representing Simpson and his donkey'.[11] Miss Robertson did not give up. She told Paul Montford, the sculptor who had the Melbourne statue of Adam Lindsay Gordon to his credit, that the appeal could be renewed at a later date in order to achieve a 'full size group'.[12] She also sought advice from W. Leslie Bowles, Honorary Secretary of the Sculptors' Society of Australia, who believed that his members would be willing to submit sketches for a memorial. Robertson was pleased and hopeful. We could put the sketches in the *Argus* window in Collins Street, she told Holtz, and announce a target of £1000 to carry out the approved design. We could reopen the appeal and it would come good yet, she hoped.[13]

The *Argus* replied that it would be a grave mistake to reopen the fund, commenting that 'it was very difficult towards the end to obtain even the amount that was received'. Another twenty or thirty pounds might be raised but anything substantial was impossible. An artist should be commissioned to get the best possible result in miniature. 'This view is emphasised', wrote Holtz, 'by the very many appeals which are constantly being made through our columns'. The implication was clear: the public was overburdened with calls upon its purse, and the financial limits of the monument were fixed.[14] Accepting this argument, the sub-committee decided to pursue 'the best possible memorial for the amount actually in hand', a sum of £385 9s. 6d. But a month later this option did not seem possible and the committee was again considering a 'plaque or tablet representing Simpson and his donkey', perhaps incorporated into a drinking fountain 'which it is understood is needed in the vicinity of the Shrine'. Robertson wrote off to the Shrine trustees to test the water,[15] but they believed that there should be no memorial to an individual near the Shrine. The Shrine was to express the egalitarian tradition of the armed forces at its most solemn: universal themes to prevail; no man to be elevated above another; all sacrifice equal. The exception was to be King George the Fifth,[16] and possibly Monash. Simpson was out of the running.

In the following months there was little change, except that the original idea was further downgraded. The Shrine trustees held firm. The Parks and Gardens Committee of the Melbourne City Council was planning its own drinking fountain near the Shrine and Robertson hoped to 'obtain permission for the Red Cross to attach to it the tablet or plaque commemorating 'The Man with the Donkey''.[17] The snag was that the City Council did not yet have control of the King's Domain. It was to take over from the Public Works Department some time in the future. Anticipating its authority, the Parks and Gardens Committee replied that there would be no Simpson memorial until it saw a satisfactory design. The situation looked bleak. The bronze group had ceased to exist; the plaque and the tablet had no resting place; the memorial was being reduced to an afterthought on a hypothetical waterspout. But the sub-committee was not prepared to give up its quest.

Before the year was out Robertson was negotiating with William Bowles of the Sculptors' Society on the terms for a competition for the design and execution of a statuette. It may have been on the sculptor's initiative that a bronze group again became a possibility, but we cannot be sure. Notes of a telephone conversation in Miss Robertson's hand indicate that at least three sculptors, including

Bowles, were in touch with her, and all three were doing their own legwork—writing, lobbying on the phone and comparing notes.[18] It was a good time for monuments but a lean time economically, so contacts and self-promotion were an essential part of the monumental sculptor's existence. There was plenty of business but the competition was tough and the sculptors were on their toes. It was out of this activity—with Philadelphia in the middle of it—that the proposal for a 'Private Simpson Memorial Competition' arose, the winning design to be submitted to the Parks and Gardens Committee for approval. The idea was taking shape in October 1934, a year after the fund had opened, and the sub-committee wanted the memorial completed and erected before Anzac Day the following April.[19] Such hopes were wildly optimistic.

From November 1934 to February 1935, seven sculptors laboured at their 'Modelled Sketch Design'. Bowles, Montford, Ola Cohn and the others competed for a first prize of £12.[20] The winner was Wallace Anderson, who had served in France and, since the war, had worked for the Australian War Museum as a sculptor and designer of dioramas. In the 1930s he went freelance but took commissions from his former employer.[21] Anderson described his work for the Red Cross as

> a pedestal in Harcourt Granite fine axed with a bowl on either end to contain either planted flowers or to be used to take running water issuing from bronzed masks set above. On the pedestal is placed the bronze of Private Simpson with his donkey supporting a wounded soldier.[22]

The Parks and Gardens Committee acted promptly. Within a fortnight of seeing Anderson's model it approved the erection of a monument on an agreed site, though not without dissension: the Chairman, Alderman Stapley, registered his opposition 'to the Gardens being used for memorial purposes'.[23] Once it had been accepted by the committee, Anderson made a plaster representation to scale, which was sent to Italy for casting in bronze by the same firm that had done Montford's statue of Adam Lindsay Gordon, Chiuruzzi of Naples. A Melbourne founder lost the commission because, according to Anderson, he 'is a little afraid of undertaking the work & is putting me off and will I think continue to do so'.[24] The modest dimensions of the work permitted additional costs, principally shipping, to be contained within the fund's strict ceiling of £386.

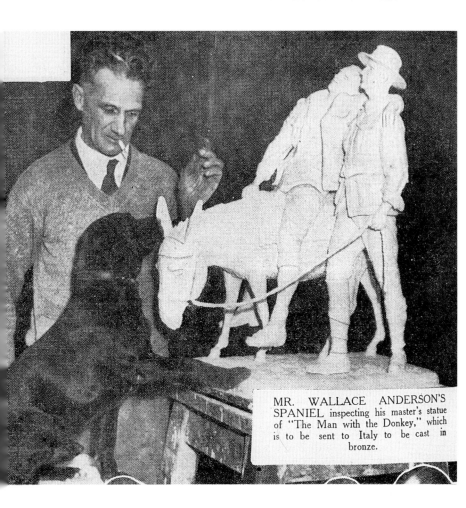

MR. WALLACE ANDERSON'S SPANIEL inspecting his master's statue of "The Man with the Donkey," which is to be sent to Italy to be cast in bronze.

Mr Wallace Anderson, his spaniel and the plaster model which was to be sent to Naples to be cast in bronze

Anderson and the Red Cross sub-committee hoped that the monument would be in place for Armistice Day of that year (1935), but they reckoned without continued strife over the location of the monument, and the effects of an international crisis. The Secretary for Lands had approved the site in March subject to approval by the chief engineer at the Public Works Department, A. D. Mackenzie, whom General Sir Harry Chauvel was lobbying to no avail three months later.[25] Already Anzac Day had passed and the Committee now looked to completion before Armistice Day. At Chauvel's instigation the parties met in the King's Domain in July, about the same time the plaster model left Australia, and inspected the site favoured by the Red Cross and the City Council, beneath an English oak near the Shrine. They inspected another site, this one favoured by Mackenzie and the Shrine trustees; it was near the gates of Government House, well away from the Shrine, perhaps on a spot marked for a drinking fountain. This location was not favoured by Robertson and her committee, who felt that the statue would lose meaning if sited too far from the Shrine; they believed it should sit within sight of the great building, basking in the glow of its reverence and solemnity. But no one shifted ground, the meeting broke up without agreement, and the matter stood in abeyance.[26]

At home there was a deadlock; from abroad there was not a word. Anderson wrote twice to Chiuruzzi. Months went by and in October there was still no news. 'There seems no prospect now of having the memorial completed by the 11th of next month (11/11)', he told Robertson. Late in October she appealed to Colonel Vaughan at the Commonwealth Bank, which was handling payment to Naples.[27] Word or rumour finally came through that the foundry was short of bronze as a result of the heavy demand in Italy for munitions and armaments; another rumour had the foundry short of staff because of call-up for service with the Italian army.[28] The committee must have pondered the irony of this.

The Italo-Abyssinian crisis then intervened. The League of Nations applied sanctions against Italy, Australia stood with the League and no money was to go to Italy. The final payment for the bronze group, which was ready early in 1936, could not now be transferred. Robertson was beset from both sides. Abroad the statue had fallen victim to big power politics; at home the fight for a site dragged on. The Public Works Department was still unmoved. In the long term its opinion was irrelevant, but Public Works and the Shrine trustees did not want Simpson where the committee wanted

him. Whatever their motives, the importance of the statue's proximity to the Shrine carried no weight with them. Robertson must
have felt that there was a shortfall of goodwill, in the quarters that
mattered, towards the man, his donkey and the Red Cross Committee which championed his memory. Surviving records suggest
that practical considerations overtook the loftier, mnemonic
concerns of Robertson and her supporters.[29]

By mid-February the *Argus* was crying 'shame'. Another Anzac
Day was approaching with no hope of a monument in place for the
ceremonies. The *Argus* was embarrassed: it had run an appeal for
money more than two years before and still had nothing to show for
it. Lobbied by the Red Cross, the Federal Treasurer exempted the
statuette from sanctions and gave permission for the final instalment of funds to be transferred to Naples.[30] That meant the statue
would soon be home, but there was still nowhere to put it.

In May, with another Anzac Day behind her, the memorial in
hand and ready, Robertson was still seeking confirmation from the
Town Clerk,[31] but Parks and Gardens was equivocating and would
make 'no definite decision yet'.[32] Control of the King's Domain now
passed to the City Council, and with it the right to make a final
decision on the location of the statue. Plumbing suggested the Red
Cross site was the more suitable 'as the memorial, which will be a
drinking fountain, will be in close proximity to the main drain,
which can take the overflow of water'.[33] The Town Clerk, on the
other hand, was worried about the safety of children: 'The site
selected by the Red Cross Society is very close to the vehicular traffic
roadway traversing the King's Domain and may be the means of
subjecting children using the fountain to risk of accident by fast
moving traffic', he wrote. The council weighed these matters; it
looked again at the site recommended by Public Works 'as a matter
of courtesy'. The main drain prevailed. The site selected by the Red
Cross was approved. 'It will be more easily seen and accessible to a
greater number of people in the area,' wrote the Town Clerk in his
letter about the main drain and the memorial as drinking fountain.
It appears that the monument as monument was hardly considered
at all.[34]

On 13 May 1936 the council finally approved the site near the
Shrine.[35] As the *Argus* put it, the 'homely figures of the plain man
and his little grey donkey' would be there to balance the stately
grandeur of the Shrine. The memorial was unveiled by the
Governor, Lord Huntingfield, on a Saturday afternoon in June

1936. He spoke to the crowd about sacrifice and patriotism and dying for one's country. Sir Harry Chauvel made a short speech and then the Reverend A. P. Blunden and Dr Victor Hurley spoke of their memories of Simpson at Gallipoli. Major Chester Reynolds read an excerpt on Simpson from his Gallipoli diary and then the acting president of the Victorian RSL placed a wreath at the foot of the statue. Robertson did not speak. She had written a poem to commemorate the unveiling, but she kept it to herself. The size of the crowd is unknown.[36]

The limits of the legend

Why did the appeal fall so far short of its original goals? One answer is that the failure of memorial subscriptions was not surprising for the 1930s. The memory of the war and the dead, and the casualties who survived, gave rise to perpetual memorialisation and welfare needs. Never to forget had become a moral duty, an element of citizenship. As a result, the Australian people in the inter-war years were faced with many calls on the hip pocket. There was not enough spare change to go around and some funds had to fail. So much money was raised for causes arising from the war that, in 1931, there were calls for an investigation of all funds being held for soldiers and other patriotic purposes, in case they were being misused. Many were lying dormant. The Victorian Branch of the RSL called for a 'searching inquiry'. A campaign headed by the *Age* newspaper floated the idea of unified control to coordinate and oversee all such moneys.[37]

Widows' charity bequests, commemorative medallions, memorial halls and leap year balls helped TB soldiers not on Commonwealth pensions.[38] Victoria had a Last Post Fund to ensure that former soldiers received a decent burial. People built memorials to AIF units and to the fighting forces of other nations. In the provinces they put up memorials, fountains and cenotaphs. Occasionally the presence of a temporary cenotaph signalled the perception of an urgent need to set memory in civic culture. Some country towns planted an 'Avenue of Honour'. There were statues to dead generals and memorial tombstones for other great soldiers. Even the donors were memorialised on one occasion: in 1934 a bronze cenotaph was erected at the Shrine, to hold the receipt slips of donations for its construction.[39] There were memorial gates at grammar schools, and drinking troughs dedicated to fallen horses. The Dog on the Tucker Box was unveiled in 1932 during Back to Gundagai Week. And there were grand plans for the greatest of military heroes, General Sir John Monash who died in 1931.[40] The memorial proposed for Monash was to equal in cost that erected for Edward VII in the Domain. This meant a figure in excess of £6000. Melba died the same year. The people remembered her voice, but also her donations to soldiers' causes. It was said she raised over £100 000 for these, and some suggested she, too, should have a worthy memorial.[41]

The Simpson appeal raised nearly £400 in seven weeks, late in the Depression and in the run-up to Christmas; it was not a bad result. If donations simply corresponded to legendary standing, the appeal should have done much better than, or at least as well as, that for Monash or Melba. But the limits of its success were set firm by the competition and several other considerations. The outcome of the appeal was complicated by the politics of the funding process, by the social character of its organisation and by the mnemonics of the Simpson legend, which worked against the appeal in several respects. Robertson and her Red Cross committee were faithful to the end, but the widespread effort that went into the Monash memorial, and the elite support behind it, did not rally for Simpson. Perhaps that was inevitable given Monash's place in Melbourne society?

The appeal for a Monash memorial flanks the Simpson appeal, beginning and end. The calls began in October 1931, soon after the general's death. There was no cause for haste. How best to perpetuate the memory of Monash was an important decision according to the *Sun* newspaper, 'every opinion and every view should be welcomed'.[42] When the appeal began is not certain, but by May 1933 it was well under way, with more than £900 subscribed.[43] By March 1934 the Monash Memorial Committee— headed by Melbourne's mayor—had nearly £4000 cash and promises that would take the total to £5382.[44] Progress then slowed. In December 1935 the *Argus* reported that subscriptions were still at the £4000 mark, and a fresh drive for the further £2000 was launched.[45] Calls appeared regularly in the Melbourne newspapers. Late in 1937 the *Argus* reported work could begin on the statue, sufficient funds were in hand.[46] The fund had been advertised intermittently in the newspapers, for about five years. Whatever doubts there may have been along the way—and there is no evidence of doubts—the committee and the newspapers saw the appeal through to the required end.

The campaign succeeded because Monash was well known to the Victorian people. Like Melba, he *was* a Victorian and had great wartime and peacetime significance for them. He was identified with both the past and the future, having headed the State Electricity Commission and developed the 'model township' of Yallourn during the 1920s.[47] His engineering background and his connection with electricity made him a symbol of modernisation. His military reputation had continued to grow in peacetime. In his biography, Geoffrey Serle writes that Monash's authority over returned servicemen grew throughout the 1920s and was unchallenged at the time of his death.[48] When he died he was a popular hero and, despite his Jewish ancestry, firmly part of the Establishment. Those who sustained the appeal for a memorial were men of similar rank and status who had admired Monash in life. Given his unique position in Melbourne society, and the codes associated with that society, those running the appeal were bound to see it through to a successful conclusion. Some had personally given substantial amounts. Sidney Myer gave £105.[49] The idea was a 'non-utilitarian' monument—no common drinking spouts or such things—funded by a loving public.[50] In this one respect—public funding—the Monash monument shared common ground with the Simpson monument. But other differences were considerable: the people had participated, recently, in the civic ritual following the death of Monash;[51] the goal—a one and a half times life-size 'non-utilitarian' statue—was never relinquished; the committee was headed by powerful men of the city and backed by others of similar status; the newspapers remained committed; the goal was achieved.

For the Monash memorial, the backing of a powerful social class made the difference and this was reflected in the horizons of the two committees. The humble monument envisaged for Simpson was in keeping with his legend. The initial goal was a mere £1000 and only local sculptors were involved, whereas the statue for Monash was chosen from an empire-wide competition, judged in London and Melbourne.[52] The Simpson Committee was not so socially elevated, though it was solid enough. It was a Red Cross-based committee celebrating a plain soldier who had enlisted in Western Australia, unknown to the people of Victoria except as legend. Most people seemed favourably disposed to a Simpson memorial, just as they were to one for the dead general, the 'soldier after Caesar's pattern'.[53] However, in the circles that mattered beyond the Red Cross, the commitment to Simpson was more sentimental than practical. No large donations came in for the Man with the Donkey and very little corporate money. The shipping firm McIlwraith, McEacharn Ltd, which had formerly employed Simpson as a greaser on a coastal collier, donated £5 5s. The Melbourne City Council declined to make a donation after being invited to do so.[54]

When the appeal began to flag, Robertson wrote to five of the generals who had served on the peninsula, asking them to rally support with a newspaper statement. Only one of these agreed and that was Sir Harry Chauvel, who was close to the Simpson Committee. Blamey told Robertson he could not help because he was not prepared to divide his commitment between Monash and Simpson. His excuse appears feeble—we are talking here about a few lines for a newspaper, a few lines for an AIF hero—and it underlines how the two appeals competed. 'I would have been very glad to do so', wrote Blamey, 'had it not been that I am so engrossed in the effort to raise funds for the erection of a memorial to General Monash'.[55]

Next, Robertson tried a little cunning. She sent a letter for publication to the *Argus*, signed 'We Will Remember Them'. It is an important letter, expressing puzzlement at the 'inadequate results' of the appeal and then addressing the lack of support from influential people:

> If some of our prominent citizens would give a suitable lead, I feel sure that thousands of wellwishers of moderate means would follow suit, and the end would soon be gained. The city would then possess a memorial worthy of it in design and appearance, and—of still greater importance—one that would show that we as a people honour the compassionate service of those who tended the sick and wounded, as exemplified in the moving record of this high minded and selfless hero.[56]

The letter was never published, suggesting that even at this early stage, the *Argus* was having doubts about the appeal, though no evidence exists to indicate that priority for the Monash memorial increased its reluctance. The *Argus* however was also handling the Monash fund, calling for and taking donations from the public, as was the Melbourne City Council and a number of municipal councils. It was a weighty network that may not have had the enthusiasm for another campaign and a less commanding figure.

Before the monument was unveiled, H. S. Gullett, ex-soldier and conservative MHR, expressed the view that 300 guineas was an excessive amount for a statue depicting Simpson, 'not for the work itself, but for the subject'.[57]

Monash fitted better into the stridently masculine core of the Anzac tradition; the representation of Simpson was not as solidly masculine, despite his unquestioned courage and heroism. He was identified with the 'feminine' qualities of care for the sick, of selfless giving, of saving rather than taking life, 'quietly succouring the wounded under fire'.[58] Comparisons with Florence Nightingale would recur during the appeal. Just as the Crimea had given rise to the 'merciful inspiration of "The Lady of the Lamp"', so out of the horrors of Anzac came the 'inspiring example' of the man with the donkey.[59] In time of war the nature of Simpson's work carried a deeper meaning, and more weight, for soldiers.

But in the 1930s it is perhaps not surprising that a somewhat different constituency was getting behind the proposal for a monument. The appeal was championed by the Red Cross, one of the core women's institutions of the day, and was largely carried by a senior member of that organisation, Robertson herself. The suggestion of a one-shilling 'Mother's Tribute' came within days of the appeal's opening and was seen as a 'graceful compliment from the mothers of Victoria to the mother of the hero of Gallipoli'.[60] The author was not to know that Mrs Kirkpatrick had died earlier in the same year. In a column written for the *Argus*, Vesta endorsed the idea, asserting that the shilling fund would

> be welcomed by every mother who remembers the early days of the war . . . The story of this simple soldier, who saw, and seized, the opportunity to render help to whom it might otherwise have been impossible to give medical attention, has touched the hearts of all women; and the picture of the man with his donkey has brought tears to the eyes of many of those who learned of his work long ago from their men among the Anzacs.

Subscription lists suggest that women contributed heavily to the appeal, sometimes through Red Cross branches but mostly as individuals. Those women donors who did not give their name frequently signified their relationship to another, usually a soldier, by such signatures as: Anzac's Mother, Soldier's Mother, Two soldier's aunts, Mother of two fallen soldiers, Sister Sue, Sisters, Soldier's Mother and Sister, British Soldier's Mother, Widow's Mite.

Women's letters also figured prominently in the correspondence on Simpson. Women's organisations, such as the Soldiers and Sailors Womenfolk branches and the Australian Women's National League, made modest donations.[61] The Returned Army Nurses Association met to commend the appeal.

The 'humble donkey' further softened Simpson's image and helped to give him a special place in folklore for kindergartens, schools and churches. Robertson believed that Simpson's gentle image would add meaning to the Shrine setting for children. The Shrine would overpower them; a Simpson monument would give rise to voluntary impulse. 'Children seeing the Shrine will be awed into reverence by its greatness', she wrote. 'Simpson, with his donkey and its pathetic burden, will appeal to the child's natural love of animals, and sympathy with all suffering.'[62] Doubling as it would as a drinking fountain, the monument was frequently represented as something for the children.[63] The *Argus* commended the appeal to all readers, but also promoted the memorial as one with special meaning for children, and to which children could donate.[64] Again the subscription lists are telling. Junior Red Cross branches and schools appeared regularly as donors. The failure of the appeal to attract support in high places makes more sense in the light of these not-so-tangible considerations of gender and age. There was a tendency to reduce the Simpson appeal in a way that Monash never suffered; to locate it on the edge of the private realm, the woman's sphere; to delegate support and enthusiasm for Simpson to the parsons and the school teachers, to the women and the children.

Ironically the egalitarian tradition associated with the AIF may have encouraged this tendency and worked further against the Simpson appeal. The Anzac legend presumed a plurality of heroes and elevated collective effort over individual achievement. It stressed universal themes and their impersonal representation. The appeal for a Simpson monument brought some of this to the surface and, although its effect is difficult to assess, there is no shortage of evidence. Robertson and her committee were always on the defensive in this respect, their concern aroused from the start by Chauvel:

Sir Harry Chauvel spoke of the desirability of emphasising the symbolical character of the proposed memorial, and this view was endorsed by the Rev. J. Danglow who pointed out that difficulties might be created by singling out for recognition the heroic record of one man when the history of the war contained many others.[65]

Sir Harry and Rabbi Danglow were right. The papers soon carried evidence of dissension in the ranks. The *West Australian* reckoned it was the general opinion among returned men that 'the memorial should be symbolical of the service given by the ranks of the AIF, particularly the stretcher-bearers'.[66] There was Colonel Tilney's expansive view that all stretcher-bearers deserved a monument or a Victoria Cross.[67] And there was the continuing pressure for the Shrine to make a solemn, collective, impersonal statement. Possibly the most telling comment came in a letter to the Editor of the *Sun* from a Gallipoli veteran:

> While quite appreciating the sentiment that is behind the suggestion to erect a memorial to the late Pte. W. [*sic*] Simpson, of the 3rd Field Ambulance, it does not seem to me quite as the men of the AIF would have it—that an individual should be singled out for this honor. I saw 'Murphy' and his 'donk' at work during those first few days ashore at Gallipoli, but later I also saw the stretcher-bearers at work on the Somme and out towards Passchendaele. Hats off to those good fellows who gave their lives in doing their jobs well, but do not single out one man because his work was a little more picturesque.—OBSERVOR (Elsternwick).[68]

Although the committee's strategy, henceforth, was to stress the typicality of Simpson's spirit and endeavour, the problem did not go away. When the flow of funds began to falter, Sir Harry again told Robertson: 'The appeal is not going too well and I think it is largely because a number of people think that there were many cases just as deserving of a memorial as Simpson's'.[69]

Monash's death had provoked similar argument. There was much discussion about his grave at Brighton Cemetery. Many soldiers thought that his headstone should be the simple stone that marked all war graves, a view which the Federal President of the RSL, G. J. C. Dyett, shared: 'Personally I think it is a beautiful idea. We were all diggers, from general to private. We are still diggers in civilian life united by the greatest of all bonds, the memory of having shared common dangers. And in death we are diggers still'. But this commitment to levelling, to avoiding glorification of any kind, to deepest solemnity, does not appear to have carried through to debate on the Shrine, where Monash was to be an exception. Late in 1931 the plans for the Shrine included two equestrian statues, one on either side of the northern portal. These were in the original design, according to Shrine architect Philip Hudson, and it was assumed one of them would be Sir John Monash.[70] About a month after his death the RSL and the Institute of Engineers (Victorian Branch) endorsed the idea; the War Memorial Committee offered no objection to the erection of a memorial to the late AIF leader.[71]

When the Shrine trustees took over in 1934, however, Monash's position was no longer secure. It is clear from the Trustees Minute Books that few details about the Shrine environs were fixed. A multitude of decisions pressed for resolution, some of which had to be settled before the dedication of the Shrine by the Duke of Gloucester on 11 November. There was the furnishing of the crypt to consider, carving contracts for the buttress groups, insurance matters, flag-poles to purchase, and the prosecution of anti-war pamphleteers was to go ahead. There were broadcasting arrangements to be made, frieze panels to be settled upon and bronze contracts to sign; the electrics were bothersome, brochures and advertisements took time, the shaft of light had to be right and, oh no—damp penetration. The interminable arrangements for the dedication ceremony included 20 000 pigeons to be released simultaneously, the benediction, and the arrival of Kipling's dedication poem. Outside there was floodlighting to take care of, the landscaping, the unemployed at work on the Reflecting Pool, and liaison with the curator of the King's Domain. He might be planting iris bulbs, taking advice on the insect enemies of shade trees, selecting plants for the Herbarium, putting down top-dressing or trying out his new Massey-Ferguson, a triple horse drawn lawn mower.[72] The trustees had to watch this front too. There was a state of perpetual adaptation as the Shrine plans entered the real world.

As these matters were settled the likelihood of a statue of Monash declined. The details are obscure though the key moments may be discerned. In January 1934 the trustees decided to move the Monash statue away from the north portal and to locate it some 270 feet from the Shrine steps.[73] They reiterated this decision in March when they realised that the excavation for the Reflecting Pool, an unemployment relief scheme, was in the wrong place.[74] Monash was 270 feet off; the Pool was to be no closer to the steps than Monash. If the debate about personal versus impersonal statuary was continuing it was then working against the general. He was about to be moved out of the Shrine precincts altogether. In mid-1935 the trustees met to discuss both Monash and Simpson on the one afternoon. They endorsed the distant location for the Simpson statue—the site that had been approved by the Public Works Department and had so disappointed Robertson. They also decided that the Monash memorial had to go. The Monash Memorial Committee was most unhappy,[75] but a year later the trustees codified their position with the following motion by Sister Wilson:

> That notwithstanding that the Trustees offered no objection to the erection of a Memorial to His late Majesty King George the Fifth within the Shrine Area, the Trustees are not favourable to the erection of personal memorials within such area.[76]

The Victorian Premier, Sir Stanley Argyle, got the job of showing the motion to Blamey, the choice of messenger perhaps indicating the final stage of a long and weighty wrangle. According to Serle, 'public opinion strongly opposed *any* individual statue there'. The Monash Committee fumed and boiled but it was a lost cause. Five months after the trustees' motion, a new site was selected at the bottom of the hill, well outside the precincts of the Shrine.[77]

Nearly three years after the Red Cross committee had first met, the statue of Simpson was unveiled, in 1936. Pilgrims have been making their way to the site ever since. The statue immediately became a ritual centre for the legend they knew so well. Soon after the unveiling, an interstate visitor wrote an evocative memoir of the ritual centre at work:

> My first opportunity to see the statue . . . occurred on the King's Birthday. It was a gloomy winter day. But at the Shrine a glorious sunshine bathed the landscape with a rare beauty. I found the memorial to Private Simpson and his donkey surrounded by school children and teachers. A gentleman who was present took from his pocket a clipping of Miss McAskell's poem ['The Man with the Donkey'], and requested one of the teachers to read it aloud, which she did to the great pleasure of all who were there, especially the children. The little memorial is a great work of the sculptor's art, and Miss McAskell's poem is a literary gem that deserves to be enclosed in a casket and affixed in some way to the monument, so that those who look on the rare beauty of the sculpture can read for themselves the classic story of its meaning.[78]

Tributes to the Gallipoli hero

Colonel Sherwin, the Red Cross Commissioner for Victoria, places a wreath on the memorial to Private Simpson and his donkey. School children look on. To the right is Major-General Sir Thomas Blamey. Blamey had declined to help with the fund-raising for this memorial, preferring to busy himself with the fund for a statue of General Monash.

In 1938 Annie Simpson Pearson paid for a wreath which was laid there on Anzac Day by members of the Red Cross. The Gallipoli Legion of Anzacs took up the idea, and the wreath-laying ceremony became part of its Anzac Day program. The ritual began at 10 a.m. with a short march, culminating at the memorial statue. There was then an address from a distinguished official, usually from the Red Cross or the Legion, followed by the laying of Annie's wreath—she sent one every year—and a wreath from the Legionnaires. In 1937 Sir Isaac Isaacs officiated and, in 1938, Major-General Sir Thomas Blamey. The ceremony ended with the Last Post and the Reveille, and thereafter the service was repeated each year for some forty years.[79]

Over these years not all who visited the memorial were pilgrims. It was repeatedly vandalised, though why, or by whom, we do not know. Despite calls to move the monument within the precincts of the Shrine, under the eyes of the permanent guard, the collective sacrifice principle of the trustees held firm.[80] Not until 1968, in the midst of another war, did they give in and permit a retreat to the precincts. Today the Man with the Donkey is located just a few strides from the steps of the Shrine. It is beyond the reach of the public, behind a small iron fence. At a glance it looks like a nineteenth-century grave, yet the size of the memorial now seems in keeping with the humble and selfless endeavours of its subject, and with the pathetic limitations of the plain soldier. The statue's own fragility seems consistent with the vulnerability of all flesh, something that Simpson knew too well. Monash is still at the bottom of the hill. His statue is awesome, but it cannot be seen from the steps of the Shrine.

Chapter Nine

Invented Anew

I have heard Charlie Chaplin complain apropos *The Gold Rush* that people only mentioned the dance with the bread rolls.

Jean Cocteau

In its Anzac Day feature for 1926, the Geelong *Advertiser* published a story about a one-armed returned soldier who sat on the sand at Eastern Beach, telling stories of the Great War to children gathered about him. He told of how 'Mother England' went to help 'little Belgium', about Australia's part in the conflict, notably the landing at Gallipoli and the example set for more Anzacs to follow in France and Palestine. Nearby an old man sat and listened, and at one point he joined in to tell the children of his sadness at having lost his son at Gallipoli, and to ask of them: 'Will you remember the Anzacs?' The children answered 'Yes' and then, turning their attention back to the returned soldier, they pleaded for another story. 'Tell us one more story—just a little one about the man with the donkey', asked one of the girls. And so, of course, he did.[1]

This was one of the rare tellings of the Simpson legend in the newspapers of the 1920s, for those papers that made the legend during the war turned their attention to other matters when it was over. But, as the report suggests, the story was alive in folklore and etched indelibly into the minds of Australia's school children. Established as part of the elementary school curriculum before the war had ended, it remained so—a feature story to be told in preparation for Anzac Day, linked to religious instruction, civic obligation and imperial patriotism. The school observance of Anzac

Day around Australia consisted of special lessons, readings and songs, speeches from members of the school committee or from a returned soldier, possibly a resident teacher, who would tell the story of the landing and of brave men such as Simpson, weaving into it the moral lessons thought to be appropriate.[2]

The sacrifice that Australian soldiers made in the course of their duty was a central theme, often expressed in terms of the children's consequent debt. Celebratory poems reminded children of how these men had happily accepted death for the best empire the world had ever seen and a cause that was thoroughly good:

> And, when the clarion sounded suddenly,
> They went, a rollicking band of boys at play,
> Tilted at doom, and there, at Anzac Bay,
> Died—but they taught the world what men there be.[3]

As one teaching manual on the 'aim and method of History and Civics' put it, 'right impulses are given from the contemplation of the "actions of the just," and warning and reproof from observing the results of the conduct of the tyrannical . . . History teaches by high examples what to scorn and what to admire, what to seek after and what to avoid'.[4]

In school texts, Private Simpson was the personification of devotion to duty and self-sacrifice in the Great War. He featured with great men of the empire such as General Gordon ('the Hero of Khartoum'), and with the heroes of ancient Greece. For the April 1919 issue of the New South Wales *School Magazine*, C. E. W. Bean wrote that Simpson 'had given his life for his fellows more gloriously perhaps than any other hero of that desperate campaign'. He stressed Simpson's bravery and reliability, noting how, in the midst of heavy shellfire and rifle fire,

> the Man with the Donkey calmly went his way as if nothing more serious than a summer shower were happening . . . [Thus] the colonel of the ambulance to which he belonged had from the first so recognised the value of his work that he was allowed to camp and work entirely on his own, almost as if he were a separate unit. All he had to do was to report once a day.

Using an excerpt from a borrowed poem, Bean related the story of how Simpson died. He assured readers that when Simpson passed on, when 'the flame in the dead eyes dimly-glassed,/shone for a second and sank again', others stepped up to take his place.[5]

The story could also succeed as a boy's own adventure combined with geography and military history, as it did in the popular school text by Charles R. Long, *Notable Deeds of Famous Men and Women* (1922) and later in Long's *British Worthies and Other Men of Might* (1934).[6] Used as a way into religious instruction, Simpson became 'The Good Samaritan of the Dardanelles' in direct comparison with the biblical good samaritan in Luke 10: 33, 34. Some versions appealed to the anthropomorphic imaginations of young children:

> Day after day the two did their noble work. The animal seemed to know that he must tread carefully to avoid the bumps and jolts over a long and tiresome road. Had he not done so the journey would very likely have meant death to a badly injured soldier.[7]

Other accounts used the man with the donkey to explain to children why Anzac Day was important, and a few linked Simpson's bravery to Australia's heroic past and to its prospects for a heroic future:

> In Australia many such brave deeds have been done and will be done. Men have risked their lives for their friends time and time again, in the depths of the mine when the fuse was sputtering, on storm-swept coasts, in dangers by flood and fire. Women [too] have been just as brave. You have only to think of Grace Bussell, of Western Australia, and Florrie Hodges, of Victoria, two names that stand for thousands of women whose deeds are less known . . . The man with the donkey showed the spirit of Anzac . . . There are boys and girls in Australia to-day who will be as brave when the test comes. It will come, let us hope, not on the battlefield, but in the battle of life. May Australians never be found wanting! . . . In what ways can boys be brave? In what ways can girls be brave? Tell any story you know of a brave boy or a brave girl.[8]

In the late 1920s it was even possible to retell the Simpson story in a way that would not antagonise anti-war feeling, perhaps reflecting worries about militarism among school teachers, as in the Victorian *School Paper* in 1928:

> The sad thing about war is that it sets the brave against the brave . . . That is why wise people all over the world are warring against war and all that causes war . . . On the 25th of April, we mourn the loss of brave men who fell at the Landing in a country far away, in the year 1915. They died in a war which they hoped was to end war.

They left the task for others to finish. In all that story of bravery and suffering . . . one of the most moving things that comes to mind is the picture of the Man with the Donkey . . .⁹

Texts on Simpson were used for instruction in spelling and pro-nunciation; they included lessons about the ancient world; and they were worked into social studies lessons on 'Arabs and the Mohammedans' and the god 'Allah (al-lah)'.¹⁰ In Notes and Exercises in the fourth grade *Victorian Readers* (1930-40), students were asked to discern a message in the kookaburra's laughter, to describe a fairy's dress, to write a composition about the life of a mouse, to find Khartoum and Gallipoli on a map. They were asked 'Was Simpson brave?' and 'What does his story teach us?', and they were then invited to write a composition entitled 'Their Mission is to Save'.¹¹

Outside the schools the legend had no regular or ritual presence in public culture. It did not figure on Anzac Day, at least not in ways that have been documented. If the war had proclaimed Simpson a hero, the peace had settled him back into less visible currents of memory and culture. The disputed photographs of 1933–34 and 1937 sparked brief and intense newspaper coverage in several States, coverage that testified to Simpson's presence in folklore, but apart from groups of returned soldiers and civilians who claimed some special link or affinity with Simpson at such times, there was nothing to lift the legend into public view in any State except Victoria where the little statue flourished in the shadow of the Shrine of Remembrance.¹²

Thus, when the Postmaster-General's Department decided on an 'Anzac' stamp issue in 1935 (the 20th anniversary of the landing), the man with the donkey was not even considered, and the idea of commemorating Gallipoli was rejected because there was 'no valid reason' for selecting that campaign 'in preference to other im-portant incidents associated with the conduct of the world-war'. The primacy of Gallipoli was not yet fixed (like a reflex) into Australian culture. Indeed, the decision to have a commemorative stamp was only taken after four years of intense lobbying by the RSL, and then not until the Postmaster-General came up with a design featuring the cenotaph at Whitehall. The design made no mention of Gallipoli and was an appropriate choice since nationalism in ruling class rhetoric still meant serving the empire, and the cenotaph, signifying Remembrance, avoided any telling suggestion of mili-tarism. There was to be one print run only and the production of the stamp was subordinate to that for the stamp issue to celebrate the King's Silver Jubilee.[13]

After the Second World War the tale was occasionally expressed in new forms, such as cartoons, in a new round of 'Anzac adventures' for young readers, and radio plays for children which also featured in school texts.[14] But its general absence from national culture continued. The statue at the Shrine might appear in Melbourne newspapers on Anzac Day when that small group of hardy supporters gathered after the dawn service; the tale was occasionally recounted in the press whenever 'a living link' with John Simpson Kirkpatrick spoke out; and the legend had a permanent place at the War Memorial in Canberra. But otherwise it had no public presence. If the legend of Simpson was to again become nationally prominent, it would first have to be recovered and then elevated from the classroom and the sphere of folklore. This process began as the 50th anniversary of the landing drew nearer. As 1965 came into view, the legend started to figure widely in popular culture and ultimately in public ritual.

Between 1960 and 1965 there was a great resurgence of interest in the deeds of the original Anzacs. The Man with the Donkey appeared in film and television programs, in new books about the events of 1915, in features in nationally distributed magazines such as *Pix*, *People* and *Everybody's*, in the *Australian Women's Weekly*, and in many newspaper articles where, among others, that unstoppable publicist Irving Benson was at work, preparing the ground for his 'biography'.[15] Significantly, it was Simpson who always featured. He was the one plain soldier who was consistently identified and who was now representative of all others, his name synonymous with Gallipoli in a way that it had never been before. In *Everybody's*, under the title 'The Day Simpson Said to Me: Ride The Donkey Mate', Peter Chick told the story of how he had been wounded and rescued only three days after the landing:

> 'Simpson was on his way back up the gully from the hospital clearing station. He saw I was limping and said: 'Ride on the donkey, mate'.
> 'But I told him I could manage—that there were others worse than me.
> 'He insisted: 'Get on, it's not far to take you back', he said.

Then Chick told the story of how, when he rode the donkey, Simpson was already a household name, how the soldiers admired his exploits—particularly the fact that he never flinched and never

THE DAY SIMPSON SAID TO ME:

"RIDE THE DONKEY, MATE"

The only known picture of John Simpson and his donkey was taken at the bottom of Gallipoli's bloody Shrapnel Gully.

Peter Chick (far right) says no medal would have been too good for his rescuer—legendary Anzac hero John Simpson.

John Simpson was a legend on Gallipoli, where he died. And Peter Chick, whose memories these are, is one of the few men to survive the trip down Shrapnel Gully with Simpson and his faithful donkey.

"I WAS shot through the foot only three days after landing at Anzac Cove. And as I limped from Quinn's Post down through Shrapnel Gully to safety I met John Simpson, the man with the donkey.

"Simpson was on his way back up the gully from the hospital clearing station. He saw I was limping and said: 'Ride on the donkey, mate.'

"But I told him I could manage — that there were others worse than me.

"He insisted. 'Get on, it's not far to take you back,' he said."

This is how 71-year-old retired sawmiller Peter Chick, of Lilydale, Tasmania, remembered the bullet-shattered morning of April 27, 1915, and the best-known hero of Gallipoli.

Now, 50 years later, Peter Chick still remembers every detail of his meeting with the man who became a legend among the troops.

"I didn't know Simpson (whose real name was John Simpson Kirkpatrick) during the voyage from Australia to the Mediterranean in the troopship Devanha, or when the destroyer Ribble took us close to the Gallipoli shores — he was in the Third Field Ambulance and I was in the 12th Battalion," said Peter Chick.

"But, by the day I was wounded, only three days after our landing, I had heard a lot about him.

"We all knew about how he was going up and down Shrapnel Valley taking wounded men back to the clearing station.

"And we couldn't help admiring him. That place was hot enough for anybody with a rifle — they could shoot back when shot at.

"But Simpson and the stretcher-bearers worked out in the open, with only their Red Cross armbands to protect them.

"A lot more Anzacs would have stayed on the beaches of Gallipoli if Simpson hadn't been there.

"Even going along Dead Man's Ridge, where Turkish snipers had a clear shot at men coming down that part of Shrapnel Gully, Simpson never flinched. He just regulated his pace to the slow walk of his donkey.

"But the shells were more dangerous to him than the bullets, because the artillery men with their big guns were so far away that they couldn't see the stretcher-bearers, nor their only protection — Red Cross armbands.

"It was just like a quiet Sunday walk to Simpson as he ambled along in his trousers, shirt, and slouch hat — there were no helmets in those days."

Because of his wound, Peter Chick was out of action for six weeks, resting in Egypt.

By JACK CLAYTON

And it wasn't until he returned to Gallipoli that he learned John Simpson had been killed by an enemy bullet.

For 22 days after rescuing Chick, Simpson and his donkey had continued the same fearless patrols before the inevitable happened.

"They said his donkey had been killed, too, but most of us believed it had been taken as a pet by the Indians in one of the mountain batteries. They'd thought a lot of him, too," said Chick.

Simpson's war had been brief and violent, but many of the men he rescued, among them Peter Chick, had to endure more years of violence.

By August, 1915, Chick had been wounded again, this time in the battle of Lone Pine.

A bomb smashed his left hand and he was sent back to England to recover before rejoining his battalion in Egypt for Christmas. From there, he was sent to a desert outpost before finally fighting in France.

"Lone Pine was the worst action I saw during the war, but the days on Gallipoli are the ones I'll always remember," said Chick.

"It was fellows like Simpson and his donkey that made the spirit of Anzac. They were always willing to help their mates and went right on helping to the end.

"That's why it's impossible to forget the Anzacs on Gallipoli."

May 12, 1

Yet another close encounter with Simpson

Peter Chick recounted the story of how he had been shot through the foot, three days after landing at Anzac Cove. As he limped down Shrapnel Gully he met Simpson who insisted that he ride the rest of the way on the donkey. The slightness of Chick's wound suggests that the story is authentic.

hurried, always regulating his pace to the slow walk of his donkey—and how he was typical of the bravery of all stretcher-bearers. 'It was fellows like Simpson and his donkey that made the spirit of Anzac', he said. 'They were always willing to help their mates and went right on helping to the end.'[16]

The resurrection of Simpson, and his new-found status as *the* popular hero of the Gallipoli campaign, is nowhere more evident than in Betty Roland's 1965 reminiscence for the *Australian Women's Weekly*. Roland recalled her tour of the Gallipoli battlefields and cemeteries in 1961, accompanied by the officer-in-charge of war graves. She had stood by a grave, close to the sea. The grave had not been identified, yet there,

> so I learnt later, is where the 'man with the donkey', Private Simpson, lies buried. I wish I had known at the time, for I would have laid some flowers on his grave in tribute to the man who went out at night with his patient little donkey and brought the wounded down to the dressing station on the beach.

Roland had been to Gallipoli in 1961 and never given Simpson a thought, but such carelessness was not possible by 1965. By then she had to feature Simpson in her reminiscence. The most poignant part of her account thus became something that never happened—the wish to decorate his grave.[17]

Before her departure for Gallipoli, Roland must have missed the film *Anzac*, inspired by Cyril Pearl and released in 1960. It billed itself as 'the story of why men march on Anzac Day' and celebrated the improvisation of the Australians, the many ways that enabled them to get a foothold on the Gallipoli Peninsula and to fight effectively—the making of bombs from jam tins, for example. Yet the improviser was personified not in the person of a fighting man or a bomb maker, but in the man who used a donkey to help with the wounded—the one plain soldier identified in the film.[18]

In the *Bulletin* and elsewhere, Simpson's image was used, without identification, to break up text and otherwise decorate accounts of the Great War. It was used as an allegory or pictorial discourse whose meanings were given by culture and required no explanation. At the top of a photo collage in 1964, *Pix* published the photograph of Dick Henderson with a donkey and the caption: 'One of the most publicised pictures of the war'. Readers would 'know' it was Simpson, even though it was not.[19] Just as the image was transmuted into words, so the name 'Simpson' was transmuted into imagery, instantly present in the mind's eye when spoken. Man, donkey and wounded soldier now constituted the *emblem* of the Gallipoli experience. A mere outline or unpretentious silhouette was enough to signify the familiar legend and the wider Anzac story of which it was a part.[20]

In the realm of official commemoration Simpson had also become *the* outstanding hero. As early as 1958 the RSL had proposed a commemorative stamp issue for the 50th anniversary of the landing. This time, unlike in the 1930s, the Postmaster-General accepted the proposal without hesitation. The Australian War Memorial was asked to supply ideas and reference material. It responded with notes on the Anzac campaign, a list of Victoria Cross winners, a bibliography of writings on Anzac, and the suggestion that the landing itself, the attacks on Lone Pine and The Nek, and Simpson with his donkey would all lend themselves to adaptation as a stamp design. The list of possible subjects was then expanded within the department along six thematic lines: individuals at Anzac, battle scenes, war cemeteries, Anzac monuments, flags, ribbons, etc., and symbolic treatments. In November 1959 the Stamp Advisory Committee selected the Man with the Donkey as 'possibly the appropriate subject'. The choice was confirmed in 1960 and over the next four years numerous designs were prepared, the final one being a drawing based on the statuette near the Shrine, with the acronym ANZAC and the dates 1915–65 beneath it.[21]

There were to be three stamps (5d, 8d, and 2s 3d), each bearing the Simpson emblem, while several other denominations carried the same design in the Australian territories. Within the committee, no other name had surfaced to rival Simpson's, and there was no argument when the press announced the choice in 1964. By this time the government was asserting the primacy of Gallipoli, with plans for a 'ceremonial way' in Canberra, from Lake Burley Griffin to the War Memorial, with a documentary film on the spirit of Anzac, and with £20 000 in assistance for a veterans' pilgrimage to Gallipoli.[22] The jubilee was to be a gala occasion and the stamp, now referred to as 'The Stamp of Courage', would fit in nicely. The Minute Paper summarising the decision emphasised Simpson's unrivalled fame, his bravery and individualism, and the significant fact that 'the motif itself is not of a belligerent character'.[23] A week after the release of the stamps, Simpson's relics were handed over to the Australian War Memorial by the Prime Minister, in a small ceremony that was reported in all capital cities.[24]

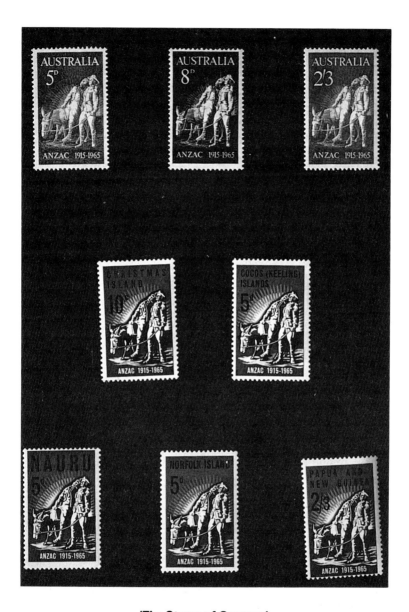

'The Stamp of Courage'

The Man with the Donkey was the subject of all eight stamps chosen to commemorate the fiftieth anniversary of the Gallipoli landing in 1965. This contrasted dramatically with 1935, when the idea of commemorating Gallipoli for the 20th anniversary was rejected by the Postmaster-General.

While the design for the stamp issue was being refined, the Commonwealth government was also considering the possibility of a Gallipoli medallion for surviving veterans of 1915 or their next-of-kin. The final decision came too late for the 1965 celebrations, but soon after it was confirmed that a medal would be struck and it would bear the image of the Man with the Donkey, bordered on the lower half by a laurel wreath and the inscription ANZAC.[25]

The proposal for a special award for being at Gallipoli went back a long way. In 1917 the governments of Australia and New Zealand had made representations to the War Office in London for the issue of a star and ribbon. A design was approved—a bronze, eight-point star, to be called the Anzac Star—but before it could be struck the War Office cancelled it on the grounds that it was unfair to single out this particular campaign. The idea of an official commemorative gesture was periodically revived thereafter, but always in the form of the Star. Only in the 1960s, when the idea resurfaced, was the Star dropped, and it was dropped in favour of the Man with the Donkey.[26] Neither the Minister for Defence, nor Prime Minister Holt, in announcing the medallion and its design, felt it necessary to explain this choice, for the 50th anniversary had already made Simpson synonymous with the Anzac tradition.[27]

Other choices were possible. There were other heroes and other ways, apart from personification, to represent the Gallipoli campaign—the range of subjects considered for the stamp issue was clear evidence of that. Some of these subjects received a great deal of attention in the press, notably the war cemeteries, which reminded readers of the cost of war and the continuing duty to remember. And the Gallipoli Star—as it was now called—would hardly have been an implausible choice. Yet there was at that time a remarkable convergence on the Simpson legend. It was recovered, popularised nationally and adopted as the official emblem, a usage that had never been likely before. The legend was invented anew, this time as the embodiment of the Gallipoli experience. The innocence, goodness and sentimentality of the tale or image cannot explain its return to popular culture, or the new-found presence in official commemoration, any more than it can explain the long absence that preceded this return. The convergence on the Simpson legend came out of the process whereby a society both remembers and forgets. In this case it was a process linking together schooling, demographic change and politics.

Schooling was important because it was the education systems of the respective States that had sustained the tale at the elementary level. While 'Anzac' signified a community of heroes, Simpson was the only plain soldier from the Great War whose name was widely known in Australia as the 50th anniversary approached. For the 10th anniversary and the 20th that was not so, and the democracy of anonymity that prevailed with respect to memorialisation was observed at least partly because it would have been so hard to find a consensus. Living heroes walked the streets, went to work, stood in parliaments (and in dole queues). Dead heroes, many of them, were known by name and deed. In 1930, the date 19 May 1915 was more widely recognised as the day Albert Jacka won his VC than the day of Simpson's death. By 1960 Jacka and many other heroes were all but forgotten, yet elementary schooling had ensured that Simpson's epic deeds were as widely known as they had been during the Great War, while the press had combined with the schools to ensure that Gallipoli was the one campaign that most Australians now knew something about.[28] The generations that had lived through the Great War, people who remembered Fromelles, Pozières, Messines, Villers-Bretonneux and Mont St Quentin as well as they remembered Gallipoli, were now depleted.

Public memory was reshaped by these changes. It was a process that thinned out the past, simplifying and accentuating what was left by means of select allegories, symbols and emblems. The primacy of Gallipoli was affirmed, the Simpson legend was rediscovered, and there was the extraordinary convergence on Simpson as the personification of the Anzac spirit. His was the most simple of epic tales: he did not play a conscious part in initiating his own myth (as did Ned Kelly), he was not widely mythologised by artists and poets (as were Burke and Wills), and the imaginative possibilities of his story were never taken up in fiction (as was the case with Leichhardt and Eliza Fraser). Yet these limits did not matter, for other less tangible forces were at work, centering and elevating Simpson within the Anzac tradition and national culture.[29]

As living memory of the Great War slipped away there was also a growing scepticism, among young people in particular, about the real meaning of Anzac Day. In 1959 Alan Seymour's *The One Day of the Year* was published and widely interpreted as a savage attack on 'digger culture'. It premiered in an Adelaide theatre in July 1960 at a time when student newspapers had also taken up the attack. At Sydney University *Honi Soit* had referred to Anzac Day as 'a glorification of war to create hysteria, maudlin sentiment and jingoism'. It described the spirit of Anzac Day as pernicious and suggested the ritual was sustained by 'pig headed militarism'. The article was supported and reprinted by *Farrago* at Melbourne University. The RSL, military leaders, churchmen and university authorities were infuriated. The proponents of Anzac Day were obliged to defend their one day. Debate raged in the editorials and the letters columns of the press for more than a month, but the wound that had opened was still open in 1965 when the Reverend Alan Walker described the RSL as 'one of the most pagan institutions in Australia' and the *Sydney Morning Herald* called together a panel to debate the subject 'Can Anzac Day Survive?'[30]

The defence of Anzac Day was carried by arguments about the nobility of sacrifice, the continuing need for an effective military force to fight Communism in Asia, and the mateship that held that force together, then and now. The prominent symbol of that mateship was the most disarming of images—it was the Man with the Donkey. For Anzac Day 1966 the Sydney *Sun* described mateship as 'an oaken creed, rooted at Gallipoli, and nourished at Tobruk, Kokoda, Pork Chop Hill and Bien Hoa'. It carried three photographs of 'mateship-in-action' which 'testify far better than words to its ruggedness and tenderness'. The first was a familiar photograph of 'Simpson and Murphy bringing in the wounded'; the second was a photograph of a 'Buna native' leading a blinded digger to safety; and the third was a photograph from the jungles of Vietnam, 'Australians comfort a wounded mate'.[31]

By the time conscription was reintroduced, in 1964, and Australian troops committed to Vietnam the following year, the Anzac tradition had been linked to all previous military engagements since the Second World War—to Korea and to campaigns in various parts of South East Asia. The link, it was commonly argued, was the defence of a democratic heritage, and close to the core of this heritage was mateship, a 'human spirit that the most terrible blows of adversity could not crush'. The politics of Anzac Day in the early 1960s were not responsible for the revival of the Simpson legend, but they dovetailed into that revival, for the legend was the quintessential expression (the high ground) of mateship as the defenders of Anzac Day wanted it to be understood.[32] When the Anzac tradition was besieged by critics, the legend of the Man with the Donkey was unassailable.

**'An Oaken Creed, rooted at Gallipoli,
and nourished at Tobruk, Kokoda, Pork Chop Hill and Bien Hoa'**

Three photographs of 'mateship-in-action', linking the Anzac tradition with the Second World War and Australia's role in Vietnam. The link, it was commonly argued, was the defence of a democratic heritage, and close to the core of this heritage was mateship, a 'human spirit that the most terrible blows of adversity could not crush'.

Since the 50th anniversary, the Simpson legend has retained its place in popular culture and public ritual, while in the classroom it is more popular than ever with teachers and has featured in numerous education kits and packs over the last fifteen years.[33] Benson's widely publicised book, and the presence of Simpson's letters and relics at the War Memorial, have enabled journalists to personalise the man, to merge the legend with their own versions of the earlier life in South Shields and Australia. Simpson's presence in the newspapers has been far more common since the early 1960s than ever it was before, with the exception of the period 1915–17. There has been a television feature, and on several occasions a donkey has been led in Anzac Day marches in Melbourne and Brisbane, in each case adorned with a Red Cross emblem and handled by a private from the medical corps. A silent, muscular, ministering Simpson got a scene in Peter Weir's film *Gallipoli*, while Abdul (the donkey) got an entry (and a photograph) in the *Animals' Who's Who* of 1982.[34]

The coffee-table book combined with the new Gallipoli 'industry' in publishing has been responsible for numerous representations of the Simpson legend. It has figured in popular works by Kit Denton, Patsy Adam-Smith, John Laird, Peter Firkins, Suzy Baldwin and others.[35] Geoffrey Dutton named him among Australia's greatest heroes; Peter Luck used him in the television series 'This Fabulous Century'; when Albert Facey wrote about his life he remembered his encounter with Simpson at Gallipoli; and when Robert Rhodes James wrote his influential account of Gallipoli, he described the Simpson tale as the most enduring episode of Australasian folklore to come out of the war.[36] In 1989 Macmillan published an illustrated version of Alan Moorehead's *Gallipoli*, which included a copy of the Moore-Jones print, a page of text and photographs on the Anzac medallion, as well as an excerpt from one of Mrs Kirkpatrick's anxiety-ridden letters to her son at the front. One curious aspect of this coverage was that the original edition, first published in 1956, contained no reference to Simpson at all. As with Sidney Nolan's Gallipoli paintings, begun in the late 1950s, Moorehead had prefigured the recovery of the Simpson legend with work that did much to rekindle the popular fascination with the events of 1915.[37]

The illustrated edition of *Gallipoli* was anticipating another round of Anzac enthusiasm with the 75th anniversary of the landing, set for 1990. It was not disappointed; nor was its emphasis on Simpson misplaced. In 1990 the legend was recounted by the press in

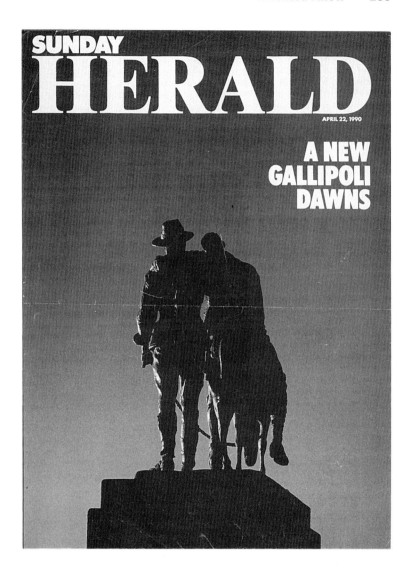

SUNDAY
HERALD
APRIL 22, 1990

A NEW
GALLIPOLI
DAWNS

Invented anew

As the 75th anniversary approached it was clear that one icon in particular had become synonymous with the Gallipoli experience.

The legend journeys on

The sculptor, Peter Corlett, said he envisaged the statue as 'not unlike the image of Christ entering Jerusalem'. The work was completed in Melbourne and trucked to Canberra with less than a week to spare before the unveiling on Anzac Day 1988. Here it is lowered into place near the entrance to the Australian War Memorial.

The unveiling in Canberra, 25 April 1988
A flock of cockatoos took up vantage points in the gums as another living link with Simpson, a Gallipoli veteran in his nineties, posed by the sculpture, while cameramen moved in.

numerous familiar ways: it figured in an April episode of 'A Country Practice', and in a Melbourne art exhibition; it was performed as a play in Sydney; the image appeared on beer coasters, drought and flood relief brochures, War Memorial postcards and greeting cards, and it was the chosen emblem for a commemorative coin set, printed by the Royal Australian Mint and released to the public in April. In the *Sydney Morning Herald* Alan Gill supported Anglican church legislation to formally recognise 'local saints' and nominated Simpson as the first choice.[38]

If, as seems clear, Simpson's current place in public culture was established, not by the Great War, but by circumstances some fifty years later, it is also true to say that his connection with national tradition reached its zenith in the bicentennial year when his commemoration was tied into two hundred years of Australian history. On the morning of Anzac Day 1988, a life-sized statue was to be unveiled in Canberra, by the front steps of the Australian War Memorial.[39] Across the valley, and in full view, the new Parliament House was nearing completion. The Dawn Service had just closed. Thousands poured out of the Memorial courtyard and down the front steps. Soldiers stood to attention around the veiled sculpture. A large crowd pressed in on them, then parted at one point to make way for the Governor-General and his entourage. There were speeches, and afterwards the Man with the Donkey was unveiled to a murmur of admiration that seemed to roll over the top of the crowd to its outer limits where adults were on their tiptoes with children on their shoulders. A flock of cockatoos took up vantage points in the gums as another living link with Simpson, a Gallipoli veteran in his nineties, on walking sticks, posed by the sculpture, while cameramen moved in. Simpson was now prominently and permanently at the nation's ritual centre. The restoration of the little epic was complete.

Postscript

The Language of *Legend* and *Myth*

'**L**anguage belongs to us all', wrote Stephen Murray-Smith, 'and we speak it as we please. Still, if you call a cabbage a clock people will have difficulty in understanding what you mean. It is worth trying to reach at least temporary agreements about the way we use words'.[1] True, but what if you call a myth a legend or a legend a myth? It does not matter, does it? People do it all the time. There's the Anzac legend or the Anzac myth, the digger legend or the digger myth. There's also *The Myth of Marilyn Monroe* and then there's *Marilyn. The Ultimate Look at the Legend.* If they are not used interchangeably these two words are clearly close cousins in meaning.

When Paul Fussell described oral tradition as 'the ancient mother of myths and legends', what distinction was he making, or was he just filling out the sentence as in 'My grandad was a great source of yarns and tales'. Probably the latter. The language purists might call this complacency, but these days linguists and lexicographers put more emphasis on describing how language is used, than on prescribing how it should be used, which is why it has been possible to leave this discussion until last.[2] The new emphasis makes for less pedantry and more joy in language, but it does not make a clock into a cabbage, nor a myth into a legend.

Some distinction between the two terms is clear. The Akan belief in a Moon-goddess called Ngame, who gave human beings souls by shooting lunar rays into them, should not be referred to as a legend. Nor should the story of the 'grub-men' who are part of the Aranda's spirit world. Similarly we would avoid describing John McEnroe's skills on the tennis court as mythical, unless we happened to be 'mythomaniacs' who wanted to see myth in everything or knew very little about tennis. When John Alexander said of McEnroe 'it is not easy to defeat a legend', he never for a moment toyed with the idea

239

of saying 'it is not easy to defeat a myth'. There are differences here that matter, and while the following 'word portraits' confirm these differences, they also suggest connections and overlap, an inter-relatedness that is important.

The documented life of the word 'legend' begins in 'the Middle English period', and is represented in several European languages from that time: in the Old French (*légende*), in Spanish (*leyenda*), in Italian (*leggenda*), and in Medieval Latin (*legenda*), meaning 'things to read' which in turn is derived from the verb *legere*. The earliest documented usage is thirteenth century, the work of Jacobus de Voragine, Archbishop of Genoa, who wrote about the lives of numerous saints under the title *The Legend* (later *The Golden Legend* or *Legenda Aurea*). *Legend* signified a collection of saints' lives or of stories of a similar character. In the fourteenth century the word acquired a singular, biographical connotation, being widely used to mean the story of the life of a saint, as in the anonymous *Life of St. Katherine* (*c.* 1430): 'Thys glorious virgyn seynt Kateryne had alle these geftes as hir legende sheweth tofore'. A broader usage, evident at the same time, probably followed from this, for legend could also mean a story, a history or an account of a life, not necessarily that of a saint. Chaucer (*c.* 1386), is an instance: 'Thanne wolde I telle a legende of my lyf, What I haue suffred sith I was a wyf'.[3]

Legend is also recorded as 'an unauthentic or non-historical story, especially one handed down by tradition from early times and popularly regarded as historical'. Thomas Brown's *Saints in Uproar* (1730), for example: 'The kingdom . . . is ten times as populous as when the legend supposes you and your sister-trollops to have lived there'. Or G. C. Brodrick's *Memoirs and Impressions* (1900): 'it was deliberately and skilfully employed to break down what has been called the Gladstonian legend'. Here the use of the term implies the passage of time and adaptation through retelling, an accretion of fiction around a nucleus of fact, such that the account, having been 'legendized', is more or less fictitious. Thus we can have 'the true legend of famous King Arthur', but there are also 'legends being growne in a manner to be nothing els but heapes of frivolous and scandalous vanities'.[4]

The Greek meanings of the word myth (*mûthos*) are, according to Liddell and Scott, numerous, perhaps so numerous as to suggest the elusiveness of discourse itself. The *mûthos* can be a 'mere word', used in Homer to distinguish between men of 'mere words' and men of fighting skill; a *mûthos* is also a public speech, or the tendering of a speech in the form of a petition; it can signify a conversation, or a message, a thing said, as in somebody has been entrusted with a *mûthos*, a message and the obligation to deliver it. A *mûthos* can be a saying, a proverb or a rumour: one can attribute a *mûthos* of this kind to an owner or a period of time; one can say this is my *mûthos*, or his *mûthos*, or this *mûthos* is very old. *Mûthos* is also the talk of men, rumour, talk that might distort or magnify a message.

Another string of meanings begins with *mûthos* as 'tale, story [or] narrative'. In Homer its use in this sense does not imply falsehood. However a second use has *mûthos* counterposed to *logos* (historic truth). Thucydides' use of myth as falsehood was a way of separating his own work, his history, from the work of the poets 'who exaggerate the importance of their themes', and of

> the prose chroniclers who are less interested in telling the truth than in catching the attention of their public, whose authorities cannot be checked, and whose subject-matter, owing to the passage of time, is mostly lost in the unreliable streams of mythology.[5]

Although *mûthos* and *logos* recur together in Greek usage, it is more common to find the former used in isolation to signify a story about the Gods, as in Epicurus who undertakes a sort of therapy of human life by putting such stories in due proportion, by indicating that they are merely stories, so people can set them aside without worrying too much about them. A *mûthos* was also a professed work of fiction, a children's story or a fable, the plot of a comedy or tragedy, or a genre of pleasing, amusing, traditional stories that, although fictional, were related to the histories of nations.[6]

Out of these origins comes the modern understanding of myth as 'a purely fictitious narrative, usually involving supernatural persons, actions, or events, and embodying some popular idea concerning natural or historical phenomena'. The *Oxford English Dictionary* goes on to 'properly distinguish' myth from legend because legend implies a nucleus of fact, though myth is 'often used vaguely to include any narrative having fictitious elements'. Which means that if we are not going to be vague, then we *can* sort myth from legend. The latter is a narrative about real people, it has biographical connotations and it contains at least a nucleus of fact, whereas myth has no foundation in fact, it is about fictitious or imaginary people and sometimes it is not about people at all, but instead is about gods or minotours or mermaids or grub-men. On these counts it is clearly more accurate to refer to the story of Anzac, and to Simpson who is a leading figure in that story, as legend rather than myth.

Of course dictionary definitions are not always the last word in meaning. As Ambrose Bierce said in his *Devil's Dictionary*, 'down to the time of the first lexicographer no author ever had used a word that was in a dictionary'. Similarly, popular and scholarly usage will alter meaning when the dictionary definition falls short as an adequate concept. When anthropologists speak of myth, for instance, they have several criteria in mind. Myth is a narrative which contains at least some events or objects that are not of this world, it is a narrative that acquires a sacred quality, and one that refers in dramatic form to origins or transformations:

> The narrative quality distinguishes a myth from a general idea or set of ideas, such as cosmology. The sacred quality and the reference to origins and transformations distinguish myth from legend and other types of folk-tale. The narration of events and reference to objects unknown outside the world of myth differentiates myth from history or pseudo-history.[7]

It is only at this general level of description that there is any scholarly agreement about myth. But this general level of description does not rule mythology out of all history. For in so far as history allows some scope to fantasy, in so far as it celebrates or highlights origins and transformations, and in so far as it acquires a sacred character, it has some of the qualities of myth. It is vestigial myth, and it might reasonably be argued that these qualities can be found in the Anzac legend.

When George Mosse wrote of 'The Myth of the War Experience', he was attempting to describe 'a vision of the war developed, above all, though not exclusively, in the defeated nations, where it was so urgently needed. The Myth of the War Experience was designed to mask war and to legitimize the war experience; it was meant to displace the reality of war'.[8] Mosse went on to indicate how this Myth enabled the memory of the war to be refashioned as a sacred experience 'which provided the nation [Germany] with a new depth of religious feeling . . . The cult of the fallen soldier became a centerpiece of the religion of nationalism after the war'. Mosse's emphasis on 'masking' and 'displacing', to say nothing of the way that he sees both as part of the political process, may mean that he would do better to speak of this vision as ideology rather than myth, for historians have generally favoured the former when referring to any scheme of ideas which has become a prescriptive doctrine, derived from class or sectional interests and advanced on behalf of society as a whole. Yet, the *Supplement to the Oxford English Dictionary* seems to endorse his use of the term when it quotes from J. S. Huxley's *'Race' in Europe* (1939):

> Napoleon, Shakespeare, Einstein, Galileo—a dozen great names spring to mind which in themselves should be enough to disperse the Nordic myth. The word *myth* is used advisedly, since this belief frequently plays a semi-religious role, as basis for a creed of passionate racialism.[9]

That is to say, myth is not here an untrue or impossible tale, but a tale the telling of which serves to justify some aspect of the social order or of human experience, a particular hierarchy of social/racial order. If this functional notion of myth is acceptable then once again the Anzac legend, and the Simpson tale within it, would qualify as being mythical in purpose. As William H. McNeill has explained 'myths are important because they can provide a society with a belief in itself, in its rightness, in its heroic character, [a belief] strong enough to get it through a crisis such as war'.[10]

According to Robert Graves, mythology is the study of whatever religious or heroic legends are so foreign to a student's experience that he cannot believe them to be true. Hence the English adjective mythical, meaning incredible, and hence the omission from standard European mythologies of all biblical narratives even when closely paralleled by myths from Persia, Babylonia, Egypt and Greece. Graves was referring to a corpus of myth that most historians know little about—to the myths of ancient civilisations and so called 'primitive' peoples, to that other spiritual world in which gods, goddesses, heroes, monsters and demons predominate. In defining mythology as he did, he clearly wanted to be difficult. It was his introduction to the *Larousse Encyclopaedia of Mythology* (1959). He wanted to remind his readers that mythology is a culturally loaded term; that in the realm of what we call belief, there is no place for a complacent distinction between fiction and fact (or between superstition and faith), and that we should not move onto questions about the social function of myth until this first principle is clear.[11]

When myth is the term applied to someone else's faith or belief it can be a term of abuse and provocation, a bit of sensationalism, which might explain why its use has become so common in journalism and why publishers like to get the word into book titles such as *The Captain Cook Myth* and *The Myth of the Blitz*.[12] In John Terrain's *The Smoke and the Fire. The Myths and Anti-Myths of War*, the author claims that his purpose is to blow away the 'smoke' of myth in order to get at the truth of 'fire'. He then proceeds to distinguish between legends and myths by judging the former to be naive and kindly, and the latter to be horrific and cruel, a distinction which is original if nothing else. The one, according to Terrain, is harmless and well-intentioned, the other inspires fear, suffering and hatred, serves a particular point of view and is, effectively, propaganda.[13] Germaine Greer also sees myths as nasty things, akin to brain-washing or propaganda. In *Daddy We Hardly Knew You*, she writes of how 'military mythology has to pretend that real men are in the majority; cowards can never be allowed to feel that they might be the normal ones and the heroes the insane.'[14]

Myth as nasty and deceptive or wrong-headed notions is now common parlance and for many people it is a handy meaning. But for historians it has its dangers. 'What seems true to one historian will seem false to another, so one historian's truth becomes another's myth, even at the moment of utterance'.[15] When history is reduced to this, the other meanings of myth are likely to be lost, which is unfortunate because those other meanings are important. They have been favoured here, over the pejorative use of myth, because my purpose has been to explain, not to debunk. Thus my word portraits can conclude as I had hoped, with a certain tale described as a legend, even if it does bear some of the markings of myth.

Notes

Introduction

[1]Thomas M. Greene, *The Descent from Heaven*; C. M. Bowra, *Heroic Poetry*.

[2]Charles Moorman, *A Knyght There Was*, pp. 27–9.

[3]Marina Warner, *Joan of Arc. The Image of the Female Heroine*, ch. 7.

[4]Sir Philip Sidney, 'An Apology for Poetry', in G. Gregory Smith (ed.), *Elizabethan Critical Essays*, Volume 1, Oxford University Press, Oxford, 1904, p. 179.

[5]George L. Mosse, *Fallen Soldiers. Reshaping the Memory of the World Wars*, pp. 16, 37.

[6]Hegel cited in Georg Lukacs, *The Historical Novel*, Merlin Press, London, 1962, p. 36.

[7]Gwyn A. Williams, *Madoc. The Making of a Myth*, esp. ch. 3.

[8]John Lehmann, *Rupert Brooke, His Life and His Legend*, ch. 15.

[9]'Among School Children', in R. J. Finnernan (ed.), *W. B. Yeats. The Poems*, Macmillan, London, 1983, pp. 215–17.

[10]George Orwell, *Nineteen Eighty-Four*, p. 196.

[11]Patsy Adam-Smith, *The Anzacs*, p. 122; G. P. Walsh, 'John Simpson Kirkpatrick', *Australian Dictionary of Biography*, Vol. 9, 1983, pp. 612–13. Much earlier, in the RSL journal *Duckboard*, (2 April 1934, p. 36) he was 'a lean Australian, sunburnt and brown/Somewhere outback lies his town'.

[12]*Queensland School Paper* (Classes V & VI), vol. 8, April 1917, p. 66. In the inter-war years the unpopularity of immigration may have helped to sustain Simpson's Australian-ness.

[13]The official historians assigned by the Australian War Memorial to adjudicate on Bowles' work were C. E. W. Bean and A. G. Butler. See C. E. W. Bean to T. H. E. Heyes, 22 April 1941; Bowles to Heyes, 8 May 1941; Bowles to Heyes, 6 April 1941; and Butler to Heyes, 2 May 1941. AWM 93, 895/2/148. The quotations are from Butler to Heyes, 2 May 1941. It was Bean who used the word 'absurd'.

[14]*Labour Call*, 8 July 1915.

[15]Lehmann.

[16]Quoted words are from Warner, p. 274.

[17]Paul Fussell, *The Great War and Modern Memory*, ch. 4.

[18]A. P. Cohen, *The Symbolic Construction of Community*.

[19] Greg Dening, *History's Anthropology: The Death of William Gooch*, esp. chs 1 & 5.

[20]Graham Seal, *The Hidden Culture. Folklore in Australian Society*, ch. 1. Seal makes this distinction between official or institutionalised legend

and folklore. See also Barry Schwartz, 'The Social Context of Commemoration.

[21]On the social and political roots of allegiance to the modern state, see Raymond Williams, *Towards 2000*, pp. 177–99. For Churchill on 'self-surrender', see *The Times*, 26 April 1915.

Chapter One

[1]E. Gibbon, *The History of the Decline and Fall of the Roman Empire*, (ed. D. Milman, M. Guizot & Sir William Smith), 8 vols, London, 1854, vol. 2, pp. 245–6.

[2]On the handing over of Simpson's relics, see, for example: Launceston *Examiner*, 22 April 1965; Melbourne *Herald*, 21 April 1965; *Sydney Morning Herald*, 22 April 1965. C. I. Benson, *The Man with the Donkey. The Good Samaritan of Gallipoli*.

[3]Benson was born in Hull on 1 December 1897. He was Superintendent of the Wesley Church Central Methodist Mission 1926–67. His contributions to the *Herald* began in 1922 and appeared regularly until 1979. (*Who's Who in Australia*, 1968, pp. 89–90).

[4]On the Lord Wardenship, see C. I. Benson to R. G. Menzies, 15 June 1967 and 7 May 1970, Menzies Papers, National Library of Australia (NLA), MS 4936 (series 1, box 4, folder 28). For the ongoing pursuit of Winston Churchill's signature see Benson to Menzies, 27 October 1954, Menzies Papers (series 2, box 55, folder 160); 16 February 1955 (series 2, box 64, folder 236); 7 April 1955, series 2, box 64, folder 236. On the love of royalty and empire, see Benson to Menzies, 26 March 1954, Menzies Papers (series 2, box 55, folder 160). Also Benson to Menzies, 21 May 1964, Menzies Papers, (series 1, box 4, folder 28). On 'the soul of the empire', see his 'Church and People' column, *Herald* (Melbourne), 27 November 1965. Benson was 'an outstanding member of the ideology-making elite in Victoria' according to Hugo Wolfsohn in his 'The Ideology Makers', in H. Mayer & H. Nelson (eds), *Australian Politics: A Second Reader*, Cheshire, Melbourne, 1969, p. 47.

[5]'The part of the mother in Empire-building and colonisation has been but little recognised', he wrote in his 'Church and People' column, Melbourne *Herald*, 13 May 1933, p. 28. Copies of the 'Church and People' column are held in the State Library of Victoria (MS 9338–1064/2 (f)).

[6]The statuette was created in 1916, by A. B. Pegram, exhibited at the Royal Academy that year, then acquired by the Tyne Dock Mason's Club of South Shields and later presented to the South Shields library. See Angela Jarman (ed.), *Royal Academy Exhibitors 1905–1970*, vol. 3, p. 293.

[7]Benson, *The Man with the Donkey*, p. 56.

[8]Benson, p. 57.

[9]Benson, pp. 60–1.

[10]Benson, p. 61. Actually the letters are in very good condition.

[11]Benson, p. 67. Elsewhere Benson says, 'this strong sense of duty to provide for his Mother is the main theme of most of his letters that have survived' (pp. 58–9). Note that Mother's Day was another World War I invention.

[12]The donated records list for these letters indicate 53 letters from Simpson to his mother and sister between 1909 and 1914; 12 letters to his mother from Blackboy Camp and Cairo, October 1914 to February 1915; five letter cards and two postcards written to his sister in 1912 and 1913. See AWM 3DRL 3424.

[13]References in this paragraph are from Benson, p. 59, 76, 71 and 68 respectively.

[14]References to this point are from Benson, pp. 68, 72–3, 80 and 76 respectively.

[15]Benson, p. 62.

[16]Benson, p. 78.

[17]Benson, pp. 16–20.

[18]Benson, p. 14.

[19]Held in the Benson Papers, AWM PR83/69.

[20]Benson, p. 67.

[21]John Simpson Kirkpatrick to his mother, 1 September 1912. Letters of John Simpson Kirkpatrick (hereafter J.S.K.), are located in AWM 3DRL 3424. All letters cited hereafter are at this location unless otherwise indicated.

[22]Benson, p. 80. J.S.K. to his mother, 4 April 1912. Note that a reference to Benson's book, as here, where one of his omissions is being quoted is a reference to the cut letter in the book, not to the quote itself. The original letter is cited thereafter.

[23]J.S.K. to his mother, 4 April 1912. On colonial labour's sense of good fortune and superiority, see Richard Glover, 'Australian Unions and the 1889 Dock Strike', *Bowyang*, no. 7, March 1982.

[24]Benson, pp. 76–7. And J.S.K. to his mother, 5 August 1911.

[25]Benson does not refer at all to this letter. See J.S.K. to his mother, 1 October 1910.

[26]Undated letter from Jack's time at or near Corrimal on the south coast of NSW, September–October 1910.

[27]Benson, p. 75. J.S.K. to his mother, 31 May 1911.

[28]Benson, p. 65. Compare with J.S.K. to his mother, 16 December 1909. And Benson, pp. 65–6. Compare with J.S.K. to his mother, 18 October 1909. The reference to scarlet fever is on p. 57.

[29]Benson, p. 43.

[30]The most evocative account of the grim and troubled Tyneside region is Ellen Wilkinson, *The Town That Was Murdered. The Life-Story of Jarrow.*

[31]Mrs Kirkpatrick to J.S.K., 3 September 1914. Note that two letters from Simpson's mother were in the collection donated to the War Memorial by Annie, and handed over by Benson. The other is a letter of 17 August 1915 in which she says 'Germany should be wiped off the Earth'.

[32]J.S.K. to his mother, 30 January 1915. In another letter dated 'Xmas Day 1914', he says he would 'like to have the pleasure of putting a

bullet through the damned old Kaiser as he is the start of the lot'. Benson used the letter but cut this sentence.

[33]Benson, pp. 61–2. J.S.K. to his mother, 26 October 1909.

[34]Benson, p. 85. J.S.K. to his mother, 9 April 1914.

[35]Benson, p. 64. J.S.K. to his mother, 30 November 1909.

[36]J.S.K. to his mother, November 1910. Letter not in Benson.

[37]Benson, pp. 79–80. J.S.K. to his mother, 1 March 1912.

[38]Perhaps not surprisingly the hundreds of published accounts that constitute the legend contain virtually no suggestion of a Simpson who could be abrupt or prickly.

[39]J.S.K. to his mother, November 1910.

[40]J.S.K. to Annie Kirkpatrick, undated. Lloyd George launched the National Insurance Scheme in 1911. The Act came into operation on 15 July 1912. For Lloyd George, see R. K. Ensor, *England 1870–1914*, Oxford University Press, Oxford, 1960, pp. 445–6. Also E. Royston Pike, *Human Documents of the Lloyd George Era*, George Allen & Unwin, London 1972, pp. 101, 109–11.

[41]The nineteenth-century Non-Conformist English origins of 'The Pleasant Sunday Afternoon' and 'The Problem of Pleasure' are outlined in K. S. Inglis, *Churches and the Working Classes in Victorian England*, pp. 74–85.

[42]J.S.K. to his mother, 29 September 1910; J.S.K. to Annie Kirkpatrick, 1 April 1913. Letter not in Benson.

[43]Benson, p. 75. J.S.K. to his mother, 31 May 1911. For the 'Poor Bugger' letter see J.S.K. to his mother, 5 August 1911.

[44]J.S.K. to Annie, 17 January 1915. AWM PR 83/69(3).

[45]Annie to J.S.K., 3 June 1915; 24 May 1915. Also 15 June 1915.

[46]Annie to J.S.K., 10 June 1915, PR 83/69 (2). Presumably Annie means to convey the idea that she and mother would share the button between them.

[47]Benson, p. 70. J.S.K. to his mother, 29 September 1910. Several of Jack's references to Sarah indicate considerable friction between them. In 1957 Benson wrote to Annie as follows: 'I do want to discuss with you in detail as to whether the letters which refer to your sister should not be withheld, at any rate, during our life-time'. Benson to Annie Simpson Pearson, 4 April 1957, AWM 83/69, items 6–7.

[48]Benson, pp. 19–20. J.S.K. to his mother, 25 December 1914, 17 and 24 January 1915. The matter becomes more complicated and difficult for Jack when he is informed he needs a specimen signature from his mother. Jack has to wait for the next letter—thus we know he was not in the habit of keeping her letters.

[49]A copy of the birth certificate is held in the John Simpson Kirkpatrick file, Australian Dictionary of Biography archive, Australian National University, Canberra. He was born on 6 July 1892. The 'informant' column on English birth certificates usually bears the name of one parent only. In this case, there are two names: 'Robert Kirkpatrick, Father', and 'S. Simpson, Mother'. Elsewhere in his book, Benson relied on the standard explanation from the legend—that Jack dropped 'Kirkpatrick' having jumped ship in order to enlist, and

fearing the shipping company would trace him if he retained his surname. But Jack dropped 'Kirkpatrick' long before the war began, and Benson knew this. 'He appears on the Electoral Roll at Coledale as John Simpson and also on the Wages Register at the mine there', he told Annie in 1965. Benson to Annie, 5 January 1965, AWM 83/69, items 6–7.

[50]Annie Simpson Pearson to Benson, 8 September 1956, AWM 83/69, items 1–2. 'Pearson' was Annie's married name. She seems to have taken on 'Simpson' some time after the death of her brother.

[51]Pearson to Benson, 9 September 1956, AWM 83/69, items 1–2.

[52]Pearson to Benson, 1964 (not otherwise dated). Also Benson to Pearson, 5 January 1965, AWM 83/69, items 6–7.

[53]Pearson to Benson, 23 February 1965, AWM 83/69, items 6–7. See also Annie's letter to Benson dated 22 January 1965, AWM 83/69, items 6–7.

[54]Benson to Pearson, 12 March 1965, AWM 83/69, items 6–7.

[55] Benson to Pearson, 26 March 1965; also 30 March 1965, AWM 83/69, items 6–7.

[56]Benson to Menzies, 12 November 1952. Menzies Papers (series 1, box 4, folder 28). Also Benson to Menzies, 7 April 1955, Menzies Papers (series 2, box 64, folder 236).

[57]Menzies regularly accepted invitations to speak at Benson's 'Pleasant Sunday Afternoons' (PSA) at the Wesley Church in Collins Street, Melbourne. See Benson to L. J. Craig (private secretary to the PM), 21 September 1953; also Benson to Menzies, 8 January 1974, Menzies Papers (series 1, box 4, folder 28). The first broadcast from a church in Australia was the PSA at Wesley Church, 22 October 1924. *Herald* (Melbourne), 6 September 1958.

[58]Benson to Pearson, 12, 23 and 30 March 1965, AWM 83/69, items 6–7. There was also a proposal to present Annie with the Anzac commemorative stamps issued for the 50th anniversary of the landing. It lapsed too. See 'FADG Postal Services' to F. P. O'Grady, Director General (PMG), 19 March 1965, and E. J. Bunting to O'Grady, 7 April 1965, in file '50th anniversary of Anzac (Landing at Gallipoli)—depicting Simpson and his donkey', PostMaster-General's Department, 281/22/306 (Part 1), Philatelic Section, Australia Post.

[59]Pearson to Benson, 8 April 1965, AWM 83/69, items 6–7.

[60]Benson to Pearson, 13 April 1965 and 5 January 1965, AWM 83/69, items 6–7.

[61]This letter has not survived. Its contents are here deduced from Benson's reply: Benson to Pearson, 17 August 1967, AWM 83/69, items 6–7.

[62]Benson did have a niece called Marjorie who lived in Yorkshire. However, his secretary at the Central Mission in Melbourne was a Marjorie Featonby and she was the Marjorie who accompanied him to South Shields. See Benson to Pearson, 3 October 1956 and 4 April 1957. Annie addressed at least one letter (30 April 1959) to 'Dear Dr. Benson and Margerie', AWM 83/69. Benson's first wife died in 1947. He married Marjorie Featonby in 1967.

[63]Pearson to Benson, 14 September 1967, AWM 83/69, items 6–7. Annie's expectations may have been raised by the manner in which Benson talked about the proposed book. In one letter to Annie (11 September 1956) he wrote of his desire to 'tell the world the full story of dear Jack, his splendid parents and devoted sister'. Other letters praised her hospitality.

[64]Annie had apparently written to Benson requesting these changes. The letter is missing but Benson's reply is extant and responds, serially, to Annie's requests. Benson to Pearson, 14 September 1964, PR83/69, 4 of 17 (item 5). Also Benson to Pearson, 1964, (otherwise undated), AWM 83/69, items 6–7. Certain passages in the extant letters suggest that other exchanges regarding censorship did take place.

[65]George Orwell, *Nineteen Eighty-Four*, p. 80.

[66]Patsy Adam-Smith, *The Anzacs*, p. 122. The 'real' St Thérèse, according to Adam-Smith, was 'as frail in spirit as any of us, as fierce as an unbroken filly and as ashamed of her shortcomings as we are'(pp. vii–viii). See also *Simpson J. 202* by Richard Beynon, played at the Ensemble Theatre in Sydney 2 May—23 June 1990 (conversation with Richard, 10 May 1990) For Petra Rees account, see *Australian*, Special Edition to commemorate the 75th anniversary of the landings at Gallipoli, 24 April 1990, pp. 1, 10.

[67]'The World in 1961', Lecture No. 125, MS 11493, Benson Papers, State Library of Victoria; Benson to Menzies, 21 May 1964, NLA, MS4936 (series 1, box 4, folder 28); also 'Church and People', *Herald*, 27 November 1965.

[68]'Church and People', *Herald*, 19 April 1952, 24 January 1953 and 25 April 1959. Benson seems always to have been a voluntarist of this kind. See transcripts to his earlier radio broadcasts under the title 'Questions and Answers', in Australian Archives (NSW), series SP1558, item SR 21/R1765 (5).

[69]On the use of the digger tradition in the conservative press during the period of the Menzies government, see Ben Pearson, Images of the Vietnam Serviceman, 1965–1990, ch. 2.

[70]'Church and People', *Herald*, 23 April 1960.

Chapter Two

[1]Paul Fussell, *The Great War and Modern Memory*, p. 310.

[2]Typed note in Tom Walsh Papers, Auckland Institute and Museum, MS. 1469: 'There was a "buzz" in Anzac that when Turk snipers heard that one of their number had shot Murphy dead they shot the culprit'.

[3]Sister E. Davies (AANS) to her mother, 15 January 1916. Later accounts echoed this view, e.g. Robert Rhodes James, *Gallipoli*, p. 176.

[4]The *Acta Sanctorum* is a vast collection of biographies and legends of the Christian saints which has been compiled by a small group of Belgian Jesuits since the seventeenth century.

[5] 3rd Field Ambulance, War Diary, AWM 4, 26/46/4. This Diary also noted Simpson's death on 19 May 1915: 'No. 202, Pte J. Simpson, shot thro heart, killed, while escorting patient'.

[6] Diary of Sgt J. E. McPhee, 4th Field Ambulance, AIF, Diary No. 1, pp. 78 and 84 (emphasis added). Also, interview with McPhee, 18 March 1976, LaTrobe Library, TMS123, MS 10495.

[7] Monash and Green cited in J. L. Legge, 'The man with the Donkey (no date, approx. 1953). For Fry's part see 'Personal Narrative of Lt-Col H. K. Fry, 3rd Field Ambulance, 1914–16', Butler Papers.

[8] Diary of L/Sgt C. F. Bosward, 4th Battalion, AIF, AWM 3DRL/4104. Also, Private Fred Knight [AASC, AIF] to 'Dear Mother', 16 September 1915. LaTrobe Library, MS 9616.

[9] Typescript of diary of Private Victor Laidlaw, 2nd Field Ambulance, AIF, 23 May and 22 July 1915.

[10] Ion Idriess, *The Desert Column. Leaves from the Diary of an Australian Trooper in Gallipoli, Sinai, and Palestine*, p. 15. Diary of Ion Idriess, 22 May 1915, folder 1. Robert Louis Stevenson's journals, original and rewritten, have been treated similarly, as two very different kinds of evidence, by Richard Holmes, who found that Stevenson's desire for a more 'romantic, raffish pose', led him to cut personal and emotional content from the original account of his famous journey through the Cevennes in France. See Holmes, *Footsteps. Adventures of a Romantic Biographer*, ch. 1, esp. p. 33.

[11] Diary of Trooper A. S. Hutton (no page numbers).

[12] Diary of Private J. H. Turnbull.

[13] On dittography and haplography, embellishment, etc., in another context, see Raymond Carr, 'Landfall of landfalls. Westwards to the East with Christopher Columbus', *Times Literary Supplement*, 1 November 1991, pp. 3–5.

[14] Diary (Anon), AWM, PR 84/288.

[15] Diary of L/Sgt C. F. Bosward.

[16] Discussion with Bill Gammage, 18 May 1989; see also Gammage, *The Broken Years. Australian Soldiers in the First World War*. The Questionnaire was sent through the Department of Veterans' Affairs, to 43 veterans. (Questionnaire and replies in author's possession.)

[17] J. G. Jackson to Major J. Treloar, 22 September 1937, AWM 93, 417/20/35.

[18] Capt. A. G. Carne, 6th Battalion, AIF, AWM 2DRL/13.

[19] 'Patterson wounded. Patterson died from loss of blood. ' Diary of Spr. R. Cornell, 3rd Fld Coy, RAE, AIF, 19 May 1915, AWM PR 83/87.

[20] Wilfred Doe to 'Dear All', 14 May 1915, AWM 3DRL/3126.

[21] A. D. Carbery, *The New Zealand Medical Service in the Great War, 1914–18*, p. 58. Another example: 'A donkey on Gallipoli would not have lasted any more than 5 minutes, from my experience'. Ralph S. Dyer in response to the Questionnaire, April 1991. Dyer indicated that he did not see Kirkpatrick at Gallipoli nor did he hear of him while there.

[22] *West Australian*, 20 July 1915, p. 5.

[23] *Weekly Press* (New Zealand), 28 July 1915, pp 7 and 9. Note the distinction between date of dispatch and date of publication.

[24] *Commonwealth Gazette* (London), no. 53, 8 June 1915, p. 1092.

[25] *Daily Malta Chronicle*, 12 June 1915, pp. 4–5; *Argus*, 19 July 1915, p. 4. The *Daily Malta Chronicle* is not available in Australia. Xeroxed copies of relevant pages in author's possession. See also Adelaide's *Register News-Pictorial*, 22 July 1915.

[26] *Argus*, 19 July 1915, p. 4.

[27] *Argus*, 24 November 1915, p. 7.

[28] For the first photograph, see *Sydney Morning Herald* (*SMH*), 26 July 1915, p. 5. For the announcement of the *Sydney Mail* photograph, see *SMH*, 28 September 1915, p. 8. The photograph appeared in the *Sydney Mail* on 29 September 1915, p. 5. Hogue was not yet on the Gallipoli peninsula when Simpson died. His account referred to Simpson as 'Murphy' and to the donkeys as 'Murphy's mules'. Hogue's journalism is discussed in Gerster's *Big-Noting. The Heroic Theme in Australian War Writing*, pp. 48–51.

[29] *Herald* (Auckland), 22 September 1937. Here Alec McClean of Waitakaruru recalls seeing, on Gallipoli, a copy of the *Weekly Times* (NZ) in which 'Murphy and his Donkey' figured. Soldiers were getting papers and letters on Gallipoli as early as 24 May. (Diary of Pte Victor Laidlaw, 2nd Field Ambulance, AIF, 24 May 1915.

[30] Soldiers reacted variously to newspaper accounts of their deeds, but there was a widely shared fascination with them.

[31] Poems and soldiers' memoirs feature in chapters to follow. The bronze was a statuette created by A. B. Pegram, an English sculptor, and exhibited at the Royal Academy in London in 1916. See *Royal Academy Exhibitors 1905–1970*, (ed. Angela Jarman), vol. 3, p. 293. The film 'Murphy of Anzac' was made in 1915–16 and has not survived; see Andrew Pike and Ross Cooper, *Australian Film 1900–1980*. For school texts see Victorian *School Paper*, No. 193, 1 November 1915, pp. 147–9. School Papers in other states followed Victoria's example in 1916 and 1917. The photolithographic print was from a watercolour painting of the Man with the Donkey by Sapper Horace Moore-Jones, a New Zealand soldier who was at Gallipoli.

[32] In London, 1915, E. C. Buley talked to many convalescent soldiers about Simpson. See his *Glorious Deeds of the Australasians in the Great War*.

[33] *Sunday Times*, 10 October 1915, p. 19. The early reports were uncertain about names.

[34] *Sun* (Sydney), 11 October 1915, p. 2. Currie had enlisted with Simpson in Perth. The story of the telling of the story was recounted in the *Advertiser* (Geelong), 30 April 1977.

[35] *Sun* (Sydney), 12 October 1915, p. 6. The *Daily Mirror* as source is acknowledged in the *Sun*.

[36] *Sydney Mail*, 29 September 1915, p. 5.

[37] *Sydney Mail*, 3 November 1915, pp. 24–5; 24 November 1915, p. 30. See also Major G. P. Dixon to ADMS, 19 May 1915, AWM 25, 367/204.

[38] *Sydney Mail*, 8 December 1915, p. 35; 26 April 1916, p. 9; 9 August 1916, p. 26.

[39] For Simpson's presence in the Indian press, see *The Statesman & Friend of India*, 24 September 1915, p. 3, which carried a feature photograph

(from the *Daily Mirror*) 'And Life is Perfected by Death' is from Elizabeth Barrett Browning's 'A Vision of Poets'.

[40]*Argus*, 2 November 1933.

[41]Excerpts from letter written by Pte Andy Carnahan, held in Tom Walsh Papers, Auckland Institute and Museum, MS1469.

[42]These photographs are discussed in detail in Chapter Seven.

[43]C. I. Benson, *The Man With the Donkey. The Good Samaritan of Gallipoli*, pp. 44–5, 46. Another Gallipoli veteran, also at the far end of that long line, told a version in keeping with the legend itself: 'We lost an inspiration and Simpson and his Donkey became a legend to be told of to reinforcements who joined us', Douglas Sutherland to Benson, 25 April 1955, AWM 83/69 (419/9/22, item 4).

[44]*Argus*, 20 July 1917, p. 7.

[45]*Coo-ee*, vol. 1, no. 1, 10 November 1916. No page number.

[46]Buley, *Glorious Deeds*, p. 3.

[47]Sister E. Davies (AANS) to 'Mum', 15 January 1916. The *NSW Red Cross Record* carried a full page photograph of the man with the donkey, with the man identified as 'Murphy', in its January 1916 issue; see vol. 2, no. 1, January 1916, p. 47.

Chapter Three

[1]R. Gerster, *Big-Noting. The Heroic Theme in Australian War Writing*, p. 12, 15.

[2]P. S. Cohen, 'Theories of Myth', pp. 337–53. Cohen suggests that mythology is a narrative laced with fantasy, one that acquires a sacred quality and is preoccupied with origins and transformations.

[3]C. E. W. Bean, *The Official History of Australia in the War of 1914–18, The Story of ANZAC*

[4]Kevin Fewster, Expression and Suppression: Aspects of Military Censorship in Australia during World War One, p. 116.

[5]George Orwell, 'Politics and the English Language', in S. Orwell and I. Angus (eds), *The Collected Essays, Journalism and Letters of George Orwell, vol. iv, In Front of Your Nose, 1945–50*, pp. 139–40.

[6]Fewster, pp. 106, 121–2, 124; *Argus*, 8 May 1915.

[7]Kevin Fewster, 'Ellis Ashmead Bartlett and the Making of the Anzac Legend', pp. 17–30.

[8]*Argus*, 12 July 1915.

[9]William Shakespeare, *The Life of Henry V*, act 4, scene iii, 35.

[10]*Argus*, 5 October 1915. On this theme see also Paul Fussell, 'Killing, in Verse and Prose', in *Thank God for the Atom Bomb and Other Essays*, p. 117.

[11]*Argus*, 11 June 1915.

[12]*Sydney Morning Herald*, 7 July 1915; *Argus*, 14 June, 23 October 1915. For the 'vicious ram' quotation, see *Argus*, 8 July 1915. In the middle of 1915 even Lloyd George could not praise the Australians without a reference to real men embracing manhood, see *Argus*, 31 July 1915.

[13]*Argus*, 30 June 1915.

[14] *Sydney Morning Herald,* 12 June 1915; *Argus,* 4, 20 October, 1, 8, 17 July and 9 June 1915. David McKee Wright, 'Gallipoli', in *Bulletin,* 2 September 1920, p. 40.

[15] *Argus,* 17 July 1915. The physiology of death could put an expression something like a smile on the face of dead men. This may have increased talk of the smiling dead. But the cases cited here are mostly of men who are smiling before they die and as they die. The death smile is an eerie extension of heroic behaviour in life; heroism beyond the veil.

[16] *Argus,* 16 December 1915.

[17] *Age,* 12 July 1915.

[18] *Argus,* 2 October 1915.

[19] Rupert Brooke, 'Peace', in *Rupert Brooke: The Collected Poems,* Sidgwick & Jackson, London, 1987, p. 312.

[20] *Argus,* 3 May 1915. For Churchill on a soldier's death, see *The Times,* 26 April 1915. Arkwright's poem was popularised as the hymn 'Oh Valiant Hearts'. Imperial patriots quite commonly called on the Greeks when the topic was sacrifice, 'self-surrender' and obedience: e.g., the Rev. J. S. Needham in an Anzac Day recruiting speech, reported in the *Daily Standard* (Brisbane), 26 April 1917.

[21] Fewster, Expression and Suppression, p. 135.

[22] Cited in Gerster, p. 24. The connection between the recruitment crisis and the origins of the myth of the digger has not been widely recognised. At least one historian managed to write an entire book on the subject without recognising this aspect of its origins. See Jane Ross, *The Myth of the Digger.*

[23] Carmel Shute, 'Blood Votes and the "Bestial Boche". A Case Study in Propaganda', pp. 14–16.

[24] The term 'print circus' is taken from Sylvia Lawson, *The Archibald Paradox. A Strange Case of Authorship,* ch. 7. Here the term is used to indicate only the totality of the pro-imperial newspaper as a political statement. For the 'sooling-on business', see *Labor Call,* 8 July 1915, p. 6.

[25] *Sydney Mail,* 3 November 1915, p. 24. Later accounts of Simpson's decision to work alone reiterated the 'shortage of men' theme from various angles: one soldier said his use of a donkey saved a stretcher squad of four men; another said that the donkey was ideal for leg wounds and so freed other bearers to attend to the badly wounded men who were lying everywhere; there was the view that Simpson had little choice because his squad was killed at the landing. A New Zealander said he recalled Simpson's response to the officers' opposition: 'To hell with them. The old donk and I can do as much work as four men. ' See Charles Love to J. Walsh (Director, AWM), 26 September 1964; Captain Victor Conrick, 'Narrative of Simpson, the Donkey Man', (n.d., apparently written in the 1960s after Conrick read newspaper accounts of Simpson that he disagreed with). Also J. G. Jackson to J. L. Treloar (Director, AWM), 22 September 1937.

[26] *Sydney Mail,* 3 November 1915, pp. 24–5.

[27] *West Australian,* 20 July 1915, p. 5.

[28] *Coo-ee* was produced at Bishop's Knoll Hospital in Birmingham. See vol. 1, no. 1, 10 November 1916 and vol. 1, no. 3, 1917; J. Gallishaw, *Trenching at Gallipoli: A Personal Narrative of a Newfoundlander within the Ill-fated Dardanelles Expedition*, p. 84. Mr Ernest Bailey, Chief Librarian, South Shields Free Library, told the tale in much the same way in 1933, cited in J. L. Legge, 'The Man with the Donkey.

[29] Sister E. Davies to 'Mum', 15 January 1916. Following from the argument in Chapter Two it is presumed Sister Davies' letter is part of the 'conversation' between the press, the wounded, the censors and the readership on the home front, that produced the Simpson legend.

[30] *Sydney Morning Herald*, 20 July 1915, p. 8.

[31] *Boy's Own Annual*, vol. 39, 1916–17, p. 330.

[32] E. C. Buley, *A Child's History of Anzac*, p. 63. For the Education Department directive on Buley's books, see *Education Gazette & Teachers' Aid*, 20 February 1917, p. 34. 'The Good Samaritan of the Dardanelles' is in the *Victorian School Paper*, no. 193, 1 November 1915, pp. 147–9; another wartime school version is *The School Paper* (Brisbane), for Classes V and VI, vol. 8, April 1917, pp. 66–70.

[33] For the politics of Cavell's martyrdom, see M. Saunders and P. M. Taylor, *British Propaganda During the First World War*, pp. 145, 203–4.

[34] *Argus*, 10 August 1915; *Sunday Times*, 22 August 1915, p. 9; *Sun*, 25 October 1915, pp. 4–5 and 29 October 1915, p. 7; *Bulletin*, 17 February 1916, p. 22. For 'Ginger Mick' by the 'Sentimental Bloke', see *Bulletin*, 10 June 1915. On the politics of 'Ginger Mick', see Ken Inglis, 'The Anzac Legend', *Meanjin Quarterly*, March 1965, pp. 25–44. Humphrey McQueen suggests that Dennis's intention was financial and satirical, rather than jingoistic, see *Gallipoli to Petrov. Arguing with Australian History*, pp. 23–34.

[35] On soldierhood as the highest expression of citizenship, a theme with deep origins in Western intellectual culture, see G. Lloyd, 'Selfhood, War and Masculinity', in C. Pateman and E. Gross (eds), *Feminist Challenges. Social and Political Theory*.

[36] *Sydney Mail*, 21 July 1915, p. 13.

[37] *Sydney Mail*, 18 August 1915, pp. 6, 11; *West Australian*, 3 July 1915, p. 7; 9 July 1915, p. 8 and 10 July 1915, p. 7.

[38] *Sydney Morning Herald*, 7 August 1915, p. 16.

[39] Typescript of the diary of Lt-Col P. C. Fenwick (NZMC), 20 June 1915, p. 68.

[40] Oliver Hogue, *Love Letters of an Anzac*, p. 218. Being 'unwounded' could be no less devastating than wounds. Hogue never regained his health and fell victim to the influenza epidemic in London in 1919.

[41] *Argus*, 24 November 1915, p. 9.

[42] E.g. 'Wounded Australians at Harefield Hospital: The House and Grounds were lent by Mr. Billyard Leake of NSW', *Australasian*, 20 November 1915, Pictorial Section, p. ii.

[43] *Sunday Times*, 8 August 1915, p. 9.

[44] A curious term, as it was used in the press to refer to the civilian population in general. It was loaded with indebtedness and duty.

[45]Quoted in Patsy Adam-Smith, *The Anzacs*, p. 87. One Australian report of Nurse Cavell's death said her execution was not for spying but for nursing men back to the battle, see *Sydney Morning Herald*, 21 October 1916, p. 10.

[46]The term 'war artist' is used here to cover only those who sketched or drew for the newspapers.

[47]E.g. *Sydney Mail*, 24 March 1915, p. 1; *Bulletin*, 29 July 1915, p. 1. Note that the wounded man fighting on was a rare *photographic* subject.

[48]*Sydney Mail*, 18 October 1916, p. 5.

[49]Undated newspaper clipping, AWM PR 84/133(12a).

[50]*Sunday Times* (Sydney), 15 August 1915, p. 9; 5 September 1915, p. 23. In New Zealand, where conscription was successfully introduced in 1916, the wounded were tied into the recruitment offensive in a similar way, see, e.g., *The New Zealand Freelance*, 23 July 1915, p. 1, and 15 October 1915, p. 1.

[51]*Sun* (Sydney), 12 March 1916. Cited in Ina Bertrand (ed.), *Cinema in Australia. A Documentary History*, NSW University Press, 1989, p. 87. Apparently 'Murphy of Anzac' was part of an attempt, by Fraser Films, its maker, to stave off liquidation in the face of competition from its more powerful rival Austrasian Films. It was not a great success.

[52]E.g. C. E. W. Bean, *The Official History of Australia in the War of 1914–18. Vol. 1. The Story of ANZAC*, pp. 435–6, 554–5.

[53]Perhaps the major accounts of conscription have missed the cult of the wounded because the visual evidence was not properly examined. Not one of these accounts has an index entry for 'wounded' and, where there is one for 'casualties', it invariably turns out to be head counting rather than analysis. The major accounts of conscription are textually preoccupied and indifferent to visual evidence.

[54]*Sydney Mail*, 7 July 1915, p. 7. In Melbourne something similar: the pictorial section of the *Australasian* juxtaposes photographs of the recruiting campaign with pictures of the returning wounded and of caring for the wounded in Egypt (14 August 1915, pp. iii–v).

[55]M. McKernan, *The Australian People and the Great War*, pp. 66–73.

[56] A photo-caption in the *Australasian* reads: 'Established on the Impregnable Gallipoli Peninsula: The Great Landing of Troops and Supplies at Gaba Tepe, and a Red Cross Station for the Wounded', *Australasian*, 10 July 1915, Pictorial Section, p. ii.

[57]Maude B. Jacob, 'Our Red Cross Boys', *Sydney Mail*, 30 June 1915, p. 36.

[58]'After the Stunt. Work of the Red Cross', *Argus*, 11 May 1918, p. 4.

[59]'The Red Cross Spirit Speaks', *New South Wales Red Cross Record*, vol. 4, no. 6, June 1918, p. 48.

[60]See, for example, the poem 'Australian Red Cross Day: July 30, 1915', *Sydney Morning Herald*, 30 July 1915, p. 7. Note that, in 1915, 30 July was also Australia Day. The day commemorating the arrival of the First Fleet—Australia Day, 26 January—was originally known as Anniversary Day and did not acquire its current title until 1931.

[61]*Australasian*, 7 August 1915, Pictorial Section, p. iv.

[62]*West Australian*, 2 July 1915, p. 7; 30 July 1915, p. 8; 31 July 1915, p. 12.

[63]Hogue, pp. 195–6.

[64]*Argus*, 24 November 1915, p. 9.

[65]P. N. Robertson, *An Anzac Budget and Other Verses*, pp. 14–21.

[66]For Robinson's role in the campaign for a Simpson monument at the Shrine of Remembrance, see Chapter Eight.

[67]*The Anzac Book*, (ed. C. E. W. Bean), p. 53.

[68]Poem by T. H. 'Crosscut' Wilson, cited in *Bulletin*, 22 September 1937, first appeared in Perth *Sunday Times* in 1916. (Wilson was an Anzac.)

Chapter Four

[1]John M. Steadman, *Milton and the Renaissance Hero*, pp. 2–20; R. Folkenflik, 'Johnson's Heroes', in R. Folkenflik (ed.), *The English Hero, 1660–1800*, esp. pp. 143–5; Robert P. Adams, *The Better Part of Valor. More, Erasmus, Colet and Vives, on Humanism, War and Peace, 1496–1535*, esp. chs 3 and 5.

[2]A. G. Butler, *The Australian Army Medical Services in the War of 1914–1918, Vol. 1. (Gallipoli, Sinai and New Guinea)* p. 159. For Tinley and Brand, see the *Argus*, 26 October 1933; for the wartime convention regarding VCs for the stretcher-bearers see, e.g., *Argus* (L), 8 July 1915, p. 7.

[3]*West Australian*, 20 July 1915, p. 5.

[4]J. L. Beeston, *Five Months at Anzac*, p. 21. The padre's talk is from E. C. Buley, *Glorious Deeds of the Australasians*. It is quoted in an essay called 'Non Combatants' in the *Victorian School Paper*, 1 April 1916, p. 41. For the belief that stretcher-bearers did little work and so put on weight, see Major C. J. Jarman to his mother and father, 7 July 1915.

[5]An acronym that apparently had its origins in the Boer War. See Captain A. G. Carne, 'Seven Months at the Dardanelles', p. 23, a narrative based on wartime diaries, AWM 2DRL/13.

[6]Colin M. Gordon, 'Life of a Hospital Orderly in Cairo and England 1915–1916'. unpublished manuscript, 13 August 1984, Stout Research Centre, Victoria University, Wellington, New Zealand. On the connection between conscientious objection and stretcher-bearing, see Paul Baker, *King and Country Call. New Zealanders, Conscription and the Great War*, ch. 7, esp. pp. 170–90.

[7]Sources for the folklore critical of Simpson, or reporting the criticisms, are numerous: Lesley Grant to Peter Cochrane, 8 May 1989 (copy in author's possession); J. G. Jackson to J. McGrath, 30 September 1953, Collection of Information regarding Simpson and the Donkey, 1914–18 War, AWM, Box 15, 417/20/35; 'Biddy' H. M. Bidmead in the *Advertiser* (Adelaide), 18 September 1937; Bill Fogharty (AWM), personal communication. The claim that he was shot by Australians was made by a veteran of World War I who said he was shot because 'he drew the crabs', meaning he drew enemy fire. There is no evidence to suggest that this claim has any validity. On Simpson's bad teeth see *Labor Daily*, 25 April 1935.

[8]Buley, p. 322. This seems to have been another conventional line with its origins in the Gallipoli campaign: 'Jokes about the band are not popular any longer. They never were very funny', *Argus*, 2 November 1915, p. 5.

[9]Diary of J. G. Jackson, 16 May 1915.

[10]Sgt C. F. Laseron in *Sunday Times* (Sydney), 11 July 1915, p. 14.

[11]Major J. S. Mackay to 'Mother', 1 December 1917.

[12]Neville Howse to R. H. Fetherston, 20 June 1917, Fetherston Papers (bundle 1, item 3). Howse was Surgeon-General at AIF Administration Headquarters and a VC.

[13]N. Boyak, *Behind the Lines. The Lives of New Zealand Soldiers in the First World War*, pp. 52–3.

[14]*West Australian*, 21 June 1915, p. 8.

[15]*Weekly Press* (NZ), 18 August 1915, p. 13.

[16]Typescript of the diary of Lt-Col P. C. Fenwick (NZMC), 5 May 1915 (p. 7 of transcript).

[17] *West Australian*, 20 July 1915, p. 5.

[18]C. E. W. Bean, *The Official History of Australia in the War of 1914–18. Vol. 1. The Story of ANZAC*, pp. 435–6, 554–5.

[19]Leonard M. Hart, typescript, p. 6. Paul Fussell speaks of the universal feeling of shame at abandoning the wounded (*The Great War and Modern Memory*, p. 124).

[20]'The Donkey Man. A Humble Hero', *Weekly Press* (NZ), 18 August 1915, p. 13. This account originated in the *Daily Malta Chronicle* article of 12 June 1915, p. 4. The *Argus* reproduced it on 19 July 1915, p. 4.

[21]*West Australian*, 28 July 1915, p. 9.

[22]Diary of L. G. Donovan, 8 May 1915.

[23]Albert Facey, 'Gallipoli', in J. Laird (ed.), *The Australian Experience of War*, pp. 56–64, esp. pp. 56, 59. See also Wendy Capper, 'Facey's *A Fortunate Life* and Traditional Oral Narratives'.

[24]Robert M. Calder to father, 4 October 1915.

[25]Diary of Major C. L. Mason, Royal Engineers, British Army, 1915 (otherwise undated).

[26]Diary of George Davidson (Diary No. 5, September 7, p. 17). For a long extract on flowers, see Diary No. 5, Nov. 15, pp. 97–105.

[27]*The Sun* (Sydney), 10 November 1915, p. 1.

[28]R. D. Baker, 'Four Months at Anzac, April–Aug 1915', p. 58.

[29]Fenwick, 3 June 1915 (pp. 57–8 of transcript).

[30]The case quoted is that of a convalescent in a London hospital, and is taken from Buley, p. 80.

[31]*Weekly Press* (NZ), 28 July 1915, p. 8.

[32]*Christchurch Press*, 22 July 1915, p. 8.

[33]Statement on behalf of the Red Cross, by Agnes S. Irvine, *Argus*, 20 October 1933. Emphasis added.

[34]Bean, pp. 435–6.

[35]Cited in Boyak, p. 73.

[36]Diary of James Gardner Jackson, 29 April 1915.

[37]*Sunday Times* (Sydney), 19 September 1915, p. 10.

[38]'Oriel', *Argus*, 28 October 1933.

[39]Eric J. Leed, *No Man's Land: Combat and Identity in World War 1*, pp. 105–14.

[40]Stephen Kern, *The Culture of Time and Space. 1880–1918*, ch. 11 ('The Cubist War'), esp. pp. 296–7.

[41]Captain A. G. Carne, 'Seven Months at the Dardanelles', p. 13, narrative based on his diaries.

[42]Diary of L/Sgt C. F. Bosward (4th Bn, AIF), 24 June 1915.

[43]Lt J. T. Hampson to his mother, 27 August 1916.

[44]Harold G. Massey. Letter addressed to the *Sydney Morning Herald*, 25 July 1916. AWM, PR82/8. Emphasis added.

[45]*Coo-ee*, vol. 1, no. 1, November 1916.

[46]J. L. Legge, 'Kirkpatrick, J. S., 3rd Field Ambulance' (n.d. approx. 1953), p. 1, AWM 27, 172. 13 (1). Also Dale Collins, *Anzac Adventure: The Story of Gallipoli for Young Readers*, p. 108.

[47]'Every day wounded men are being brought into the military hospitals of Egypt, and every day some new story of battle is told that cannot fail to make the Australian proud of his country and the type of man it gives the Empire' (*Argus*, 17 July 1915).

[48]*Christchurch Press*, 8 July 1915, p. 7. (A photograph of the wounded Cavill features in the *Sydney Mail*, 23 June 1915, p. 26.)

[49]*Weekly Press*, 29 September 1915, p. 10. Of course soldiers could and did engage in this sort of bravado too.

[50]This paragraph is based on a report in the *Canterbury Times*, 7 July 1915, p. 15.

[51]*Sydney Mail*, 16 June 1915, p. 10; *Weekly Press*, 16 June 1915, p. 10.

[52]The quotation is from the *School Journal* (NZ) (Classes V & VI), Vol. ix, No. 6, July 1915, pp. 173–80. See also *School Paper* (Vic), (For Classes V & VI), 1 April 1916, p. 41. The Simpson story was first told in the *School Paper* in Victoria, in November (1 November 1915, p. 148). An article and poem about Simpson also figures in the *Boy's Own Annual*, vol. 39, 1916–17, p. 330. For Kipling's 'Gunga Din', see *Rudyard Kipling's Verse: Inclusive Edition, 1885–1932*, London, 1933, pp. 339–401. The Simpson legend's more or less permanent place in the schools after the war is discussed in Chapter Nine.

[53]Bruno Bettelheim, *The Uses of Enchantment. The Meaning and Importance of Fairy Tales*, pp. 143–50.

[54]The notable improvements in arrangements were to some extent due to fewer casualties.

[55]E.g. *Weekly Press*, 9 June 1915, p. 11.

[56]*West Australian* (L), 4 June 1915, p. 8. See also Richard Graves' epic poem, AWM PR 83/127 (p. 5). Also the diary of Pte Fred Robson (15th Bn, AIF), 27 April 1915.

[57]*Weekly Press* (NZ), 16 June 1915, p. 10.

[58]Fenwick, 30 April 1915.

[59]*Weekly Press*, 16 June 1915, p. 10.

[60]Taken from E. C. Buley's *A Child's History of Anzac*. Cited in the Victorian *School Paper*, 1 April 1918, p. 41.

[61]Bean, pp. 7, 15.

[62]In this instance the poem ('The Pullyerleg Brigade'), and Sir John Monash, were responding to Robert Graves' accusations in *Goodbye to All That, Herald*, 15, 16 January 1930; *Sun*, 15 January 1930. For 'Oh Valiant Hearts', see 'Anzac Day Hymn', St. Peter's Church, East Maitland [1921], National Library of Australia [JAFp, REL,802]. For

this reference to 'a touch like a woman's', see *Reveille*, 29 November, 1930, p. 7 (emphasis added). For the Reverend Rowland's speech, at the graveside of Jacka, see the *Age*, 20 January 1932.

[63]Alistair Thomson, 'Steadfast until Death'? C. E. W. Bean and the Representation of Australian Military Manhood', *Australian Historical Society*, vol. 23, no. 93, October 1989, p. 465. Thomson argues that Bean's history contains an evident strategy for the rendering of Anzacs as both fierce and civilised. On the fierce language of the Australians, for instance, he points to Bean's argument that 'the Australian soldier was more humane in his deeds than his words' (cited on pp. 463–4).

[64]*Age*, 27 July 1915, p. 8.

[65]Herbert Grattan, 'Grieve Not for the Anzacs' (n.d.). Copy in T. Walsh Papers, Auckland Institute and Museum, MS1469. Copy in author's possession.

[66]*Argus*, 23 October 1915.

[67]*Argus*, 4 October 1915.

[68]*Otago Witness*, 21 July 1915, p. 11; *Weekly Press*, 7 July 1915, p. 13.

[69]*Lone Hand*, vol. 7, no. 1, 1 December 1916, p. 22.

[70]'The Australians have made a great name here especially amongst the navy who have no time for anybody not Australian. We have a reputation of being great fighters now—nicknamed The White Ghourkas for we charged and fought our way up these hills as the Ghourkas have in the hills of India. ' Diary of L/Sgt C. F. Bosward, 7 May 1915, 4th Battalion AIF. See also Bill Gammage, *The Broken Years. Australian Soldiers in the Great War*, p. 84.

Chapter Five

[1]*Canterbury Times*, 11 August 1915, p. 30.

[2]Robin Gerster, *Big-Noting. The Heroic Theme in Australian War Writing*, pp. 12, 27.

[3]Private Dick Finch to Marjorie Finch, 27 May 1915.

[4]Diary of Private W. J. Hutchison, 4th Battalion, AIF, died 20 June 1915.

[5]Bill Gammage, *The Broken Years. Australian Soldiers in the Great War*, p. 102.

[6]*Sydney Morning Herald*, 16 December 1915, p. 8. Also Gerster, pp. 46–52.

[7]Bean on Monash and Bridges is discussed in Gerster, p. 70.

[8]*Sun* (Sydney), 28 December 1915, p. 1.

[9]*Age*, 7 July 1915, p. 8.

[10]Diary of J. G. Jackson, 10 May 1915..

[11]C. E. W. Bean, *The Official History of Australia in the War of 1914–18. Vol. 1. The Story of ANZAC*, pp. 134, 136, 215, 234–5, 297.

[12]*Christchurch Press*, 28 July 1915, p. 8.

[13]Bean, pp. 122–3.

[14]C. E. W. Bean (ed.), *The Anzac Book*, pp. 102–3.

[15]*Sunday Times* (Sydney), 19 September 1915, p. 10.

[16] *Bulletin*, 27 January 1916, p. 47.
[17] *Sydney Mail*, 24 November 1915, p. 30.
[18] Sydney de Loghe, *The Straits Impregnable.*
[19] *Argus*, 21 August 1915.
[20] Bean cited in J. L. Legge, 'The Man with the Donkey. Compiled from AWM Records', AWM Archives, 417/20/35; for Ashmead Bartlett: *Mirror* (Perth), 4 November 1933 (Simpson press cuttings).
[21] E. C. Buley, *A Child's History of Anzac*, pp. 61–4.
[22] Joseph Bowes, *The Young Anzacs*, pp. 112–13, 182–6.
[23] *Bulletin*, 7 October 1915, p. 48.
[24] *Argus*, 6 January 1916, p. 5.
[25] *Advertiser* (Adelaide), 27 April 1938.
[26] *West Australian*, 1 November 1933, 30 August 1934.
[27] Sunday *Sun*, 22 April 1934.
[28] From the *South Shields Gazette*, n.d. Cited in the *Christchurch Star*, 3 April 1965, p. 5.
[29] E.g. *Sun*, 11 October 1915. This column was headed 'Man with the Donkey. Rescue Under Fire. Men Held Spellbound'.
[30] Paul Fussell, *The Great War and Modern Memory*, p. 123.
[31] Eric J. Leed, *No Man's Land. Combat and Identity in World War One*, ch. 4, esp. pp. 116–17, 127–8. Also Gammage, p. 184.
[32] *Bulletin*, 19 August 1915, Red Page.
[33] *Age*, 25 August 1915, p. 12.
[34] *Argus*, 7 July 1915, p. 7.
[35] *Weekly Press*, 13 October 1915, p. 12.
[36] Lance Corporal A. E. (Alf) Weymouth to sister May, 12 November 1915.
[37] Diary of A. C. Aitken, Vol. 1, p. 58.
[38] Gammage, op. cit., p. 261.
[39] C. E. W. Bean, *The Official History of Australia in the War of 1914–18, Vol. 1. The Story of Anzac*, p. 298.
[40] *Weekly Press*, 20 October 1915, p. 11.
[41] *Christchurch Press*, 17 July 1915, p. 7.
[42] Diary of P. C. Fenwick, 14 May 1915.
[43] The charmed lives of animals at Gallipoli is discussed in detail in Chapter Six.
[44] *Sun*, 11 October 1915.
[45] P. Stanley, 'An Entente . . . Most Remarkable': Indians at Anzac', p. 20. For a later instance see the statement of Lt-Cl Bell, MHR, in the *Argus*, 30 October 1933.
[46] 'Correspondence re whereabouts of 'Murphy', late Pte Simpson's donkey after evacuation of Anzac', Bean Collection, AWM 91, 3DRL 8042, series 5.
[47] E. C. Buley, *The Glorious Deeds of the Australasians*, p. 4.
[48] *Daily Malta Chronicle*, 12 June 1915, p. 4.
[49] Pte W. Lowes to Mrs S. Kirkpatrick, 28 November 1915.
[50] Chauvel and Brand cited in *Argus*, 22 November 1933.
[51] 'Murphy. A Tale of Anzac', a poem by John Lea, *Boy's Own Annual*, Volume 39, 1916–17, p. 330.

52*Duckboard*, 1 November 1933, p. 6. (*Duckboard* was the journal of the Melbourne branch of the Returned Sailors and Soldiers Imperial League of Australia.)

53War Diary excerpts cited in Legge.

54Information regarding the Routine Order supplied by Christopher Pugsley, Wellington.

55Buley, p. 3.

56*Argus*, 27 October 1933.

57*Bulletin*, 2 July 1936.

58The Menin Gate Memorial to the missing presumed dead was unveiled at Ypres on 24 July 1927. See *Menin Gate at Midnight. The Story of Captain Will Longstaff's Great Allegorical Painting*, Australian War Memorial, Melbourne, 1932, p. 26. For Sassoon's poem 'On Passing The New Menin Gate', see *The War Poems of Siegfried Sassoon* (arranged and introduced by R. Hart-Davis), p. 153.

59'Displacement' meaning a 'shift of emotion from the person or object toward which it was originally directed, to another person or object' (B. J. Wolman, *A Dictionary of Behavioural Science*, Van Nostrand, Reinhold Co., New York, 1973, p. 103).

60Buley.

61*The Egyptian Mail* (Special Gallipoli issue), 25 April 1917, p. 1.

62*Sunday Times* (Sydney), 13 August 1915, p. 9.

63*Sunday Times* (Sydney), 12 December 1915, p. 24.

64*Sunday Times* (Sydney), 19 September 1915, p. 10 (emphasis added).

65Byron, *Childe Harold's Pilgrimage*, canto iii, l xviii.

66*Argus*, 20 June 1936, p. 22. The day of the unveiling.

67The resistance to the Simpson legend is discussed in more detail in Chapter Eight.

68Charles Love to T. Walsh, 26 September 1964.

69Letter to the *Sydney Morning Herald* by an unnamed and wounded private from Victoria, AWM PR82/8. He spoke of how the Indians worked on regardless, 'with bullets whistling all around them, as calm as if they were at dinna [*sic*].

70Diary of Russell Weir, 10 May and 18 May 1915.

71Aitken, p. 66.

72*Sunday Times*, (Sydney), 19 September 1915, p. 10.

73*Sydney Mail*, 26 April 1916, p. 9.

74Shakespeare used the phrase 'turn Turk' in the sense of turning renegade: 'Would not this, Sir, and a forest of feathers—if the rest of my fortunes turn Turk with me', *Hamlet*, act 3, scene 2, 265–6.

75*Bulletin*, 24 June 1915, p. 24.

76I am indebted to Michael Sharkey for providing the relevant biographical pieces of Wright's background and for information regarding those other poems by Wright that are discussed here (Michael Sharkey to Peter Cochrane, 19 March, 12 April 1991, correspondence in author's possession). For Wright's pseudonyms, see *Australian Literary Pseudonyms: An Index*, comp. Bruce Nesbitt and Susan Hadfield, LBSA, Adelaide, 1972, p. 133. Also *Australian Dictionary of Biography*, vol. 12, pp. 584–5.

Chapter Six

[1] Zechariah 9: 9–10.

[2] Matthew 21: 5–16.

[3] G. K. Chesterton's 'The Donkey' being one of the best known instances, having become one of the most widely anthologised of his poems. See *The Essential G. K. Chesterton*, (Introduced by P. J. Kavanagh), p. 1.

[4] M. McKernan, *The Australian People and the Great War*, p. 20; George Mosse, *Fallen Soldiers. Reshaping the Memory of the World Wars*, p. 7; Luke 17: 16. Compare with the donkey associated with the Australian contingent in the Sudan (1885), in Ken Inglis, *The Rehearsal. Australians at War in the Sudan, 1885*, pp. 127, 131, 140–6.

[5] *Sydney Mail*, 3 March 1915, p. 19.

[6] *Sydney Mail*, 29 March 1916, p. 17.

[7] John Meredith, *The Coo-ee March. Gilgandra to Sydney, 1915*, p. 44.

[8] *Sydney Mail*, 29 December 1915, p. 21.

[9] *Australasian*, 22 May 1915, p. v; 15 January 1916, p. iii; 18 March 1916, p. vi; *Otago Witness*, 30 June 1915, p. 39; *Weekly Press*, 22 December 1915, p. 35; *Daily Mail* (London), 26 April 1916. For the dog 'Rags', see E. W. Bush, *Gallipoli*, p. 139 and photograph opposite p. 256.

[10] *The Statesman & Friend of India*, 9 September 1915, p. 3; *Weekly Press* (NZ), 2 June 1915, p. 42; *Sydney Mail*, 3 February 1915, p. 17, 13 October 1915 p. 16, 29 March 1916, p. 17. Egyptian donkeys, and the donkeys of the Greek islands, were part of the collective travel experience—useful for games and transport (*Otago Witness*, 3 November 1915, p. 46; *Sydney Mail*, 13 October 1915, p. 16). They figured in the courtship of French and English 'girls' (*Sydney Mail*, 13 October 1915, p. 14). Also *Anzac Bulletin*, 21 February 1917, p. 12.

[11] Wilfred Collinson Smith to his wife, 17 April 1917. Quoted in J. Phillips, N. Boyak and E. P. Malone (eds), *The Great Adventure. New Zealand Soldiers Describe the First World War*, pp. 206–7.

[12] J. L. Beeston, *Five Months at Anzac*, pp. 7–8, 37.

[13] John Keegan, *The Face of Battle: A Study of Agincourt, Waterloo and the Somme*, p. 217. See also Jill Cooper, *Animals in War*, p. 134. Cooper also noted that in France when it was bitterly cold, soldiers sometimes took donkeys into dugouts for extra warmth while sleeping (p. 156).

[14] *West Australian*, 20 July 1915, p. 5.

[15] Wilfred Doe to 'Dear All', 14 May 1915.

[16] J. G. Jackson to J. McGrath, 30 September 1953, p. 6, AWM 93, 417/20/35.

[17] Diary of J. G. Jackson, 23 April 1915.

[18] 'Anzac Diary, 24 April to 27 June 1915', Typescript of the diary of Lt-Col Percival C. Fenwick (NZMC), p. 11.

[19] Quoted in T. Walsh, *The Man with the Donkey. A Narration of the Undaunted Chivalry of John Simpson Kirkpatrick (Murphy) in the Gallipoli Campaign, 1915*, pp. 10–11. Tom Walsh Papers, Auckland Institute and Museum, MS 1469. Walsh's booklet recounted his association

with Bush-King and featured 'A Padre's Recollections', excerpts from Bush-King's diary. The diary has not been traced.

[20] *Sydney Mail*, 9 August 1916, p. 26.

[21] *Sydney Morning Herald*, 2 September 1915, p. 8.

[22] Oliver Hogue, *Love Letters of an Anzac*, p. 180.

[23] *Dinkum Oil*, 4 July 1915.

[24] C. E. W. Bean (ed.), *The Anzac Book*, p. 53.

[25] Fred Knight to mother, 2 September 1915. Knight was with No. 3 Co., AASC.

[26] Alf Weymouth to May, 12 November 1915.

[27] *Standeasy* (Journal of NZRSA), July 1964.

[28] J. G. Jackson to J. Treloar, 22 September 1937, pp. 20–1. Jackson wrote two very long letters to the Australian War Memorial, one in 1937 (quoted here), the other in 1953 (quoted earlier). These letters figure prominently in the next chapter.

[29] *Sunday Times* (Perth), 24 May 1936.

[30] Eric J. Leed, *No Man's Land. Combat and Identity in World War One*, pp. 127–8.

[31] Diary of Private Victor Laidlaw, 1 May 1915 (transcript, p. 33). Laidlaw was with the 2nd Field Ambulance.

[32] *Sydney Morning Herald*, 2 September 1915, p. 8. Hogue was orderly to Colonel Ryrie who was later photographed beside a donkey foal.

[33] Hogue, p. 180.

[34] Bean, *TheAnzac Book*, p. 53.

[35] *Simpson and his Donkey 'Murphy'*, Hill & Plumber, Auckland, n.d. (*c.* 1918), AWM 93, 417/20/35. These superstitions were perhaps fortified by English folklore which celebrated the donkeys' forecasting powers with respect to other calamities: 'Tis time to cock your hay and corn,/When the old donkey blows his horn'. And: 'Hark! I hear the asses bray;/We shall have some rain today' (Richard Inwards, *Weather Lore*, 1893, p. 127.)

[36] *Sydney Mail*, 3 November 1915.

[37] Diary of G. Davidson (Diary no. 2), pp. 68–9.

[38] *Otago Witness*, 22 September 1915, p. 36.

[39] R. D. Baker, 'Four Months at Anzac, April–August 1915', p. 18.

[40] Fenwick, pp. 5, 10 (of transcript).

[41] Fenwick, 8 May (p. 13 of transcript).

[42] *Sun*, 19 October 1915, p. 5. For a cartoon along these lines, see 'Ain't These Mules Cows', in *Aussie. The Australian Soldiers' Magazine*, no. 10, 1919, p. 2. See also, diary of Davidson, 17 June 1915.

[43] Fenwick, p. 7 of transcript.

[44] Diary of G. Davidson, 7 June 1915.

[45] Diary of J. G. Jackson, 4 May 1915.

[46] A. D Carbery, *The New Zealand Medical Service in the Great War, 1914–1918*, p. 58. Also H. de Balzac, *The Wild Ass's Skin*, pp. 226–7.

[47] Beeston, p. 34.

[48] W. R. Birdwood to R. E. Bush, 2 December 1916. Cited in *Coo-ee*, vol. 1, no. 3, 1917.

[49] C. E. W. Bean, *The Official History of Australia in the War of 1914–18, Vol. 1. The Story of ANZAC*, p. 573.

[50] *Sunday Times* (Perth), 10 May 1936.

[51] *Sunday Times* (Perth), 17 May 1936.

[52] *Telegraph* (Sydney), 18 May 1936.

[53] *Sunday Times* (Perth), 24 May 1936.

[54] J. G. Jackson to J. McGrath, 30 September 1953, pp. 6–7. Neither photo can now be found in the AWM photographic collection. However the first of these is in the Jackson Papers, Hocken Library.

[55] Jackson to McGrath, p. 7.

[56] Quoted in T. Walsh, pp. 10–11.

[57] *Bulletin* (Sydney), 24 June 1936.

[58] *Sunday Times* (Sydney), 5 September 1915, p. 23.

[59] Bean, *The Anzac Book*, p. 53.

[60] 'Last Link with the Anzac Legend Ends', *North Shore Times Advertiser* (NZ), 12 October 1985, p. 12 (copy in AWM 419/1/5). In the *School Paper* in Queensland it is the second day of the occupation: 'The man had carried two heavy men in succession down the awful slopes of Shrapnel Gully and and through the Valley of Death. His eye lit on the donkey. "I'll take this chap with me next trip," he said; and, from that time, the pair was inseparable'. (For Classes V and VI, vol. 8, April 1917, p. 67.)

[61] C. I. Benson, *The Man with the Donkey. John Simpson Kirkpatrick. The Good Samaritan of Gallipoli*, pp. 56, 76.

[62] Benson, p. 56.

[63] A. R. Davidson to J. L. Treloar, 28 March 1938, AWM 93, 417/20/35. See also A. R. Davidson's address to the Soldiers' Institute in Perth in November 1933, quoted in *West Australian*, 16 November 1933, and in J. L. Legge, 'The Man with the Donkey, p. 5, as is the letter to Treloar (p. 3). A similar interpretation can be found in *Reveille*, 1 August 1961.

[64] 'Heroes of the Red Cross. Private Simpson, DCM and His Donkey at Anzac, 1915', AWM 93, 895/2/148. This document appears to be the text associated with the display of Sapper H. Moore-Jones 'Simpson' painting, in London 1918. See Chapter Seven. The story had at least two precedents: a similar account in the *Sunday Times*, 10 October 1915, p. 19, and in the *Anzac Bulletin*, no. 7, 21 February 1917.

[65] *Sunday Times* (Sydney), 5 September 1915, p. 23.

[66] Walsh, p. 18.

[67] Benson, p. 40.

[68] Davidson to Treloar. Also *West Australian*, 1, 16 November 1933. In his 1937 letter to the AWM, James G. Jackson explained that it had become increasingly difficult for the donkeys to get forage as there was no grass, Jackson to Treloar, 22 September 1937, pp. 4–5.

[69] *Herald*, 21 April 1965. Copy in AWM PR83/69, 419/9/22.

[70] Walsh, p. 18; also *Coo-ee*, November 1916, and the retelling of the *Coo-ee* tale in the *Herald*, 28 August 1936.

[71] *Sydney Mail*, 3 November 1915, pp. 24–5. Also *Sunday Times* (Sydney), 10 October 1915, p. 19. This account features Simpson smuggling the

donkey ashore at Gallipoli in a wool bale slung over his shoulder, and
has him working at night with a lantern, searching for the wounded.
[72]Walsh, p. 11.
[73]*Duckboard* (official organ of the Melbourne branch of the Returned
Sailors and Soldiers Imperial League of Australia), 1 November 1933,
p. 6.
[74]C. Love to T. Walsh, 26 September 1964.
[75]The earliest instance being in *School Paper* (Queensland), Classes V
and VI, vol. 8, April 1917: 'The donkey was a little mouse-coloured
animal no taller than a Newfoundland dog. His master called him
Abdul' (p. 66). Stevenson's description of his donkey is quoted by
Richard Holmes in his *Footsteps. Adventures of a Romantic Biographer*, p.
17.
[76]*Sydney Mail*, 3 November 1915, p. 24.
[77]Carbery, p. 58.
[78]Diary of Sgt J. E. McPhee, 19 May 1915 (Diary no. 1), p. 78. McPhee
figured in Chapter Two.
[79]Peter Stanley, 'An Entente . . . Most Remarkable, p. 20.
[80]*Sydney Morning Herald*, 28 September 1915, p. 8.
[81]Excerpts from letter written by Pte Andy Carnahan to his family,
September 1915, held in Tom Walsh Papers, Auckland Institute and
Museum, MS1469. A returned soldiers' publication for Anzac Day
1916 confirmed that taking Murphy to Australia had been discussed,
but that 'nothing was decided upon and the movement [to bring the
donkey home] was allowed to drop'. See *Anzac Memorial*, published by
the Returned Soldiers Association, Sydney, 25 April 1916, pp. 80–1.
[82]All letters responding to Bean's circular are held with 'Correspondence re whereabouts of Murphy, late Pte Simpson's donkey after
evacuation of Anzac', Bean Collection, AWM 91, 3DRL 8042, series 5,
item 91. For Bean's letter to General White, see AWM 3 DRL7953,
item 23. Carey Evans' photograph of 'Murphy' does not seem to have
survived.
[83]*Anzac Bulletin* (London), no. 7, 21 February 1917. This Bulletin was
issued to Australian soldiers and sailors in England, France and
elsewhere. Also, *Anzac Memorial*, pp. 80–1.
[84]*Argus* (L), 20 October 1933.
[85]*Mufti*, 5 December 1959.
[86]'Albert Jacka', in *Australian Dictionary of Biography*, vol. 9, pp. 452–3.
Jacka's name was also used by Keith Murdoch in association with the
conscription campaign, but Mr Jacka senior promptly announced that
'Bert' had never declared himself in favour of conscription.
[87]'Trophies and Recruiting', AWM 16, 4386/1/24. These papers also
reveal that Lieutenant General Birdwood, another enthusiast for
Murphy's repatriation, was working hard for the return of 'Australian
captures' to aid the recruitment campaign. Bean's views on conscription for the Great War are unclear. He may have been reticent on this
matter, knowing of the strong feeling against conscription among
Australian soldiers in Europe. Before the war, in 1907, he had joined
the National Defence League, an organisation which advocated
compulsory training.

Chapter Seven

[1]See, for example, C. E. W. Bean, *In Your Hands, Australians*, pp. 59–60.

[2]A. G. Butler to W. O. Garland, 28 May 1918. Also Garland to Butler (including report to Butler entitled 'Pte Simpson and "Murphy"'), 4 June 1918, AWM 41, Item 5/43.

[3]H. S. Gullett (Director, AWM) to Editor, *Sydney Mail*, 9 March 1920, AWM 93, 17/1/52. See *Argus*, 18 April 1922.

[4]*Argus*, 6 March 1918, 11 March 1921; also *Age*, 7 March, 2 April 1921; and *Mail* (Brisbane), 23 October 1921.

[5]Australia at the War. Catalogue of exhibition of War Photographs in Color', Jan–Feb. 1920, Fergusson Collection (Ferg/3608), National Library of Australia (NLA).

[6]*Age*, 13 August 1921, also 15, 17, 20 August 1921.

[7]*Age*, 17 September 1921.

[8]R. G. Casey to J. L. Treloar, 17 August 1921; Treloar to Casey, 23 August 1921; Casey to Treloar, 26 August, 9 September 1921; Treloar to Casey, 1 December 1921, AWM 93, 17/3/250. See also 'Australia at the War. Catalogue of Exhibition of War Photographs in Color'.

[9]R. J. Clark to Treloar, 25 June 1922; Treloar to Clark, 30 June 1922, AWM 93, 17/3/255. Clark had returned to Australia in April 1916, then re-embarked, again with the medical corps, in May (Biographical Card Catalogue for Clark, prepared by the Official Historian, AWM).

[10]C. E. W. Bean and H. Gullett, *Official History of Australia in the Great War of 1914–18. Volume 12. Photographic Record of the War.*

[11]*Advertiser* (Adelaide), 15 September 1937. In this report, arising from a later controversy, Treloar reflects on earlier events.

[12]Some years later Treloar revealed he had called publicly for Clark to come forward, see *Star* (Melbourne), 2 November 1933.

[13]It appears Treloar wanted to send a copy of Ralph Clark's photo to Mrs Kirkpatrick but for some reason did not. See A. W. Bazley to Treloar, 27 June 1922, AWM 93, 17/3/255. Here Bazley sends Treloar Mrs Kirkpatrick's address. Yet later in the decade the Museum would contact her to ask for copies of Simpson's letters and other written material.

[14]*Herald* (Melbourne), 2 November 1933.

[15]*West Australian*, 1 November 1933. Note the reference here to the Australian War Museum which was the Australian War Memorial's original name.

[16]*Star*, 2 November 1933.

[17]*Sun* (Melbourne), 6 November 1933; for the Friday edition, see *Sun*, 3 November 1933.

[18]A photo of the Auckland Commercial Travellers' Club painting appeared in the *Auckland Star* on 10 September 1937. McCann, Sir Charles Francis Gerald (1880–1951).

[19]*Australasian*, 18 November 1933. The comparison with Longstaff's famous 'Menin Gate' painting and the reference to sales in 'great

numbers' at the end of the war is to be found in a Memo, Anne Gray to Director, 10 October 1985, AWM 895/4/52.

[20]W. J. Bryce to Agent-General for South Australia, 17 September 1937. Also Agent-General to Treasurer (SA), 18 September 1937, State Records of South Australia, GRG 55/15/30.

[21]A. Wallace Fraser quoted in *Sydney Morning Herald*, 13 September 1937.

[22]W. E. Curran in *Argus*, 14 September 1937.

[23]*Star*, 17 September 1937.

[24]A. A. Schmidt in *Herald* (Auckland), 17 September 1937.

[25]*Mail* (Adelaide), 18 September 1937; F. B. Cox in the *Age*, 14 September 1937.

[26]*Telegraph* (Sydney), 13 September 1937; *Advertiser*, 13 September 1937. See also J. McGrath to Clark, 28 September 1953, AWM 93, 417/20/35.

[27]*Advertiser*, 13, 15 September 1937.

[28]*Argus*, 20 September 1937. For McCann, see *Advertiser*, 15 September 1937.

[29]*Telegraph* (Sydney), 15 September 1937.

[30]*Telegraph*, 14 September 1937.

[31]*Telegraph*, 16 September 1937.

[32]*Advertiser*, 14 December 1937. Annie did see the painting, according to the Agent-General. Agent-General to Treasurer (SA), 29 October 1937, State Records of South Australia, GRG 55/15/31.

[33]British Section Notes'. Compiled by Nobby Clark. Copy in author's possession.

[34]Undated clipping from *Auckland Weekly News* (signed 'Nikora').

[35]*Complete Index to the First Series of Sketches Made at Anzac by Sapper H. Moore-Jones*, Hugh Rees Ltd, London, 1916, p. 6. (Subsequent editions, from 1917, published by W. J. Bryce of London.)

[36]Anne Gray, 'Moore-Jones' Gallipoli'. Also Una Platts, *Nineteenth Century New Zealand Artists: A Guide and Handbook*, Avon, Christchurch (NZ), 1980, pp. 172–3.

[37]Cited in *NZ Listener*, 21 April 1984, p. 66.

[38]John Barr (Director, ACAG) to the Mayor, 23 September 1918, Auckland City Art Gallery (ACAG) Archive.

[39]*Dominion*, 2 May 1919; 'Kiwi apathy "sickens" family. Battle to win recognition for unsung hero', *Sunday Star*, 23 April 1989, p. A9; also 'Unofficial History', *RSA Review*, vol. 64, no. 2, April 1989, p. 10. Moore-Jones sketches also feature on pages 97, 113 and 145 of Alan Moorehead's *Gallipoli* (illustrated edition), 1989.

[40]Records in respect of C. E. W. Bean, AWM 3 DRL 6673. Also *ABC Weekly*, 20 August, 17 September 1955, for an account of the paintings of 'Gallipoli Jones' in the AWM.

[41]*Paintings and Drawings by Horace Moore-Jones*. From the foreword by Douglas Seymour; J. G. Jackson to Treloar, 22 September 1937, p. 8, AWM 93, 417/20/35.

[42]Simpson and his Donkey "Murphy". Reproduced from the Original Water-Color by Sapper H. Moore-Jones by Hugh Rees, Ltd, Publishers, London', Hill & Plummer, Auckland, n.d.

⁴³Treloar to Jackson, 3 November 1937, AWM 93, 417/20/35.

⁴⁴As for note 43.

⁴⁵A. R. Davidson to J. L. Treloar, 28 March 1938. Also A. R. Davidson to J. L. Treloar, 28 March 1938. (Davidson wrote Treloar two letters on this date), AWM 93, 417/20/35.

⁴⁶J. G. Jackson to J. L. Treloar, 22 September 1937, AWM 93, 417/20/35 (emphasis added).

⁴⁷As for note 46. Indented quotations from the Jackson letter are from pages 5, 8–9, 10 and 15 respectively. 'Hullo Dig' quote, p. 4, and 'Sapper Moore-Jones received two identical photos . . . ', p. 11.

⁴⁸Treloar to Jackson, 12 November 1937, AWM 93, 417/20/35.

⁴⁹Today it hangs in the Gallipoli Gallery at the Australian War Memorial.

⁵⁰'The real "Murphy". Modest Hero, Red Cross Worker Dies in Waikato', *Red Cross News*, December 1950, pp. 1–3.

⁵¹Unreferenced New Zealand press clipping dated 17 April 1950. In author's possession.

⁵²*News* (Adelaide), 19, 25 April 1950.

⁵³Quoted in Chapter Two.

⁵⁴Beverley S. May to J. McGrath (Director, AWM), 19 October 1953, AWM 93, 417/20/35. McGrath was the new Director after the death of Major Treloar in 1952.

⁵⁵*Sydney Mail*, 29 March 1916, p. 3.

⁵⁶May to McGrath, 19 October 1953, AWM 93, 417/20/35. May was speaking to the press on Little's behalf, as Little was incapacitated.

⁵⁷McGrath to Clark, 28 September 1953, AWM 93, 417/20/35. This is the letter indicating that the War Memorial had at last traced and reestablished contact with Ralph Clark.

⁵⁸J. L. Legge, 'The Man with the Donkey. Compiled from AWM Records'.

⁵⁹McGrath to Jackson, 15 September 1953, AWM 93, 417/20/35. The absence of the relevant records at John Fairfax Ltd. was confirmed in 1990.

⁶⁰J. G. Jackson to J. McGrath, 30 September 1953, AWM 93, 417/20/35. Jackson's 1937 letter attributed the captions to his brother, Jack, and cited instances of his first-hand knowledge reflected in the captions. It also said the Dick Henderson caption was 'Murphy and his Donk'. But in 1953 Jackson reveals that he has checked the caption this time and has it before him as he writes.

⁶¹Diary of James Gardner Jackson, 4 May 1915 (Johnstone Papers).

⁶²Clark to C. E. W. Bean, 2 July 1922 (emphasis added), AWM 3 DRL/7953, item 19.

⁶³The Ras-El-Tin Convalescent Depot, Alexandria, opened on 5 July 1915 with a capacity for 200 soldiers and was disbanded in July 1916. A. G. Butler, *The Australian Army Medical Services in the War of 1914–18, Vol. 1: Gallipoli*, pp. 201, 269, 646. Clark's hospitalisation details in Alexandria are from Central Army Records Office, Melbourne.

⁶⁴Diary of C. E. W. Bean, no. 17, 21 September–4 October 1915, pp. 19–20, AWM 38/3DRL. Also K. Fewster, Expression and Suppression: Aspects of Military Censorship in Australia during World War One, pp. 61–6, 82.

Chapter Eight

[1]*Argus*, 18 October 1933.

[2]*Argus*, 19 October 1933.

[3]'On the wallaby', an abbreviation of 'on the wallaby track', an Australian colloquialism meaning tramping the outback or bush country in search of work (as though following the track made by the wallabies).

[4]C. E. W. Bean, *Anzac To Amiens*.

[5]*Argus*, 24 April, 25 July 1933; *Age*, 2 June, 3,10 August, 14, 28 November 1933; *Argus*, 23 May 1934; *Age*, 10 August 1935. The battalion histories referred to are as follows: N. Wanliss, *The History of the Fourteenth Battalion A. I. F.*; *The Thirty Ninth*, ed. by the 39th Battalion Historical Committee, Melbourne, 1934; H. Williams, *The Gallant Company. A Soldier's Story of 1915–18.*

[6]*Argus*, 20 October 1933, (L) 25 October 1933, (L) 17 November 1933.

[7]Simpson's parents were Scottish born.

[8]*Argus*, 20 October 1933.

[9]The committee's typed Minutes indicate a regular membership of five people: Mr. O. Morrice Williams Esq., OBE (Chairman, Vic. Red Cross Executive); Rabbi J. Danglow, St Kilda Hebrew Congregation & Jewish Chaplain to the AIF, WWI; Maj. Gen. C. H. Brand, CB, CMG, CVO, DSO; Miss E. Ballantyne (Assist.-Sec.); Miss P. N. Robertson, OBE. General Sir Harry Chauvel, a member of the Victorian Red Cross Council, was not on the Committee. However, he liaised with it on a regular basis. A. E. Kane of the Melbourne City Council appears to have attended one meeting only. A representative of the *Argus* attended several meetings.

[10]Roy S. Curthoys (Editor, *Argus*) to Robertson, 5 December 1933, Simpson Collection, Red Cross Archives, Victorian Division, South Melbourne (emphasis added). Mr. A. C. C. Holtz was General Manager of Wilson and Mackinnon, proprietors of the *Argus*.

[11]Holtz to Robertson, 14 December 1933, Simpson Collection.

[12]Robertson to Paul R. Montford, 1 December 1933, Simpson Collection.

[13]Minutes of Meeting of Sub-Committee Appointed by the Victorian Red Cross Council to Deal with the Question of a Memorial to 'The Man with the Donkey', 2 March 1934 (hereafter referred to as Red Cross Committee or Simpson Committee; also Robertson to Holtz, 5 March 1934, Simpson Collection.

[14]Holtz to Robertson, 9 March 1934, Simpson Collection.

[15]Robertson to J. Barnes, Secretary to the Trustees, Shrine of Remembrance, 11 April 1934.

[16]Shrine of Remembrance Trustees, Minute Book, Vol. 1, p. 318, Meeting of 31 May 1934. The Minute Book for a later meeting on 14 October 1936 (p. 114) contains a motion endorsing a memorial to 'His late Majesty King George the Fifth' within the Shrine area.

[17]Robertson to H. Linaker Esq., Repatriation Sanatorium, Mont Park, 17 August 1934, Simpson Collection. (Linaker was State Superintendent of Parks and Gardens.)

[18]W. L. Bowles to Robertson, 19 November 1934, with note attached in Philadelphia Robertson's hand, same date, Simpson Collection.

[19]Minutes of Meeting of Sub-Committee for Erection of Memorial to 'The Man with the Donkey', 22 October 1934, Simpson Collection.

[20]Bowles to Secretary, Red Cross Society, 8 February 1935, and Robertson to W. McCall (Town Clerk), 14 February 1935, Simpson Collection. Other competitors were: G. W. Allen, Lyndon Dadswell, Charles Oliver and Wallace Anderson.

[21]Ken Scarlett, *Australian Sculptors*, pp. 10–14.

[22]Anderson to Secretary, Red Cross Society, 8 February 1935, Simpson Collection. Anderson also indicated that the statue was 'modelled on a size to suit an indoor site as insufficient funds were available to make it a size satisfactory altogether for out of doors'. Anderson to C. E. W. Bean, 13 September 1935, Australian War Memorial (AWM) 93, 7/1/22.

[23]Town Clerk to Councillor Kane, 14 September 1934.

[24]Anderson to Secretary, Red Cross Society, 16 July 1935. Also Anderson to Secretary, Red Cross Society, 16 July 1935, Simpson Collection, Red Cross Archive.

[25]Minutes of Meeting of Red Cross Sub-Committee for Memorial to 'The Man with the Donkey', 27 May 1935, Simpson Collection, Red Cross Archive.

[26]Minutes of Meeting of Sub-Committee for Memorial to 'The Man with the Donkey', 9 July 1935, Simpson Collection.

[27]Anderson to Robertson, 14 October 1935; Robertson to Colonel P. W. Vaughan, 25 October 1935, Simpson Collection.

[28]*Argus*, 17 October 1935.

[29]*Argus*, 11, 13 February 1936. Mr MacKenzie was supported, perhaps advised, by Mr H. Linaker the State Superintendent of Parks and Gardens, who had laid out the King's Domain. *Argus*, 12 February 1936.

[30]*Argus*, 11, 13 February 1936.

[31]Robertson to Town Clerk, 5 May 1936, Town Clerk's Correspondence Files, City of Melbourne Archives.

[32]Town Clerk to Parks and Gardens Committee, Town Clerk's Correspondence Files.

[33]Town Clerk to Secretary for Lands (Dept of Lands and Survey), 8 May 1935, Town Clerk's Correspondence Files.

[34]Town Clerk's Correspondence Files.

[35]Parks and Gardens Committee Minute Book, vol. 4, 13 May 1936, pp. 35–6, City of Melbourne Archives.

[36]The unveiling took place on 20 June 1936. Major Reynolds' reading was reported in the Brisbane *Courier Mail*, 23 June 1936. Robertson's poem is in her *Red Cross Yesterdays*, pp. 71–2. Also *Argus*, 22 June 1936; *Age*, 22 June 1936; *Argus*, 26 June 1936.

[37]*Age*, 24 January 1931.

[38] *Age*, 12 May 1936; *Argus*, 3 November 1933.

[39] *Age*, 17 July 1934. The receipt slips numbered between 30 000 and 40 000 in all. The enthusiasm for monuments was 'so energetically promoted (in) the inter war years that it was not immediately apparent that its potency was waning'. See G. Davison,'The Use and Abuse of Australian History', p. 61.

[40] Closely followed by Captain Albert Jacka who died in January 1932, *Argus*, 26 January 1932.

[41] *Age*, 8 July 1931.

[42] *Sun*, 15 October, 14 December 1931.

[43] *Age*, 4 May 1933.

[44] *Argus*, 8 March 1934. Other known members of the committee were: Brig.-Gen. J. P. McGlinn (organiser), Major-Gen. Thomas Blamey, deputy chairman to the mayor.

[45] *Argus*, 21 December 1935.

[46] *Argus*, 10 September 1937.

[47] On Monash's post-war career, see Geoffrey Serle, *John Monash. A Biography*, chs 16 and 17, pp. 435–511. An Appendix discusses the Memorial Fund briefly (p. 531).

[48] Serle, p. 475.

[49] *Age*, 4 May 1933.

[50] *Sun*, 14 December 1931. Most of the money seems to have come through in small amounts gathered through municipal council subscription lists and soldiers' and other patriotic organisations. For example, the Heidelberg Council report in the *Age*, 1 March 1934.

[51] *Herald*, 10 October 1931; *Age*, 10 October 1931; *Smith's Weekly*, 10 October 1931.

[52] *Age*, 8 March 1934; *Argus*, 8 March 1934. The total prize money for the Monash competition amounted to £350, almost as much as the total funds raised for the Simpson monument. Also *Argus*, 8 March 1934.

[53] *Sun*, 9 October 1931.

[54] Correspondence file re erection of a Bronze Monument to the Man and the Donkey, File No. 4392, 6 October 1934, Town Clerk's Office, City of Melbourne Archives. The McIlwraith, McEachern Ltd donation appears in the *Argus*, 23 October 1933.

[55] T. A. Blamey to Robertson, 9 November 1933, Simpson Collection. Blamey's typed letter is on a Police Department letterhead (Chief Commissioner's Office), indicating a secretarial service that could just as easily have typed a paragraph or two for the *Argus* or the *Age*.

[56] We Will Remember Them' to The Editor, *Argus*, 15 November 1933. This is a typed letter. The pseudonym is in pencil, in Robertson's handwriting. Pencilled in above the letter, are the words 'Not published'.

[57] Gullett's comment was made in reference to a statuette depicting the legend, commissioned by the AWM in 1936. Gullett to Treloar, AWM 93, 895/2/148.

[58] *Argus*, 20 October 1933.

[59] *West Australian*, 1 November 1933.

[60] L. A. R. ' to Ed., *Argus*, 25 October 1933.

[61]The column by 'Vesta' appeared in the *Argus*, 27 October 1933. The *Argus* also published subscription lists, routinely, for the duration of the appeal.

[62]*Argus*, 24 October 1933.

[63]Robertson to W. McCall (Town Clerk), 19 September 1934, Simpson Collection.

[64]'All members of the Fun Family, especially those who belong to the Junior Red Cross, will be interested in the record of the Man with the Donkey. I suppose you know all about this great hero, Private Simpson?' *Argus*, 4 November 1933.

[65]Minutes of Special Meeting of the Victorian Red Cross Council, 19 October 1933, Simpson Collection.

[66]*West Australian*, 16 November 1933.

[67]*Argus*, 26 October 1933.

[68]*Sun*, 28 October 1933.

[69]Chauvel to Robertson, 18 November 1933, Simpson Collection. The Committee worded a second inscription, to appear on the other side of the pedestal, to the 'valour and compassion' of Australian soldiers in general.

[70]*Herald*, 12 October 1931. See also Serle, p. 473, on Monash's objection. Jack Barnes, the Shrine Secretary, claimed that the Trustees had frequently discussed the erection of the two statues and the public generally believed that one of them would be of Sir John (*Herald*, 12 October 1931).

[71]*Age*, 3 November 1931. It appears that the War Memorial Committee together with the State Government approved a Monash monument for the Shrine. The Shrine Trustees took control over such decisions in 1934.

[72]These examples are taken from Shrine Trustees Minute Books covering 1934.

[73]Shrine of Remembrance Trustees, Minute Book, vol. 1, 11 January 1934, p. 23, City of Melbourne Archives. The 270-feet decision looks like an attempt at a compromise.

[74]Minute Book, 23 March 1934, pp. 20–1.

[75]Minute Book, 13 June 1935, p. 95. For the Minute indicating the disappointment of the Blamey Committee, see 5 September 1935, p. 99.

[76]Minute Book, 14 October 1936, p. 114.

[77]Serle, p. 531. According to Serle the MCC selected the new site in May 1937, Minute Book, vol. 1, 14 October 1936, p. 114. The Minute Book makes no mention of a new site until their meeting of 13 October 1937, City of Melbourne Archives (emphasis added).

[78]*Argus* (L), 2 July 1936. For the McAskell poem, see *Argus*, 20 June 1936 (the day of the unveiling).

[79]*Age*, 26 April 1937; *Argus*, 26 April 1937, 14, 26 April 1938. Also correspondence between the secretary of the Gallipoli Legion of Anzacs and the Red Cross Society (Victorian Division), 1940–1943, Simpson Collection. New Zealand contingents were involved in this ceremony on occasions after the Second World War.

[80]The permanent guard, himself a sort of statue—a policeman dressed as a light horseman, thanks to Blamey's position as Commissioner of Police.

Chapter Nine

[1]*Advertiser* (Geelong), 26 April 1926.

[2]*Argus*, 25 October 1933.

[3]'Anzac', *The School Magazine*, (Class III), NSW Dept of Education, 1 April 1926, p. 44; 'Our Debt to the Soldiers', in *Supplement to the School Paper* (Grades V and VI), 1 April 1916, p. 1.

[4]C. R. Long, *The Aim and Method of History and Civics*, p. 17.

[5]C. E. W. Bean, 'The Man with the Donkey', in *The School Magazine* (Class VI), 1 April 1919, pp. 37–40. The legend lends itself to the sequence which Bettelheim has suggested is intrinsic to a successful children's story: fantasy, recovery (or rescue), escape and consolation. Bruno Bettelheim, *The Uses of Enchantment. The Meaning and Importance of Fairy Tales*, p. 143.

[6]C. R. Long, *Notable Deeds of Famous Men and Women Including Some Done by Australians in the Great War*, C. R. Long, *British Worthies and other Men of Might*, Melbourne, 1934, pp. 125–33. The Simpson excerpts from Long's *Notable Deeds . . .* were also used in other school texts, e.g. *The School Paper* (for Grades V and VI), WA Education Department, 1 April 1924, pp. 37–9. The story also appeared in this form in Victoria for, at this time, the WA *School Paper* was merely a copy of the Victorian one.

[7]*The Victorian Readers. Fourth Book*, Government Printer, Melbourne, 1930, p. 108.

[8]*The School Paper* (Grade III), Dept of Education, Melbourne, 2 April 1928, pp. 37–8.

[9]*The School Paper* (Grade III). Ken Inglis noted Simpson's utility with respect to disputes over teaching the war in his 'Reluctant Retreat from All Solemn Observance', *Sydney Morning Herald*, 25 April 1964, p. 2. See also A. W. Hannon, Patriotism in Victorian State Schools 1901–1945, chs 5 and 6.

[10]Long, *British Worthies . . .* , (Appendix), p. 195.

[11]*The Victorian Readers. Fourth Book*, Government Printer, Melbourne, 1930, pp. 106–9, 170–1; in the 1940 edition, see pp. 126–9.

[12]The legend's military following has been sustained to the present, as chapters Seven and Eight suggest. Its consistent retelling in military journals, and other soldiers' publications, is another indication. The one *regional* monument that featured the man with the donkey at this time was erected in Ararat in 1930, *Ararat Advertiser*, 12 August 1930, pp. 1, 3.

[13]The campaign for an Anzac or Gallipoli stamp issue began in 1931 when the RSSILA began to press the Postmaster-General's Department. In 1935 the PMG was still resisting an Anzac or Gallipoli stamp because any reference to war might offend the general public

and current efforts towards 'disarmament . . . between all nations' (General-Secretary [RSSILA] to PMG, 5 December 1931; PMG to Gen.-Sec. 17 December 1931; Minute Paper (PMG), 16 January 1934; Sir Harry Lawson (Acting PMG) to J. Webster (RSSILA), undated (*c.* April 1934); Archdale Parkhill (PMG) to J. Webster, 7 June 1934; J. L. Treloar (AWM) to Director-General (PMG), 10 January 1935. On the priority of the King's Silver Jubilee stamps see John Ash to H. P. Brown, 21 February 1935. For all correspondence cited here see 'Stamps Special (1935)' file, PostMaster-General's Department, 37/13767, Philatelic Section, Australia Post. The decision not to commemorate the landing was applauded by the General Secretary of the Australian Branch of the League of Nations in the *Sydney Morning Herald*, 5 July 1934. See also H. McQueen, 'The Australian Stamp: Image, Design and Ideology', *Arena*, no. 84, 1988.

[14]For cartoons, see 'The Man with the Donkey' in *Silver Jacket*, June 1954, p. 13; also 'The Man with the Donkey' in *The Victor*, 5 September 1964. The most popular version of Anzac adventures was Dale Collins, *Anzac Adventure: The Story of Gallipoli Told for Young Readers*, pp. 108–10; also T. A. Miles, *The Anzac Story for Boys and Girls*, Shakespeare Head Press, Sydney, 1957, pp. 22–3. Radio plays appeared in 1964 and 1966: Elizabeth Parsons, 'The Man with the Donkey. A Play for Anzac Day', was written for the ABC and reproduced in the NSW *School Magazine* (Part 4), April 1964, pp. 67–74. This was replete with instructions on how to adapt the play for participation of children in the classroom. The second play, 'Simpson and his donkey', was published in the Victorian *School Paper* (Grades III & IV), April 1966, pp. 36–8.

[15]See Benson Papers, AWM, PR 83/69 (419/9/22[4]).

[16]*Everybody's*, 12 May 1965, p. 7. For another 'first hand account', see Tom Yeoman's story in *Sydney Morning Herald*, 21 April 1965. Simpson also appeared in a book of war photographs published in this period: B. A. Harding, *Windows of Fame: A Heroic Chronicle of Australians at War*, p. 32.

[17]*Australian Women's Weekly*, 28 April 1965, pp. 8–9. In New Zealand the Moore-Jones version of the man with the donkey appeared on the cover of the NZ *Weekly News* for Anzac Day 1965.

[18]Anzac, Zanthus Films, 1960 (held in Australian National Library).

[19]*Pix*, 25 April 1964, p. 50.

[20]*Bulletin*, 25 April 1964, pp. 23–5; *Pix*, 25 April 1964, p. 50.

[21]K. V. Newman (Nat. Sec. RSL) to Hon. C. W. Davidson (Postmaster-General), 18 December 1958; Davidson to Newman, 13 January 1959; R. C. Stradwick (Dir-Gen, PMG) to J. McGrath (Dir., AWM), 10 June 1959; J. McGrath to Stradwick, 16 June 1959; Stradwick to General Manager, Reserve Bank of Australia (Note Printing Branch), 29 July 1960. All correspondence, see file: '50th Anniversary of Anzac (Landing at Gallipoli)—depicting Simpson and His Donkey', Postmaster-General's Department, 281/22/306 (Part 1), Philatelic Section, Australia Post. See also *Philatelic Bulletin* (Australia Post), 12(4), February 1965, pp. 25–30.

[22] *Commonwealth Parliamentary Debates*, 15 April 1964, pp. 1127–8; 30 October 1964, p. 2603. The documentary film was made by the Australian Commonwealth Film Unit and titled 'Anzac: a nation's heritage'. See also *Sun* (Melbourne), 16 April 1964.

[23] Minute Paper, 26 May 1964. See file: '50th Anniversary of Anzac (landing at Gallipoli) . . . , *Age*, 9 April 1965. On 14 April 1965 the PMG also released a first-day issue envelope featuring the man with the donkey.

[24] E.g. *Age*, 22 April 1965, p. 11.

[25] The reverse of the medallion bore a relief map of Australia and New Zealand superimposed by the Southern Cross.

[26] *Commonwealth Parliamentary Debates*, 14 March 1963, p. 1345; 15 April 1964, pp. 1127–8; 23 April 1964, p. 1385; 24 March 1966, pp. 556–8; 29 September 1966, p. 1515; 16 March 1967, p. 738. For the Gallipoli Star, originally known as the Anzac Star, see *Reveille*, 30 November 1931, p. 26, 31 December 1931, p. 6; *Mufti*, 3 October 1964, p. 6.

[27] The first medallion struck was presented to Annie Simpson Pearson at Australia House in London on 16 May 1967, Benson Papers, AWM PR83/69, 1 of 17 (items 1–2). As with the stamp, New Zealand followed suit here, issuing the same medal for the occasion, see *Review* (Official RSA[NZ] Journal), no. 6, April 1967, p. 9.

[28] Members of the Gallipoli Legion of Veterans were still visiting schools in the 1960s, see *West Australian*, 1 August 1964.

[29] Tim Bonyhady, *Burke and Wills. From Melbourne to Myth*, esp. Part 4; Graham Seal, *Ned Kelly in Popular Tradition*, Jim Davidson, 'The Mythologisation of Eliza Fraser', pp. 449–61; Tim Bonyhady, 'From inept bushman to mighty spirit', *Age*, 31 March, 1990, p. 9 (Books Extra); also, Manning Clark, 'Heroes', pp. 57–84; David Marr, *Patrick White—A Life*, Random House, Sydney, 1991, ch. 15.

[30] About 700 of the 16 000 original Anzacs were thought to be still alive in 1960. *Sun-Herald*, 24 April 1960. On the *Honi Soit/Farrago* controversy see *Canberra Times*, 23 April 1960; *News* (Adelaide), 14 July 1960; *Sydney Morning Herald*, 23, 25 April 1960. For letters see *Age*, 7, 10, 14, 16, 17 and 18 May 1960. For Alan Walker's criticism, see *Mercury* (Hobart), 8 April 1965; *News* (Adelaide), 12 April 1965. Also '50 Years after Gallipoli. A Panel Debates Can Anzac Day Survive', *Sydney Morning Herald*, 17 April 1965.

[31] *Sun*, 25 April 1966. The integration of the Anzac tradition with post Second World War defence policy and anti-Communism is discussed in Ben Pearson, ch. 2. On the disquiet over Anzac Day and the Vietnam War, see Peter Cochrane, 'At War at Home', in G. Pemberton (ed.), *Vietnam Remembered*, pp. 164–85.

[32] For a slightly earlier statement making the connection between the Simpson legend and the legitimacy of Anzac day, see C. H. Currey, 'Anzac: Memorial Reference by the President', *Royal Australian Historical Society: Journal and Proceedings*, 42(2), 1956, pp. 49–50.

[33] For example: 'Education Age Lift-Out: Gallipoli', *Age*, 21 May 1975; Mary Small, *Simpson and Duffy*, Harcourt Brace Jovanovich, Sydney, 1989; *Explore*, Ministry of Education (Schools Division) Victoria, no. 1,

1989, p. 20; Brian McKinlay, *Young Anzacs. The Contribution of Victorian Schools to the Gallipoli Campaign, 1915*, Ministry of Education, Victoria, 1990, pp. 92–3; 'Gallipoli '75: Schools and Communities Remembering' (compiled by Robyn McLachlan, AWM, 1989).

[34]For the donkey in Anzac Day parades, see *Age*, 26 April 1977, p. 5; *Courier Mail*, 26 April 1979; and *Age* (Anzac Feature), 24 April 1991, p. 8. Mike Willesee's documentary series on great Australians (1988) featured a half-hour program reconstructing the tale. *The Animals' Who's Who: 1,146 Celebrated Animals in History, Popular Culture, Literature and Lore*, Routledge & Kegan Paul, London, 1982, p. 1.

[35]Patsy Adam-Smith, *The Anzacs*, esp. pp. vii–viii, 122–7; Kit Denton, *Gallipoli Illustrated*, pp. 107–8, & *Gallipoli: One Long Grave*; Suzy Baldwin (ed.), *Unsung Heroes and Heroines of Australia*, pp. 146–7; John Laird (ed.), *Australians at War*, Peter Firkins, *The Australians in Nine Wars: Waikato to Long Tan*, pp. 13, 51; also Michael McKernan, *Padre. Australian Chaplains in Gallipoli and France*, and Suzanne Welborn, *Lords of Death*. The glossy cover of Laird's book featured the Moore-Jones print.

[36]Albert Facey, *A Fortunate Life*, pp. 260–1; Peter Luck, *This Fabulous Century*, Lansdowne Press, Sydney, 1980, pp. 28, 129–30; Robert Rhodes James, *Gallipoli*, p. 176; Geoffrey Dutton, *The Australian Heroes: A Rousing Call of 47 of Australia's Greatest Heroes and Heroines*, pp. 49–55.

[37]Alan Moorehead, *Gallipoli*, pp. 137, 198, 295; Gavin Fry, *Nolan's Gallipoli*, esp. pp. 10–11 where Fry outlines Nolan's debt to Moorehead's work. Also Charles S. Spencer, 'Myth and Hero in the Paintings of Sidney Nolan', *Art in Australia*, 3(2), 1965.

[38]For Gill, see *Sydney Morning Herald*, 28 May 1990. On the play, *Simpson J. 202*, by Richard Beynon, see *Sydney Morning Herald*, 28 April 1990, p. 3; on the Melbourne art exhibition, see the *Age*, 10 March 1990 (Extra, p. 3); on the commemorative coin set, see *West Australian*, 6 April 1990, p. 7.

[39]Peter Corlett, a well-known figurative sculptor from Melbourne, was commissioned to do this work in 1987, *Sun* (Melbourne), 10 June 1989, p. 29. Also *Canberra Times*, 13 April 1985, p. 1, 13 January 1987, p. 3, 20 April 1988, p. 9. This account of the unveiling ceremony is a personal reminiscence.

Postscript

[1]Stephen Murray-Smith, *Right Words. A Guide to English Usage in Australia*, Penguin, Ringwood, 1990, ix–x.

[2]Paul Fussell, *The Great War and Modern Memory*, Oxford University Press, London, 1977, p. 115; John Herouvim, 'Does it Matter How We Speak and Write?', pp. 100–5.

[3]Cited in *Oxford English Dictionary* (*OED*), Second Edition (Prepared by J. A. Simpson and E. S. C. Weiner), Clarendon Press, Oxford, 1989.

[4]Cited in *OED*.

[5]Thucydides, *The Peloponnesian War*, Book 1, Ch. 1, translation by Rex Warner (Penguin Classic, 1954). He went on: 'We may claim instead, to have used only the plainest evidence and to have reached conclusions which are reasonably accurate'.

[6]*A Greek-English Lexicon*, (1843: compiled by H. G. Liddell and R. Scott), Oxford, 1973, p. 1151.

[7]Percy S. Cohen, pp. 337–53.

[8]George Mosse, *Fallen Soldiers. Reshaping the Memory of the World Wars*, Oxford University Press, 1990, p. 7.

[9]Cited in *Supplement to Oxford English Dictionary*, vol. 2, Clarendon Press, Oxford, 1976. The *Supplement*'s definitions of 'ideology' include 'a systematic scheme of ideas, usually relating to politics or society, or to the conduct of a class or group, and regarded as justifying actions . . . '

[10]William H. McNeill, 'Mythistory, or Truth, Myth, History and Historians', p. 6. McNeill's view is of course a distinctly conservative one as he goes on to emphasise: 'Belief in the virtue and righteousness of one's cause is a necessary sort of self-delusion for human beings, singly and collectively. A corrosive version of history that emphasizes all the recurrent discrepancies between ideal and reality in a given group's behaviour makes it harder for members of the group in question to act cohesively and in good conscience'.

[11]The attack on the conventional opposition between myth and history, a sceptical probing of the epistemological status of all historical knowledge, has subsequently been carried by Claude Lévi-Strauss, Hayden White and others.

[12]In keeping with the elusiveness of language it might be noted that the term 'ideology' also carries a similar pejorative meaning indicating a prescriptive doctrine that is not supported by rational argument, as in Seeley's essay on Napoleon Bonaparte (1881): 'He . . . put aside the whole system of false and confused thinking which had reigned since 1792, and which he called ideology' (Cited in *OED*).

[13]John Terraine, *The Smoke and The Fire. The Myths and Anti-Myths of War. 1861–1945*, ch. 1.

[14]G. Greer, *Daddy We Hardly Knew You*, p. 187.

[15]McNeill, p. 1.

Bibliography

Archives: Commonwealth

Australia Post (Post Master-General's Department), Philatelic Section

'50th Anniversary of Anzac (Landing at Gallipoli)—depicting Simpson and his Donkey', file no. 281/22/306 (Part 1), 1958–65
Post Master-General's Correspondence, file no. 281/22/306 (Part1), 1931–37
'Stamps Special (1935)' file, 37/13767

AA/VIC (Victoria)

Department of the Army Correspondence files, Multiple Number Series (1919–1942), CRS B 1535, file no. 746/8/1194
Department of Defence Correspondence files, Multiple Number Series (1913–1917), CRS A 2023, file no. A45/1/24
Department of Defence Correspondence files, Multiple Number Series (1914–1917), CRS B 539, file no. AIF144/1/274A
Department of Defence (1919–1937), Series MP 367, Bundle 31, file no. 448–6–2554

Archives: State

South Australia

Agent-General, Correspondence, 1937, GRG55/15/30–31
Chief Secretary's Office, Correspondence, 1937, GRG24/4–9,31

Archives: Other

Auckland City Art Gallery

Horace Millichamp Moore-Jones file
Correspondence of John Barr (Director)

City of Melbourne

Correspondence File re erection of a Bronze Monument to the Man and the Donkey, file no. 4392, 1934

Town Clerk's Correspondence Files, MCC 163/1
Parks and Gardens' Committee Minute Books, 1933–36
Shrine Trustees Minute Books, 1934–6

Red Cross

Simpson Collection (1933–65), Red Cross Archives, Victorian Division, South Melbourne

Books and Articles

Adams, Robert P. *The Better Part of Valor. More, Erasmus, Colet and Vives, on Humanism, War and Peace, 1496–1535.* University of Washington Press, Seattle, 1962.
Adam-Smith, Patsy. *The Anzacs.* Nelson, Melbourne, 1978.
Adcock, A. St. J. *Australasia Triumphant.* Simpkin, Marshall, Hamilton, Kent and Co., London, 1916.
Agulhon, Maurice. *Marianne into Battle. Republican Imagery and Symbolism in France, 1789–1880.* Cambridge University Press, Cambridge, 1982.
Alexander, H. M. *On Two Fronts. Being the Adventures of an Indian Mule Corps in France and Gallipoli.* Heinemann, London 1917.
Altman, Dennis. *Paper Ambassadors—the Politics of Stamps.* Angus & Robertson, Sydney, 1991.
Arkwright, J. S. *The Supreme Sacrifice and Other Poems in Time of War.* Skeffington & Son, London, 1919.
Australians in Action: The Story of Gallipoli. Department of Public Instruction, New South Wales, 1915.
Baker, Paul. *King and Country Call. New Zealanders, Conscription and the Great War.* Auckland University Press, Auckland, 1988.
Baldwin, Suzy (ed.). *Unsung Heroes and Heroines of Australia.* Greenhouse Publications, Sydney, 1988.
Balzac, H. de. *The Wild Ass's Skin.* Penguin, Harmondsworth, 1977.
Barthes, Roland. *Camera Lucida. Reflections on Photography.* Flamingo (Fontana), London, 1984.
Baxter, Archibald. *We Will Not Cease.* Victor Gollancz, London, 1939.
Bean, C. E. W. *Anzac To Amiens.* Australian War Memorial, Canberra, 1946.
———. *In Your Hands, Australians.* Cassell & Co., London, 1918.
——— (ed.). *The Anzac Book.* Cassell, London, 1916.
———. *The Official History of Australia in the War of 1914–18, The Story of ANZAC.* Angus & Robertson, Sydney, 1921 (2 vols).
Bean, C. E. W. and Gullett, H. *Official History of Australia in the Great War of 1914–18. Volume 12. Photographic Record of the War.* Angus & Robertson, Sydney, 1923.
Beeston, J. L. *Five Months at Anzac.* Angus & Robertson, Sydney, 1916.
Benson, C. I. (ed.). *A Century of Victorian Methodism.* Spectator Publishing, Melbourne, 1935.
———. *The Craft of Prayer, D...* Pettigrew, Sydney, 1939.

——————. *The Man With The Donkey. The Good Samaritan of Gallipoli.* Hodder & Stoughton, London, 1965.

Bettelheim, Bruno. *The Uses of Enchantment. The Meaning and Importance of Fairy Tales* (1976). Penguin, Harmondsworth, 1985.

Bonyhady, Tim. *Burke and Wills. From Melbourne to Myth.* David Ell, Sydney, 1991.

Bowes, Joseph. *The Young Anzacs.* London, 1918.

Bowra, C. M. *Heroic Poetry.* St. Martin's Press, New York, 1961.

Boyak, N. *Behind the Lines. The Lives of New Zealand Soldiers in the First World War.* Allen & Unwin, Auckland, 1990.

Buley, E. C. *A Child's History of Anzac.* London, 1916.

——————. *Glorious Deeds of the Australasians in the Great War.* Andrew Melrose, London, 1915.

Bush, E. W. *Gallipoli.* Allen & Unwin, London, 1985.

Butler, A. G. *The Australian Army Medical Services in the War of 1914–1918, Vol. 1 (Gallipoli, Sinai and New Guinea).* Melbourne, 1930.

——————. *The Digger: A Study in Democracy.* Angus & Robertson, Sydney, 1945.

Capper, Wendy. 'Facey's *A Fortunate Life* and Traditional Oral Narratives', *Australian Literary Studies,* 13(3), May 1988.

Carbery, A. D. *The New Zealand Medical Service in the Great War, 1914–18.* Whitcombe & Tombs, Auckland, 1924.

Cavill, H. W. *Imperishable Anzacs.* William Brooks & Co, Sydney, 1916.

Church, Hayden. 'Sapper Moore-Jones', *The Lone Hand,* 1 September 1916.

Clark, Manning. 'Heroes', in Stephen R. Graubard (ed.), *Australia: The Daedalus Symposium.* Angus and Robertson, Sydney, 1985.

Cochrane, Peter. 'Deliverance and Renewal: the Origins of the Simpson Legend', *Journal of the Australian War Memorial,* no. 16, April 1990.

——————. 'Legendary Proportions. The Simpson Memorial Appeal of 1933', *Australian Historical Studies,* vol. 24, no. 94, April 1990.

Cohen, A. P. *The Symbolic Construction of Community.* Ellis Horwood, Chichester and Tavistock Publications, London, 1985.

Cohen, P. S. 'Theories of Myth', *MAN (N.S.),* vol. 4, no. 3, 1969.

Collins, Dale. *Anzac Adventure: The Story of Gallipoli for Young Readers.* Angus & Robertson, Sydney, 1959.

Complete Index to the First Series of Sketches Made at Anzac by Sapper Horace Moore-Jones. Hugh Rees Ltd., London, 1916. (No author cited.)

Cooper, Jill. *Animals in War.* Heinemann, London, 1983.

de Loghe, Sydney. *The Straits Impregnable.* John Murray, London, 1916.

Davidson, Jim. 'The Mythologisation of Eliza Fraser', *Meanjin,* vol. 49, no. 3, 1990.

Davison, Graeme. 'The Use and Abuse of Australian History', in Janson, S. & Macintyre, S. (eds), *Making the Bicentenary,* Australian Historical Studies (Special Issue: vol. 23, no. 91), Melbourne, October 1988.

Dening, Greg. *History's Anthropology: The Death of William Gooch.* (Association for Cultural Anthropology in Oceania, Special Publication No. 2). University Press of America, Lanham, 1988.

Denton, Kit. *Gallipoli Illustrated*. Rigby, Adelaide, 1981.
————. *Gallipoli: One Long Grave*. Time Life Books and John Ferguson, Sydney, 1986.
Dutton, Geoffrey. *The Australian Heroes: A Rousing Call of 47 of Australia's Greatest Heroes and Heroines*. Angus & Robertson, Sydney, 1981.
Dutton, Philip. 'Moving images? The Parliamentary Recruiting Committee's poster campaign, 1914–1916', *Imperial War Museum Review*, no. 4, 1989.
Ensor, R. K. *England 1870–1914*. Oxford University Press, London, 1960.
Facey, Albert. *A Fortunate Life*. Penguin, Ringwood, 1981.
Fewster, Kevin. 'Ellis Ashmead Bartlett and the Making of the Anzac Legend', *Journal of Australian Studies*, no. 10, June 1982, pp. 17–30.
Firkins, Peter. *The Australians in Nine Wars: Waikato to Long Tan*. Rigby, Adelaide, 1971.
Folkenflik, R. (ed.). *The English Hero, 1660–1800*. Newark: Delaware University Press, London and Toronto, 1982.
Fry, Gavin. *Nolan's Gallipoli*. Rigby, Adelaide, 1983.
Fussell, Paul. *The Great War and Modern Memory*. Oxford University Press, London, 1977.
————. *Thank God for the Atom Bomb and Other Essays*. Ballantine Books, New York, 1990.
Gallishaw, J. *Trenching at Gallipoli: A Personal Narrative of a Newfoundlander within the Ill-fated Dardanelles Expedition*. A. L. Burt & Co, New York, October 1916.
Gammage, Bill. *The Broken Years. Australian Soldiers in the First World War*. Penguin, Ringwood, 1987.
Gerster, R. *Big-Noting. The Heroic Theme in Australian War Writing*. Melbourne University Press, 1987.
Gordon, M. 'Brief Biography and Obituary of Rabbi Jacob Danglow', *Australian Jewish Historical Society. Journal and Proceedings*, vol. 5, part 7, 1963.
Grant, Michael. *Myths of the Greeks and Romans*. Mentor, New American Library, New York, 1962.
Graves, Robert. *Goodbye To All That*. Jonathan Cape, London, 1929.
Gray, Anne. 'Moore-Jones' Gallipoli', *The Australian Connoisseur*, no. 4, 1983.
Greene, Thomas M. *The Descent from Heaven*. Yale University Press, New Haven, 1963.
Greer, G. *Daddy We Hardly Knew You*. Hamish Hamilton, London, 1989.
Harding, B. A. *Windows of Fame: A Heroic Chronicle of Australians at War*. Lansdowne Press, Melbourne, 1963.
Hart-Davis, R. (ed.). *The War Poems of Siegfried Sassoon*. Faber & Faber, London, 1983.
Herouvim, John. 'Does it Matter How We Speak and Write?', *Bulletin*, 2 May 1989.
Hill, A. J. *Chauvel of the Light Horse*. Melbourne University Press, 1978.
Hobsbawm, E. and Ranger, T. (eds). *The Invention of Tradition*. Cambridge University Press, Cambridge, 1984.

Hogue, Oliver. *Love Letters of an Anzac.* Andrew Melrose, London, 1916.
—————. *Trooper Bluegum at the Dardanelles.* London, 1915.
Holmes, Richard. *Footsteps. Adventures of a Romantic Biographer.* Penguin, London, 1986.
Idriess, Ion. *The Desert Column. Leaves from the Diary of an Australian Trooper in Gallipoli, Sinai, and Palestine.* Angus & Robertson, Sydney 1932.
Inglis, Ken. 'Anzac and the Australian Military Tradition', *Current Affairs Bulletin,* April 1988.
—————. 'The Anzac Legend', *Meanjin Quarterly,* March 1965.
—————. *The Australian Colonists.* Melbourne University Press, 1974.
—————. *Churches and the Working Classes in Victorian England.* Routledge & Kegan Paul, London, 1963.
—————. *The Rehearsal. Australians at War in the Sudan, 1885.* Rigby, Adelaide, 1985.
James, Robert Rhodes. *Gallipoli.* Angus & Robertson, Sydney, 1965.
Jarman, Angela. (ed.). *Royal Academy Exhibitors 1905–1970,* Vol. 3. Hilmarton Manor Press, London, 1987.
Jauncey, L. C. T*he Story of Conscription.* Allen & Unwin, London, 1935.
Kavanagh, P. J. *The Essential Chesterton.* Oxford University Press, London 1987.
Keegan, John. *The Face of Battle: A Study of Agincourt, Waterloo and the Somme.* (1976), Baine & Jenkins, London, 1988.
Kent, D. A. 'The Anzac Book and the Anzac Legend: C.E.W. Bean as editor and image-maker', *Historical Studies,* vol. 21, no. 84, April 1985.
Kern, Stephen. *The Culture of Time and Space. 1880–1918.* Harvard University Press, Cambridge, Massachusetts, 1983.
'La Coche'. 'The Stretcher Bearers', *The Lone Hand,* 1 December 1916.
Laird, J. (ed.). *The Australian Experience of War.* Mead & Beckett, Sydney, 1988.
Larousse Encyclopaedia of Mythology. Batchworth Press, London, 1959.
Lawson, Sylvia. *The Archibald Paradox. A Strange Case of Authorship.* Penguin, Ringwood, 1987.
Leed, Eric J. *No Man's Land: Combat and Identity in World War 1.* Cambridge, England, 1979.
Lehmann, John. *Rupert Brooke, His Life and His Legend.* Quartet, London, 1981.
Lewis, Brian. *Our War.* Penguin, Ringwood, 1980.
Liddle, P. *Gallipoli, 1915: Pens, Pencils and Cameras at War.* Brasseys Defence Publishers, London, 1985.
Lloyd, G. 'Selfhood, War and Masculinity', in Pateman, C., and Gross, E. (eds). *Feminist Challenges. Social and Political Theory.* Allen & Unwin, Sydney, 1986.
Long, C. R. *British Worthies and other Men of Might.* Robertson & Mullens, Melbourne, 1934.
—————. *Notable Deeds of Famous Men and Women Including Some Done by Australians in the Great War.* (Stories for Children, Grade III, Victoria). Angus & Robertson, Sydney, 1922.

————. *The Aim and Method of History and Civics*. Macmillan, Melbourne, 1909.

McKernan, M. *Padre. Australian Chaplains in Gallipoli and France*. Allen & Unwin, Sydney, 1986.

————. *The Australian People and the Great War*. Nelson, Melbourne, 1980.

McKinlay, Brian. *Young Anzacs. The Contribution of Victorian Schools to the Gallipoli Campaign, 1915*. Ministry of Education, Victoria, 1990.

Mackinnon, E. and Monie, A. (eds). *Poems and Pictures for the Red Cross*. Winn & Company, Sydney, 1918.

McNeill, William H. 'Mythistory, or Truth, Myth, History and Historians', *American Historical Review*, vol. 9, 1986.

McQueen, Humphrey. 'The Australian Stamp: Image, Design and Ideology, *Arena*, 84, 1988.

————. *Gallipoli to Petrov. Arguing with Australian History*. Allen & Unwin, Sydney, 1984.

Margolis, Éric. 'Mining Photographs: Unearthing the Meaning of Historical Photos', *Radical History Review*, no. 40, 1988.

Masefield, J. *Gallipoli*. Heinemann, London, 1916.

"Menin Gate at Midnight". The Story of Captain Will Longstaff's Great Allegorical Painting. Australian War Memorial, Melbourne, 1932.

Meredith, John. *The Coo-ee March. Gilgandra to Sydney, 1915*. Macquarie Publications, Dubbo, 1981.

Miles, T. A. *The Anzac Story for Boys and Girls*. Shakespeare Head Press, Sydney, 1957.

Mitchell, G. D. *Backs to the Wall*. Angus & Robertson, Sydney, 1937.

Moorehead, Alan. *Gallipoli* (1956). Rev. ed., Macmillan, Melbourne, 1989.

Moorman, Charles. *A Knyght There Was*. University of Kentucky Press, Lexington, 1967.

Mosse, George L. *Fallen Soldiers. Reshaping the Memory of the World Wars*. Oxford University Press, New York, 1990.

Orwell, George. *Nineteen Eighty-Four*. Clarendon Press, Oxford, 1984.

————. 'Politics and the English Language', in S. Orwell & I. Angus (eds), *The Collected Essays, Journalism and Letters of George Orwell, vol. iv, In Front of Your Nose, 1945–50*. Secker & Warburg, London, 1968.

Paintings and Drawings by Horace Moore-Jones. Waikato Society of Arts, Hamilton, 1964. (Foreword by Douglas Seymour. No author cited.)

Patterson, J. H. *With the Zionists in Gallipoli*. Hutchinson, London, 1916.

Pedersen, P. A. *Images of Gallipoli. Photographs from the collection of Ross J. Bastiaan*, Oxford University Press, Oxford, 1988.

Pemberton, G. (ed.) *Vietnam Remembered*, Weldon, Sydney, 1990.

Phillips, J. *A Man's Country? The Image of the Pakeha Male—A History*. Penguin, Auckland.

Phillips, J., Boyak, N., and Malone, E. P. (eds). *The Great Adventure. New Zealand Soldiers Describe the First World War*. Allen & Unwin/Port Nicholson Press, Wellington, 1988.

Pike, Andrew and Cooper, Ross. *Australian Film 1900–1980*. Oxford University Press 1980.

Pugsley, Christopher. *Gallipoli: The New Zealand Story.* Hodder & Stoughton, Auckland, 1984.

Rickard, John. *Australia. A Cultural History.* Longman Cheshire, Melbourne, 1988.

Robertson, P. N. *An Anzac Budget and Other Verses.* Australian Author's Agency, Melbourne, 1916.

————. *Red Cross Yesterdays.* Melbourne, 1950.

Roe, Jill. 'Chivalry and Social Policy in the Antipodes', *Historical Studies*, vol. 22, no. 88, April 1987.

Ross, Jane. *The Myth of the Digger. Australian Soldiers in Two World Wars.* Hale & Iremonger, Sydney, 1985.

Rule, E. J. *Jacka's Mob.* Angus & Robertson, Sydney, 1933.

Saunders, M. and Taylor, P. M. *British Propaganda During the First World War.* Macmillan, London, 1982.

Scarlett, Ken. *Australian Sculptors.* Nelson, Melbourne, 1980.

Schwartz, Barry. 'The Social Context of Commemoration: A Study in Collective Memory', *Social Forces*, vol. 61, no. 2, December 1982.

Seal, Graham. *Ned Kelly in Popular Tradition.* Hyland House, Melbourne, 1980.

————. *The Hidden Culture. Folklore in Australian Society.* Oxford University Press, Melbourne, 1989.

Serle, Geoffrey. *From Deserts the Prophets Come.* Heinemann, Melbourne, 1973.

————. *John Monash. A Biography.* Melbourne University Press, 1982.

Shute, Carmel. 'Blood Votes and the "Bestial Boche". A Case Study in Propaganda', *Hecate*, no. 2, July 1976.

Sketches Made at Anzac By Sapper Horace Moore-Jones. Hugh Rees, London, 1916.

Small, Mary. *Simpson and Duffy.* Harcourt Brace Jovanovich, Sydney, 1989.

Smith, F. B. *The Conscription Plebiscites in Australia, 1916–17.* Victorian Historical Association, Melbourne, 1974.

Smith, Terry. 'Populism and Privilege in Australian Painting,' in S. L. Goldberg & F. B. Smith (eds). *Australian Cultural History.* Cambridge University Press, Melbourne 1988.

Stanley, P. 'An Entente . . . Most Remarkable': Indians at Anzac', *Sabretache*, vol. 22, no. 2, April–June 1981.

Steadman, John M. *Milton and the Renaissance Hero.* Oxford University Press, Oxford, 1967.

Sturgeon, G. *The Development of Australian Sculpture, 1788–1975.* Thames & Hudson, London, 1978.

Terraine, J. *The Smoke and the Fire. The Myths and Anti-Myths of War, 1861–1945.* Sidgwick and Jackson, London, 1980.

"The Times" History of the War, vol. 5. Times Printing House, London, 1915.

Thomson, Alistair. 'Steadfast until Death'? C. E. W. Bean and the Representation of Australian Military Manhood', *Australian Historical Society*, vol. 23, no. 93, October 1989.

Throssell, Ric. *My Father's Son.* Heinemann, Melbourne, 1989.

Treloar, J. L. (ed.). *Australian Chivalry. Reproductions in Colour and Duo-Tone of Official War Paintings.* Australian War Memorial, Canberra, 1933.
Waite, Fred. *The New Zealanders at Gallipoli.* Whitcombe & Tombs, Auckland, 1921.
Walsh, T. *The Man with the Donkey. A Narration of the Undaunted Chivalry of John Simpson Kirkpatrick (Murphy) in the Gallipoli Campaign, 1915.* Auckland, 1948.
Wanliss, N. *The History of the Fourteenth Battalion A.I.F.* Arrow Printery, Melbourne, 1929.
Warner, Marina. *Joan of Arc. The Image of the Female Heroine.* Weidenfeld & Nicolson, London, 1981.
Welborn, Suzanne. *Lords of Death.* Fremantle Arts Centre Press, 1982.
Williams, H. *The Gallant Company. A Soldier's Story of 1915–18.* Sydney, 1933.
Williams, Gwyn A. *Madoc. The Making of a Myth.* Eyre Methuen, London, 1979.
Williams, Raymond. *Towards 2000.* Penguin, Harmondsworth, 1983.
Wilkinson, Ellen. *The Town That Was Murdered. The Life-Story of Jarrow.* Victor Gollancz, London, 1939.
Wolfsohn, Hugo. 'The Ideology Makers', in H. Mayer & H. Nelson (eds). *Australian Politics: A Second Reader.* Cheshire, Melbourne, 1969.

Private Papers: Soldiers' Diaries, Letters and Personal Narratives

Aitken, A. C. Diary. Hocken Library, University of Otago, Dunedin, New Zealand
Anon. Diary. Australian War Memorial (AWM) PR84/288
Baker, R. D. Narrative. Alexander Turnbull Library, Wellington, New Zealand, MS1560
Bollinger, George. Diary. Stout Research Centre, Victoria University, Wellington, New Zealand
Bosward, C. F. Diary. AWM 3DRL/4104
Calder, R. M. Letters. LaTrobe Collection, State Library of Victoria, MS9003
Carne, A. G. Diary. AWM 2DRL/13
Cates, Charles. Diary. Alexander Turnbull Library, MS2368
Colbran, Ben. Diary. Alexander Turnbull Library, MS1431
Conrick, V. Narrative. AWM 3DRL/3329
Cornell, R. Diary. AWM PR83/87
Davidson, G. Diary. Alexander Turnbull Library, MS579
Davies, E. Letters. AWM3DRL/3398B
Doe, W. Letters. AWM 3DRL/3126
Donovan, L. G. Diary. Alexander Turnbull Library, MS2299
Fenwick, P. C. Diary. Alexander Turnbull Library, MS72
Finch, R. Letters. AWM PR84/58

Godfrey, G. W. Narrative. AWM 3DRL/3318
Gordon, Colin M. Narrative. Stout Research Centre
Hampson, J. T. Letters. AWM1DRL/331
Hanna, Phillip. Diary. Alexander Turnbull Library, MS1647
Hart, Leonard, M. Narrative. Alexander Turnbull Library, MS2157
Hassell, N. E. Narrative. Alexander Turnbull Library, MS2295
Hillier, Herbert. Diary. AWM 1DRL/352
Hutchinson, W. J. Diary. AWM 1DRL/372
Hutton, A. S. Diary. AWM 3DRL/3371
Idriess, Ion. Diary. AWM1DRL/373
Jackson, J. G. Diary. Johnstone Papers, Hocken Library, University of
    Otago, Dunedin, New Zealand, MS34/89
Jarman, C. J. Letters. AWM3DRL/3235
Kerse, C. A. Letters. Alexander Turnbull Library, MS591
Kirkpatrick, John Simpson. Letters. AWM3DRL/3424
Knight, F. Letters. LaTrobe Collection, MS9616
Laidlaw, V. Diary. LaTrobe Collection, MS11827
Law, Joseph. Diary. Auckland Institute and Museum, MS13/387
Love, C. Letters. AWM93, 417/20/35
Mackay, J. S. Letters. AWM1DRL/442
McPhee, J. E. Diary. AWM 3 DRL/2610
Mason, C. L. Diary. AWM 3DRL/2917
Robson, F. Diary. AWM PR84/172
Turnbull, J. H. Diary. AWM PR91/015
Watts, T. W. Diary. Alexander Turnbull Library, MS2359
Weir, Russell. Diary. Alexander Turnbull Library
Weymouth, A. E. Letters. AWM PR85/171

Private Papers: Other

ANZAC Fellowship of Women. Papers. NLA MS2864
Barr, John. Letters. Moore-Jones file, Auckland City Art Gallery
Bean, C. E. W. Papers. AWM 91, 3DRL/6673 & 3DRL/8042
Benson, C Irving. Papers. LaTrobe Collection, State Library of Victoria,
    MS11493
Benson, C. Irving. Papers. AWM, PR83/69
Butler, A. G. Papers. AWM41 (2/7.15)
Fetherston, R. H. Papers. AWM3DRL/251
Menzies, Sir Robert. Papers. NLA MS4936
Monash, John. Papers. NLA MS1884
Walsh, Tom. Papers. Auckland Institute and Museum, MS1469

Military Journals

Anzac Bulletin (London) 1917
Aussie 1919

Coo-ee (Birmingham) 1916–17
Dinkum Oil 1915
Duckboard various
Mufti 1959–65
Reveille various
Standeasy (New Zealand) 1964–65

School Journals, Papers and Readers

Adelaide Reader, Education Department (Ed. Dept), Adelaide, various
School Journal, Ed. Dept, Wellington, New Zealand, various
School Magazine, Ed. Dept, Sydney, various
School Paper, Ed. Dept, Melbourne, various
School Paper, Ed. Dept, Brisbane, various
School Paper, Ed. Dept, Perth, various
Tasmanian Reader, Ed. Dept, Hobart, various
Victorian Readers, Ed. Dept, Melbourne, various
Western Australian Reader, Ed Dept, Perth, various

Journals and Magazines

Boy's Own Annual 1916–17
New South Wales Red Cross Record 1914–18
New Zealand Stamp Collector 1964–65
Philatelic Bulletin (Melbourne) 1964–65
Theatre Magazine (Sydney) 1916

Newspapers

Age (Melbourne), various
Advertiser (Adelaide) 1937
Advertiser (Geelong) 1920–30, 1933, 1977
Ararat Advertiser 1930–33
Argus (Melbourne), various
Auckland Star, 1937
Australasian (Melbourne), various
Australian (Melbourne) 1988–90
Bulletin (Sydney), various
Canterbury Times (Christchurch) 1915, 1936–7
Christchurch Press 1915–17
Courier Mail (Brisbane) 1936
Daily Malta Chronicle (Valetta) 1915
Egyptian Mail (Cairo) 1917

Epsom District Times and Country Post, (Epsom) 1917
Examiner (Launceston) 1937
Herald (Melbourne) 1915–18, 1922–25
Labor Call (Melbourne), various
Lone Hand (Sydney) 1907–20
New Zealand Freelance 1915–17
New Zealand Herald (Auckland) 1937
Otago Witness (Dunedin), various
Statesman & Friend of India 1915
Sun (Sydney), various
Sun (Melbourne), various
Sunday Times (Perth) 1915–16
Sunday Times (Sydney) 1915–18, 1933–37
Sydney Mail (Sydney), various
Sydney Morning Herald (Sydney), various
Weekly Press (Christchurch) 1915
Weekly Times (Auckland) 1937
West Australian (Perth) 1915–18, 1930–33, 1937

Theses and Unpublished Papers

Chinn, D. A. 'The Gallipoli Star'. Unpublished Staff Paper, Department of Defence, Canberra, 1990.
Fewster, Kevin. Expression and Suppression: Aspects of Military Censorship in Australia during World War One. PhD, University of New South Wales, 1980.
Hannon, A. W. Patriotism in Victorian State Schools 1901–1945. MA, La Trobe University, 1977.
Huppauf, Bernd. 'Problems of Representing War in Photographs and Film'. Paper Presented to the Conference on 'Coming to Terms with the Photographic Image', Humanities Research Centre, Australian National University, Canberra, 1989.
Legge, J. P. L. '"The Man with the Donkey"–No. 202 Pte. John Simpson Kirkpatrick', AWM 93, 417/20/35.
McGregor, P. 'John Simpson Kirkpatrick. The Man With The Donkey'. Unpublished Bibliography, LaTrobe Collection, State Library of Victoria.
Pearson, Ben. Images of the Vietnam Serviceman, 1965–1990. BA Hons, University of Sydney, 1990.

Index

Holt, Harold, 36, 230
Holtz, A. C. C., 204
Homer, 89
Honi Soit, 231
Hugh Rees Ltd., 182, 184
Hughes, W. M., 163
Hutchinson, Private Billy, 114
Hutton, Trooper A. S., 46–7

iconography, 1, 4; official icon,
  8, 164
Idriess, Ion, 46, 48
imperial patriots, 2, 4, 9, 26, 56,
  61, 65, 82, 86, 221
imperial-patriotic press, 3–4, 51–
  7, 63–74 passim, 77, 81, 94,
  102, 105–6, 108, 114–15, 128;
  battlefield journalism of, 8;
  Indian press, 56
Isaiah, 39
Italo-Abyssinian crisis, 208

Jack, *see* Kirkpatrick, John
  Simpson
Jacka, Albert, 109, 163, 179, 231
Jackson, James Gardner, 101,
  116, 146, 153, 164, 186–200
  passim
Joan of Arc, 3
Johnson, Les (fruit-barrow
  man), 173
Johnson, Samuel, 10, 89
Johnstone née Jackson, Betty,
  197
journalists, 3, 8, 52, 64, 113–14,
  234
Joynt, Captain W. D., 166

Keegan, John, 142
Kelly, Ned, 85, 231
Kern, Stephen, 104
kings of Israel, 138
King's Own Yorkshire Light
  Infantry, 140
Kipling, Rudyard, 39, 107, 202–
  3, 217
Kirkpatrick, Annie, 10–40
  passim; 55, 220
Kirkpatrick, John Simpson
  Anglo-Scottish origins, 6, 26;

as 'Bahadur', 57; as local
hero, 44, 48; as typical digger,
5, 6, 7 and passim; as
spectacle, 122; belligerence,
19, 26, 36; birth certificate
detail, 31; 'braggart' Simpson,
133–6; brawling, 16, 21, 35;
call for sainthood, 234;
charmed life, 41, 46, 59, 125,
149; class consciousness, 7;
clothing, 179; comrades in
Perth, 170; death, 1, 4, 16, 41,
46–8, 50, 55, 63, 89, 100, 158,
197, 231; devotion to his
mother, 26, 29–30; Egypt, 16,
22, 27, 30; encounter with
James Jackson, 186;
enlistment, 16, 63; fame, 4;
family background, 10, 13, 17,
20–1; flesh and blood
allusion, 126–33; food, 13, 14;
Genoa, 23; grammar, 19;
grave, 42–3, 57, 121–2; heroic
typicality, 117, 128, 202; his
'girl', 58, 87; itinerant life, 14,
20; last words, 122; leaves
home, 23, 26; legend's link
with Vietnam War, 38–40,
220, 232–3; manliness, 35–7;
many pets, 156; memorial
statue for, 201–20 passim;
milk cart, 22; misspelling, 35;
not a hero in his own time,
42–51; not an alcoholic, 93;
on Lloyd George's Insurance
bill, 26; pet possum, 140;
political views, 17–19, 21–2,
24; rescues, 73; Simpson as
surname, 30; smuggles
donkey on board ship, 156;
S.S. *Heighington*, 21; S.S.
Kooringa, 16, 27; story from
childhood, 123; swearing, 35;
time in Australia, 13–31
passim; underclothing, 14;
unionism, 18; volunteer, 6;
wages and prices, 20;
unemployment, 21; views on
women, 22, 27, 30; 'Was it
Simpson' (poem), 134;